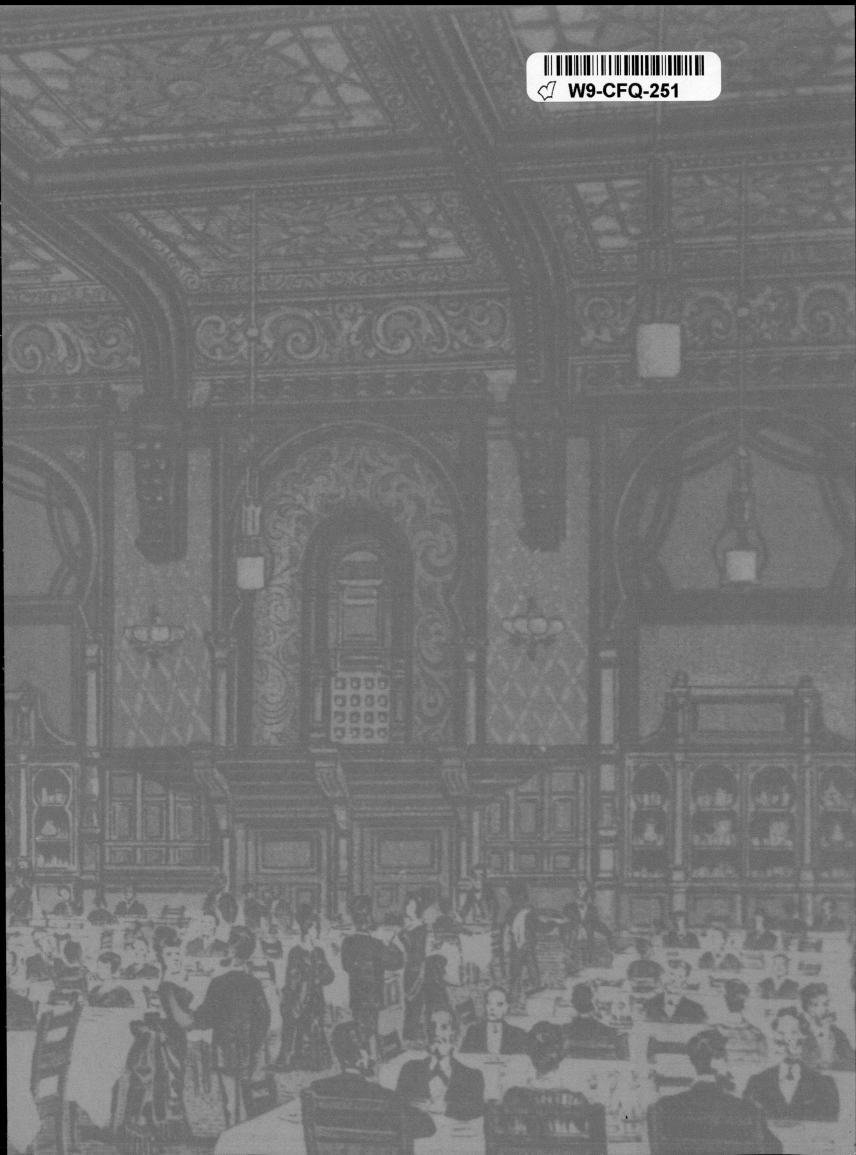

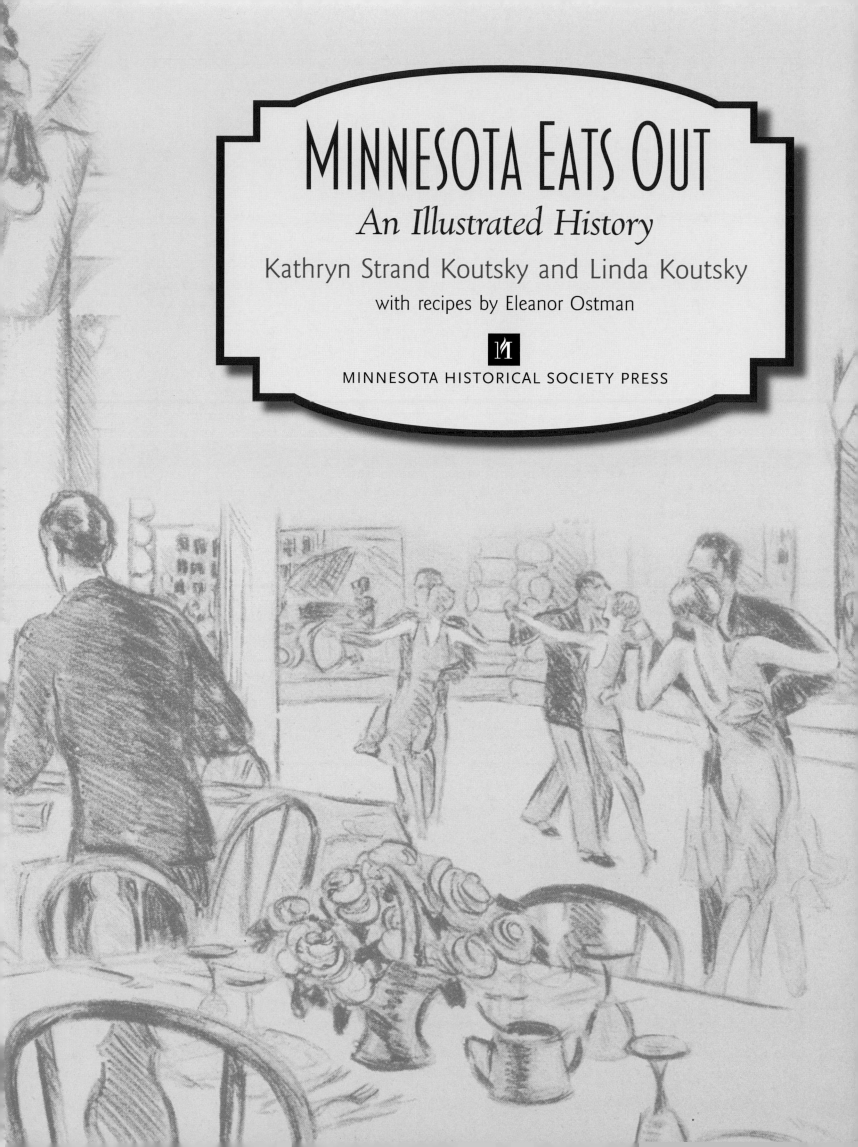

MINNESOTA EATS OUT

An Illustrated History

Kathryn Strand Koutsky and Linda Koutsky

with recipes by Eleanor Ostman

MINNESOTA HISTORICAL SOCIETY PRESS

We are grateful for the sage advice and spicy stories from hundreds of Minnesotans who reminisced of bygone dining pleasures and provided us with lively descriptions of their favorite menus and eating places.

SPECIAL THANKS TO Dean Koutsky, who dubbed himself "manservant" and chased after artifacts, tracked down missing items, and learned to cook "period" meals for famished midnight authors; to editor Shannon M. Pennefeather, who cheerfully fixed our fractured sentences and passive voices, banished all conflicting grammar from the table, and kept track of thousands of vital details along the way; to "volunteer research assistant" Madeline Betsch, who tastefully handled innumerable letters to contacts all over the state; to editor Roz Stendahl, who added spice with her exuberant prose; and to all the relatives of early restaurant workers who searched their dusty family records and ancient photo albums, enabling us to compile a truly comprehensive picture of dining out in Minnesota.

We are indebted to seasoned dining experts who shared their valuable time, priceless collections, and vast expertise. Thanks to Barbara Flanagan, Cy DeCosse, Jack Lindstrom, Dean Borghorst, Mark McGinley, David Duff, and the special collections staff at the Minneapolis Public Library.

Finally, our appreciation goes to statewide historical society volunteers and staff who helped us locate and date dozens of old photos and artifacts. In St. Paul, curators at the Minnesota Historical Society cleared the way for us to include illustrations of priceless antiques, menus, and place mats preserved in the archives at the History Center.

www.mnhs.org/mhspress

The Minnesota Historical Society Press is a member of the Association of American University Presses.

Typefaces used in this book are Village, Anna, Scala Sans, and Goudy Sans. Blakely Light on page headers and Coquette drop caps were designed by Minnesota typographer Mark Simonson. Jacket and book design by Linda Koutsky

Manufactured in China by Pettit Network, Inc., Afton, Minnesota
10 9 8 7 6 5 4 3 2 1

∞ This book is printed on a coated paper manufactured on an acid-free base to ensure a long life.

International Standard Book Number 0-87351-452-1 (cloth)

Library of Congress Cataloging-in-Publication Data

Koutsky, Kathryn.
Minnesota eats out : an illustrated history / Kathryn Strand Koutsky and Linda Koutsky ; with recipes by Eleanor Ostman.
p. cm.
ISBN 0-87351-452-1 (cloth : alk. paper)
1. Restaurants—Minnesota—History—19th century.
2. Restaurants—Minnesota—History—20th century.
3. Cookery. I. Koutsky, Linda. II. Ostman, Eleanor. III. Title.
TX909.K68 2003
647.95776'09'034—dc21
2003046404

"The Age of Elegance: Agnes and Gladys and pink drapes and Deep Purple," by Garrison Keillor. Copyright ©1997 Time Inc. Reprinted by permission.

"Talking Camping," by Charlie Maguire. Copyright ©1991 and 2002 Mello-Jamin Music BMI. All Rights Reserved.

Photographs: front endsheet, Moorish Room at the West Hotel, Minneapolis; p. i, employee stacking dishes in the dining car warehouse of the Great Northern Railway, 1930; p. ii–iii, brochure illustration from Breezy Point, Pequot Lakes; p. v, Donaldson's Grill, 1948; back endsheet, the Ladies Ordinary at the West Hotel

Menu

As family and friends arrived for Christmas Eve dinner at Linda's house, they found the tables set with historic restaurant china. One place setting included a century-old plate from the Tonka Bay Hotel alongside a fifty-year-old cup from the Elks Club, a bread plate from Charlie's Cafe, and flatware from the Forum Cafeteria. Linda's sister Lisa arrived with an antique glass and silver water pitcher from Breezy Point Resort. Kathy exclaimed that she had pictures of every one of these now-historic restaurant interiors in her antique postcard collection. Everyone looked at each other in amazement: there must be a book here. And so it began.

Backed with a research grant from the Minnesota Historical Society, Linda and Kathy contacted or visited historical societies, libraries, and collectors throughout the state. The response was awesome—and overwhelming. Photos, artifacts, and stories flooded in. There were lavish restaurants, elegant department stores, fancy soda fountains, showy supper clubs, restful resorts, comfy cafés, and ditsy diners. Fragile menus embellished with beautiful engravings told of sumptuous nineteenth-century feasts. Could we use a walking stick carved from the window frame of the town's first restaurant or bullet-shaped salt-and-pepper shakers made by Minnesota State Prison Industries? Stories of U.S. presidents, beloved movie stars, sinister mobsters, and famous personalities had become main street folklore. Collections at the Minnesota Historical Society provided dozens of menus from the 1850s and bold place mats from the 1950s, along with restaurant ware and endless, fascinating images from the photo archives.

Cup and saucer, Hotel Lowry, St. Paul

Eleanor Ostman joined us in searching for recipes and added her valuable insights on historic food and dining. And just when we thought our search over, Barbara Flanagan wrote in her Minneapolis *Star Tribune* newspaper column that we were looking for pictures and stories of readers' favorite old restaurants. Within hours we were inundated with a new flood of calls as eager Minnesotans related anecdotes about adored eateries.

We now had information on thousands of dining places in every conceivable style located throughout Minnesota. The earliest documentation began shortly after statehood in 1858, and we decided that the book must end about a century later, in the 1960s. Then began the humbling task of selecting images from that vast period in Minnesota's history.

Many eating places had disappeared, escaped our search, or lacked photographic documentation. For example, in turn-of-the-century Minneapolis, the popular Regan Brothers Restaurant and Bakery served 1,500 people each day. Then the restaurant burned to the ground and only a few photos of the bakery survived. Space was not sufficient to include the immense number of early taverns, which would fill a book of their own. With room for only several hundred pictures, we selected those we thought best represented the vast range of dining opportunities through the years and throughout the state and sadly packed away the rest—perhaps another day, perhaps another book.

Minnesota restaurants are powerfully linked, historically and emotionally, to their people and their towns. Food represents happiness, prosperity, celebration—all shared with family and friends. Our favorite memories are often associated with those special times when we dine out. The poignant history that unfolded before us stirred our imaginations, melted our hearts, and whetted our appetites—as we hope it will yours.

ELEANOR OSTMAN *on food and recipes*

"**S**ure," I said when Kathy asked me to participate in this book project, but realization soon surfaced that the recipes she wanted likely didn't exist, especially from the oldest hotels and dining salons. We were seeking specifics from eateries defunct for decades, even a century or more, and most of them hadn't had formal formulas in the first place. The oldest menus listed fanciful, elaborate dishes that were likely loosely interpreted by the kitchen masters, based on their own cooking experience and rudimentary cookery books. What they left us as a record were tattered, spotted, handwritten notes—or, more often, nothing.

New York Building Cafe, Sixth and Minnesota, St. Paul

I checked historical cookbooks to concoct directions for such pioneer mainstays as Indian Pudding. Is my version an exact match to the dessert mentioned on earliest menus? No guarantee, but it's close enough. And who's left to argue the precise proportions of molasses or cornmeal?

Amazingly, most of the recipes in this book are directly attributable to historic dining establishments. We found some in old cookbooks such as a binder of Minneapolis restaurant specialities collected post–World War II by Minnegasco. Others were unearthed in historical society records. But mostly we asked around. It was amazing what our contacts remembered and were willing to share. From my three decades as a food writer, I recollected recipes I'd gathered for newspaper stories; they were recycled into this new project. Sometimes my informants would only describe a collection of ingredients, and I had to reconstruct specifics that would function in the modern kitchen—in proportions for the average family. I fried onion rings and stirred batches of borscht until they matched flavor memories.

Recipes you'll see on the following pages don't even come close to being trendy—although in their time, they were probably the latest rage. They are the foods of our forebears, the comfort fare, the fondly remembered dishes of meals eaten long ago. Most of the restaurants that served them are gone, but these classics survive to recapture a taste of Minnesota's dining history.

Teapot, West Hotel, Minneapolis

LINDA KOUTSKY *on restaurant collectibles*

Restaurateurs have long appreciated the power of marketing and the value of good design. It isn't always enough to simply serve delicious food. Entire industries have grown up to appeal to the *visual* palates of diners. Interior designers envision attractive environments while graphic designers create distinctive logos and eye-catching graphics for menus, advertisements, and matchbooks. Early bills of fare were printed on papers of every color, had unusual folds, and often were tinted by hand. They were treasured souvenirs for many. Hotelier Elmore Lowell traveled throughout the state and saved his menus, now in the collections of the Washington County Historical Society. These fragile, fringed silk menus are hand-painted, tied with dainty bows, and promote entrées we don't even recognize today. Mid-twentieth-century menus lightened up a bit with colorful illustrations, a sense of humor, and an occasional celebrity.

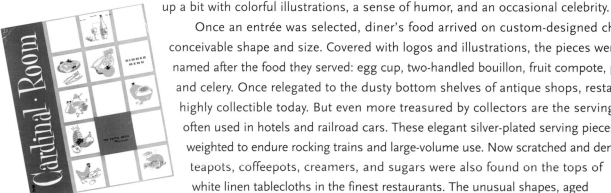

Menu, Cardinal Room, Curtis Hotel

Once an entrée was selected, diner's food arrived on custom-designed china in every conceivable shape and size. Covered with logos and illustrations, the pieces were frequently named after the food they served: egg cup, two-handled bouillon, fruit compote, pickle, sherbet, and celery. Once relegated to the dusty bottom shelves of antique shops, restaurant ware is highly collectible today. But even more treasured by collectors are the serving pieces most often used in hotels and railroad cars. These elegant silver-plated serving pieces were heavily weighted to endure rocking trains and large-volume use. Now scratched and dented, these teapots, coffeepots, creamers, and sugars were also found on the tops of white linen tablecloths in the finest restaurants. The unusual shapes, aged patina, deeply engraved logos, and crossover appeal to railroad collectors make these hard-to-find serving pieces sought-after and expensive.

Today the ephemeral nature of restaurant memorabilia appeals to collectors as they search for enticing graphics, attractive and nostalgic serving pieces, and forgotten dining memories. May the artifacts in this book stir *your* desire to collect!

ood food was the main reason people ate out, but stimulating interior design and architecture attracted diners as well. Although pioneers found bare-bones dining rooms with plaster walls, plank floors, and a few scattered windows, environments changed quickly after Minnesota became a state. As towns grew along river routes, Mississippi riverboats steamed in, their holds filled with exotic foods. Fluted columns animated the upper decks and filigree brackets surrounded fanciful on-board cafés. By the 1890s, luxurious Pullman dining cars arrived in the Midwest, their elegant interiors gleaming with stained glass, polished mahogany, and shiny brass, the perfect setting for gourmet meals.

Imperial Garden, Leamington Hotel, Minneapolis

Diners now ate in style. Lavish Victorian taste transformed restaurants into palaces of visual clutter. Old-world memories were re-created in cafés with European decorations or with intricate Asian fretwork. Architecturally imposing hotels boasted of banquet rooms in classically inspired French and Beaux Arts fashion with stately carved columns and coffered ceilings. And just for fun, light and airy soda fountains provided contrasts in scale and ambiance with enormous log dining halls at piney resorts. Although Art Nouveau structures were rarely seen in the Midwest, the beautiful fluid lines of this style graced a fortunate few restaurant façades in some major cities.

After the turn of the century, popular dining environments were fashioned in the Arts and Crafts or Prairie School Style of midwestern architect Frank Lloyd Wright. It was the perfect combination of comfortable furnishings, natural materials, and artful workmanship. Customers enthusiastically embraced the warm and inviting dining environments locally as well as nationally.

The introduction of Art Deco at the 1928 Paris Exhibition influenced dining environments for decades to come. The sprightly forms of zigzags and faceted mirrors were considered "flashy" in the Midwest, yet stunning examples could be seen in a few stoic buildings in Minnesota. Art Deco shapes later evolved into aerodynamic forms of speed and streamlining, and nearly every Minnesota town boasted of a Streamline Moderne café. With rounded walls, shiny metal and glass surfaces, chrome and vinyl seating, and jazzy jukeboxes, these cafés welcomed hordes of customers who knew it was cool to dine modern.

Donaldson's Tea Rooms, Minneapolis

By the 1950s, many beautiful old restaurant façades disappeared behind International Style's lackluster philosophy of "less is more." Restaurants that dared to embellish their spaces did so with helter-skelter modernistic and futuristic images. Automobiles and fast-food design dominated the era, and by the 1960s, the appetite for the striking surroundings of the past was gone. Still, people ate out in increasing numbers, and the hunger for appealing architecture and design would return.

Picture postcards, first published in the late nineteenth century, provide fascinating records of the evolving architecture and design of restaurants. When Minnesotans traveled, visited relatives, or ate out, they sent postcards back to their families or pasted them on pages in postcard albums to show their friends. Since cameras were not common, shopkeepers provided picture postcards of their establishments, and these became unique chronicles of the times. Postcard collecting is a rapidly growing hobby, providing rare original scenes, picturesque views, and artful designs for a wide variety of interests.

Join us for a fascinating trip through our state's rich dining history. Our journey of a hundred years will pause along the way for tastes of pioneer meals and lavish feasts, glimpses of collectible dinnerware and spirited graphics, and views of beautiful interiors and eye-catching architecture. Discover the state's history as it appeared on our restaurant tables.

Please be seated.

Charlie's Cafe Exceptionale, 701 Fourth Avenue South, Minneapolis, 1950s

Charlie's Cafe Exceptionale staff fills the main stairway. Cheers!

CHAPTER ONE

Restaurants

Beginning in the sixteenth century, a rich, restorative soup called *restaurant* was sold throughout France. Touted as a remedy for stomachaches and other ailments, this delicious beef bouillon was served at long communal tables, and strict guidelines were applied to its preparation. In 1765 a Parisian named Boulanger began selling a soup that did not conform to the official recipe, but he claimed it had identical health benefits and insisted on calling it *restaurant*. His competitors sued. Boulanger won, and he promptly added more healthful soups to his offerings. His *traiteur*—a cook shop that sold only take-out food—became the rage of Paris. Others quickly copied his winning formula, and the variety of soups expanded. When non-soup items began to appear on the menu, *restaurant* as a soup was replaced with "restaurant" as a place. Customers ordered from handwritten menus and were served at small individual tables. The restaurant as we know it was born.

A continent away, in 1850s territorial Minnesota, the first eating places were located in boarding houses or taverns furnished with big communal tables. Diners passed around platters piled high with meat and potatoes. By the late 1800s, the famous "boarding house reach" gave way to more refined manners in establishments deserving of the name "restaurant." Lumbering, mining, and railroad industries prospered, and Minnesota milling became world famous. As settlers and workers poured into the region, new and more sophisticated customers found their way to the state's restaurant tables.

During the century's final decade, known as the Gay Nineties, the economy of the Upper Midwest flourished and patrons sampled a variety of dining styles. While on the East and West Coasts lavish restaurants were becoming commonplace, dining in the Midwest, though stylish, was understated and perhaps a bit homey. Even so, exotic new foods arrived from other parts of the country and from all over the world. Minnesotans considered their state to be the land of milk and honey.

Then, in rapid succession, came World War I, Prohibition, the Great Depression, years of drought, and World War II. These events had nearly catastrophic effects on many industries, including restaurants, which scrambled to revise menus and recipes, adjusting for changes dictated by food shortages and economizing diners. While some restaurants could not overcome these challenges, many survived to welcome a new generation of customers.

Of course there were good times, too: the Roaring Twenties, energetic national patriotism, women's right to vote. People continued to eat out. Minnesota restaurants improvised and grew stronger in the '30s and '40s, and the fabulous '50s swept in with stunning new developments in food preparation, equipment, and recipes. The price of a meal followed the nation's inflation rate: a complete roast beef dinner in 1880 cost about 35¢, in 1900 under 60¢, by 1920 almost $1.00, in 1940 roughly $1.50, and by 1960 around $5.00. Restaurant design and architecture evolved from the purely practical to the richly embellished, and interiors were often themed for amusement. Dining out would be fun again!

RESTAURANT PIONEERS

City Restaurant, Wadena, 1879

Chicago Restaurant, Stillwater, 1881

Iona Restaurant, Iona, 1880s

Working men looking for supper found a variety of choices inside local eateries. The Iona Restaurant specialized in lunches at all hours and offered a full line of soft drinks, confections, fruits, vegetables, French bread, nuts, cigars, tobacco, and postcards. And the proprietor was a licensed auctioneer.

Restaurant and post office, Chandler, 1902

While the food was healthy and hearty, it was not something hungry men wrote home about—despite this post office's convenient location inside the restaurant.

hroughout the mid-1800s Minnesota's newborn cities were building their main streets. Local eateries occupied simple wooden buildings, often located on dirt streets with boardwalks. Dining rooms were utilitarian in the extreme, tables and chairs functional at best. Pork and chicken anchored most meals, served with a limited variety of seasonal fruits and vegetables, but there were always second and third helpings on the potatoes and beans—and the beer.

Deutche's, Willmar, 1880s

Family members operated many early restaurants, and it was a long day from sunrise breakfasts to after-dark suppers. Wood-fired ovens roasted meats and potatoes or baked breads and Indian puddings. Pies were plentiful thanks to bountiful native fruits, including wild cranberries, strawberries, blackberries, gooseberries, plums, raspberries, crab apples, and blueberries.

The Grill, First Avenue and Marquette, Minneapolis, 1898

Mobile customers touring by bicycle were enticed inside by the fanciful awning, hand-lettered signage, and menu listings on this storefront.

"A man seldom thinks with more earnestness of anything than he does of his dinner."
SAMUEL JOHNSON

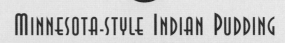

MINNESOTA-STYLE INDIAN PUDDING

On Minnesota's frontier, dessert was prized but ingredients were often limited. Most kitchens had milk, molasses, and cornmeal to make Indian pudding, a concept borrowed from Native Americans.

1 quart milk

1 cup sugar

1 teaspoon salt

1 teaspoon cinnamon

1 teaspoon ginger

1 cup cornmeal (yellow or white)

1 cup black molasses

2 eggs

In a large pan, bring milk to a slow simmer. Add dry ingredients gradually, stirring constantly. In a bowl, beat molasses with eggs. Add slowly to hot milk mixture. Continue to stir over medium heat until thickened. Pour mixture into a buttered casserole or baking pan. Cover. Bake in a 250-degree oven for 3 hours. The molasses should create its own layer if the pudding isn't stirred during baking. Serve with cream or ice cream. Makes 6 to 8 servings.

estaurant fare gradually improved, and customers sampled venison, elk, bear, pheasant, duck, prairie chicken, and wild turkey supplied by area hunters. In addition to this bounty, more than 150 varieties of fish could be found in the upper waters of the Mississippi River.

Kitchen, Oscar Sarin's Restaurant, Hibbing, 1905

Water for cooking and washing was hauled in from outdoor pumps. With only icehouse refrigeration available, meat and produce were brought in fresh and served within a day or two.

THE GOLDEN AGE

ictorians called the 1890s the Golden Age, and Minnesota's population increased as local industries prospered. Trains steamed in with barrels of iced oysters from New York, lobster from Maine, clams from Little Neck, and crab from Washington. Oranges arrived from Florida, grapefruit from Texas, potatoes from Idaho, lemons from California, and onions from Bermuda. Riverboats from the south transported Louisiana shrimp, New Orleans oysters, and fresh produce from farms located along riverbanks.

Sugar consumption grew to a whopping sixty-five pounds per person per year. Chocolates, pies, and cakes along with sweetened coffee and tea provided a sugary start for the new century. It was chic to be plump— President Taft weighed a hefty three hundred pounds—and America was bountiful with newfound confidence, prosperity, and wealth.

DelMonico's, Hibbing, 1890s

Throughout most of the 1800s, ladies did not eat at restaurants with men, but by the turn of the century, women began dining out together. Restaurants enthusiastically accommodated them by adjusting their menus to lighter fare and designing feminine-friendly environments. DelMonico's in Hibbing surrendered its dining room to the vivacious new customers above, who may have been planning their votes for a future president. The most famous restaurant at the turn of the century was Delmonico's in New York City, and owners of cafés that shared this name capitalized on a perceived connection to the notable eatery.

Keystone Restaurant, Rochester, 1898

Restaurants became landmarks in midwestern towns. Diners were attracted to the stoic buildings with decorative columns, graceful arched windows, and intricate brickwork.

Berg's Bakery and Restaurant, Red Wing, 1890s

Bakeries were often located alongside restaurants, and aromas wafting from their hot ovens tempted passers-by. Yeasty breads, sweet cakes, and flaky pastries appeared by the baker's dozen within buildings of solid American-Gothic or fussy Victorian style. Large awnings kept everyone cool.

Clam fishing on the Mississippi River, 1904

The upper Mississippi River was home to one of the most diverse mollusk populations in the world, yielding tons of mussels and clams. Some were shipped to restaurants and grocers, but most went to riverside button factories, and Mississippi River pearl buttons became world famous.

Along the East Coast, oyster palaces boomed, and they featured clams, mussels, and oysters not only as appetizers but as meals in themselves. During this "decade of the oyster," midwestern cooks prepared them steamed or fried or in endless varieties of sauces, stews, and chowders. The all-American oysters Rockefeller, clams casino, lobster à la Newburg, and shrimp scampi were created during this period. The food was sumptuous, the dining rooms lavish, and the lifestyle extravagant: Mark Twain called it the Gilded Age.

Menu, Delmonico Cafe, Duluth, 1907

The Delmonico Cafe's huge menu offered an astonishing variety of clam and oyster preparations. And if oysters were not a favorite dish, menu browsers could contemplate nine additional pages of heartland flavors. One can only imagine the size of the kitchen and the skill of the chef required to produce all the items on this extensive menu—in Duluth in 1907.

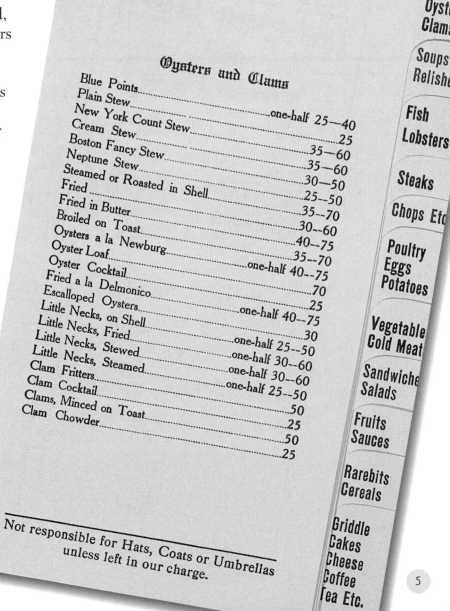

Commutation Tickets, $5.00 for $4.50

Oysters
Clams

Soups
Relishes

Fish
Lobsters

Steaks

Chops Etc

Poultry
Eggs
Potatoes

Vegetables
Cold Meat

Sandwiches
Salads

Fruits
Sauces

Rarebits
Cereals

Griddle
Cakes
Cheese
Coffee
Tea Etc.

Oysters and Clams

Blue Points	
Plain Stew	one-half 25—40
New York Count Stew	.25
Cream Stew	35—60
Boston Fancy Stew	35—60
Neptune Stew	30—50
Steamed or Roasted in Shell	25—50
Fried	35—70
Fried in Butter	30—60
Broiled on Toast	40—75
Oysters a la Newburg	35—70
Oyster Loaf	one-half 40—75
Oyster Cocktail	.70
Fried a la Delmonico	.25
Escalloped Oysters	one-half 40—75
Little Necks, on Shell	.30
Little Necks, Fried	one-half 25—50
Little Necks, Stewed	one-half 30—60
Little Necks, Steamed	one-half 30—60
Clam Fritters	one-half 25—50
Clam Cocktail	.50
Clams, Minced on Toast	.25
Clam Chowder	.50
	.25

Not responsible for Hats, Coats or Umbrellas unless left in our charge.

5

PROHIBITION

lthough the twentieth century rang in with great optimism, World War I brought a halt to lavish dining, and Prohibition ended public drinking. Many restaurants barely survived both events, and Americans tightened their belts. The 1914 war effort restricted food products such as butter and meat, and sugar bowls disappeared from restaurant tables. In 1919 Minnesota's senator Andrew Volstead introduced legislation forbidding the sale of alcoholic beverages, leading to the eighteenth constitutional amendment. While some of the gaiety melted away, the Roaring Twenties arrived in the Midwest with a clandestine new style of dining out—the speakeasy.

"Once, during Prohibition, I was forced to live for days on nothing but food and water."
W. C. FIELDS

Hollyhocks Inn, 1590 South Mississippi River Boulevard, St. Paul, 1920s

The Hollyhocks Inn was an elegant speakeasy with a peephole in the front door. Private dining areas occupied the first floor, but favored patrons could pass by the tuxedoed guard at the main stairway to gamble and sip a drink or two upstairs. The infamous St. Paul gangsters of the 1920s and '30s made Hollyhocks the place to be seen, and, sensing glamorous and risqué adventure, St. Paul's social set followed them there. In case of a raid, customers could scramble to the secret passageway leading from the third floor to the basement.

Bergsing Café, 24 North Sixth Street, Minneapolis, 1920s

Described as a "gentle speakeasy," the Bergsing Café, Buffet, and Restaurant provided libations to diners who had the proper connections. Patrons not in the know were more than satisfied with the home cooking, great soups, outstanding pot roasts, and nearly endless desserts. To no one's surprise, the place was usually packed. Cashiers behind the teller's cage not only collected for meals; they also cashed paychecks and provided simple banking services.

DINNER — $1.00

Chicken Giblet Noodle Creole or Pea Soup
Jellied Cold Consomme or Marinate Herring
Radishes   Young Onions

Fried Filet Pike, Tartar
Steamed Smoked Alaska Cod
Fried Large Fresh Mountain Trout
Reindeer Steak or Chops, Jelly
Chicken Fricassee, Steamed Rice
Two Breaded Veal Chops
Cold Meat, Potato Salad
Roast Prime Ribs of Beef au Jus
Broiled Large Squab on Toast, Bacon, Jelly
Boiled Ham Shank, New Cabbage or
New Spinach
German Pot Roast, Potato Pancakes
Creamed Asparagus
Baked, Mashed, Au Gratin, Hashed Brown
or French Fried Potatoes

New Cabbage Salad

Any 15c Pie   Apple Strudel
Ice Cream and Cake   Strawberry Shortcake

Menu, Bergsing Café, 1920s

Columbia Restaurant, 225 Hennepin Avenue, Minneapolis, 1920s

SOUPS
Pea Soup (Served with Dinner)
FISH
Lutefisk with Cream Gravy or Drawn Butter ......
Baked Northern Pike, Egg Sauce ....
Half Dozen Oyster Stew ....
Half Dozen Fried Oysters ....
Fried Pike (to order) ....
Boiled Salt Mackerel ....
Pickled Herring (Swedish Style) ....
Imported Norway Herring (Any Style) ....
ENTREES
SPECIAL TO-DAY:— Mutton Chop on Toast with
   Green Peas
Spareribs and Sauerkraut ....
Lamb Stew with Green Peas ....
Chicken Giblets with Rice ....
Baked Meat Loaf, Green Peas ....
Little Pig Sausage, Mashed Potatoes and Gravy ...
Pickled Pig's Feet ....
Pork and Beans ....

Menu, Columbia Restaurant, 1928
Cook Erick Johnson

Located where Nicollet and Hennepin Avenues merge, the Columbia made good use of both street addresses. Passengers from the nearby Great Northern Depot could order their first meal in town, and cook Erick Johnson, fresh from Sweden, felt right at home with Scandinavian fish on the menu. The oldest restaurant in the Gateway District was open twenty-four hours a day for travelers and hometown diners alike. The family-owned eatery promoted its quality food, clean dining room and basement, and pressed linen napkins.

ew "processed" foods began sweeping the country in the form of Kellogg's, Quaker, C. W. Post, and Campbell's brands. Aunt Jemima's became a familiar face, and Oreo cookies rolled out in cellophane packages. One-dish recipes, savory stews, hearty soups, and cheese and macaroni casseroles provided flavorful meals. People still ate out, often on special occasions, and many restaurants—particularly those that were family-oriented or already had non-drinking customers—survived into the middle of the century and beyond.

MENU
GRIDDLE SPECIALTIES
(300) Butter Cakes 10
(370-450) GRIDDLE CAKES WITH BUTTER AND SYRUP.. 15
   (Wheat, Buckwheat or Virginia Cornmeal)
(170-250) Toast, Dry or Buttered 10
(289) Milk Toast 20
BEVERAGES
(85) Coffee .... 10 | (108) Malted Milk 10
(70) Postum .... 10 | (180) Milk, per glass... 10
(60) Cream, Five Cents per ounce (1, 2, 4 or 7 oz. portions)
(18) Individual Pot of Tea 10
(150) Hot Chocolate, with whipped cream.... 15
Goose Liver Sausage Sandwich 20
Sandwiches
(415) Minced Ham..... 15 | (270) Oyster 20
(275) Sliced Ham...... 20 | (275) Fried Egg ... 15
(260) Roast Beef ...... 20 | (240) Sliced Chicken.. 3
(275) Corned Beef ..... 20 | (620) Club ....
OYSTERS
(85) Fried Oysters ....
(325) Oyster Stew ....
(110) Broiled Oysters .... *+ Potatoe Salad*
Fried Oysters SPECIALS
(320) FRESH COUNTRY SAUSAGE...................
(310) Corned Beef Hash 25
(360) Liver and Bacon with Potatoes............. 25
(560) Bacon, Broiled 25
   FRIED OR BROILED HAM....................... 30
(625) Fresh Country Sausage, Apple and Griddle Cakes.. 30
(440) Broiled Lamb Chop 25
(165) Two Eggs, Boiled, Fried or Poached....... 30
(310) Hamburger Steak 30
(180) PLAIN OMELET 25
(180) Scrambled Eggs 30
   Fresh Country Sausage with Buckwheat Cakes.. 35

Childs

ACCORDING TO CARLYLE—

The biggest gold nugget ever found was not half as useful to the world as one good mealy potato.

Now, the mealiness which makes the potato more useful than a nugget of gold is solely a matter of proper cooking.

So, quite naturally, prospecting for deliciously mealy potatoes leads to CHILDS, the house of good cookery.

Potatoes served in golden French fried nuggets in mounds of fluffy whiteness, or in the good old home fried style.

Menu, Childs, 414 Nicollet Avenue,
Minneapolis

Childs restaurants promoted the potato's virtues on their menu cover, and daily specials and price changes were handwritten inside. The menu shows "the approximate calories as computed by an expert in nutrition," but today's calorie counters may question the numbers at left. Childs in New York City was one of the first "chain" dining concepts, and the Minneapolis restaurant was one of many located throughout the country.

CARLING'S

29 WEST FIFTH STREET, ST. PAUL

Meals were served on heavy china plates printed with a stag head and Carling's motto, *tout droit,* "straight ahead." Dinners started with salads doused in savory dressings, continued with meats seasoned by French sauces and vegetables bathed in herb butters, and ended with a finale of blazing desserts served from rolling carts.

Carling's, 1900s

Banquet room, Carling's

Red Cross meeting at the former Carling's, 1917

Red Cross workers temporarily replaced dining tables with sewing machines and work surfaces to prepare supplies for World War I.

Carling's was a St. Paul landmark for nearly forty years. Its exterior featured designs rarely seen in Minnesota architecture: Art Nouveau–style windows of colored glass supported by iron in curvilinear lines and organic contours. Patrons passed under a wrought metal and glass awning to enter dining rooms resplendent with gilded ceilings, embroidered window valances, and classical moldings. Equal to the elegant surroundings, seating was provided on velvet chairs at tables set with starched linens, embroidered napkins, custom china, and shimmering silver.

SCHIEK'S CAFE

45 SOUTH THIRD STREET, MINNEAPOLIS

Fred Schiek began his business in 1862, opening Schiek's Cafe in Minneapolis in 1887. The café operated in various locations and, later, under other owners for more than one hundred years. Sumptuous Victorian interiors sparkled with beveled glass, carved fretwork, intricate tile, and ornate plasterwork. Dark and moody by design, the fanciful environment enveloped diners while they contemplated an extraordinary dinner menu or the equally long and diverse list of after-theater and midnight-snack offerings. Originally a German restaurant, Schiek's first served hearty sauerbraten, potato pancakes, and sauerkraut accompanied by lively German music. In later years, diners delighted in nightly entertainment by the famous Schiek's Sextet and ordered the house seafood specialties. Schiek's hosted local and national celebrities throughout its illustrious life, and vivacious Minneapolis newspaper columnist Barbara Flanagan remembers interviewing notorious actor George Jessel there: "He only wanted to chase me around the table."

There were two entrances to Schiek's: one opening onto the main barroom, and one at the side for ladies only. Innocent feminine eyes viewed a long, dark corridor leading to the rear of the restaurant, protecting them from glimpsing the unseemly drinking taking place at the front.

SCHIEK'S RICE PUDDING

After a robust meal at Schiek's, a soothing rice pudding was the favorite of many customers. Some skipped the entrée and simply ordered this dessert.

6 eggs, beaten

1/2 teaspoon cinnamon

1/2 teaspoon nutmeg

1/2 teaspoon salt

1 teaspoon vanilla

4 tablespoons butter, melted, divided

1 cup sugar, divided

1 quart whole milk, heated

2 cups cooked rice

1 cup raisins plumped in hot water, then drained

Combine the beaten eggs, cinnamon, nutmeg, salt, vanilla, 2 tablespoons melted butter, and 1/2 cup sugar in a large bowl. Gradually add the hot milk. Combine the rice, raisins, and remaining sugar and butter in a well-greased 9x9-inch baking pan or casserole. Pour the egg mixture over the rice mixture. Set the pan or casserole in a larger pan; add hot water halfway to the depth of the pudding pan. Bake in a 325-degree oven for about 1 hour or until a knife inserted in the center of the pudding comes out clean. Serve warm with a dollop of whipped cream. Makes 4 generous servings.

This handwritten menu from 1899 lists many of the items served throughout Schiek's hundred-year history.

DEPRESSION AND DROUGHT

The sobering Great Depression began with the calamitous decline of the U.S. stock market in October 1929. The crash brought hardship to all American businesses, including restaurants. Then a severe drought hit most of the country in the '30s, and food supplies became scarce. The National Biscuit Company (Nabisco) created mock apple pie—the filling made from Ritz crackers, lemon juice, sugar, and cinnamon—so that people could enjoy pie without using expensive apples. In 1937, in Austin, Minnesota, Hormel Foods invented SPAM luncheon meat, and few kitchens survived without it. One-pot meals such as chili, stew, chicken potpie, and the infamous Minnesota "hot dish" became standard fare on local menus.

The Seville, Rochester, 1930s

A holiday in Spain could be had for the price of a meal as restaurants adjusted their décor to offer depression-era "vacations." As people continued to eat out during the lean times, foods from other cultures became favorites, and restaurant designers were challenged to provide interiors to match.

Restaurant interior, 1930

Patterns, fringes, and braid from the Victorian era were popular decorations; oriental rugs sometimes covered floors, walls, and ceilings. Table lamps with pleated shades and tassels added warm ambiance.

CHILI CON CARNE

Chili was considered spicy in the era when most food was minimally seasoned. Today's cooks might want to add minced garlic to this recipe. If you don't like the texture of kidney beans but want the fiber and flavor they contribute, briefly whirl the beans in a food processor until they are broken up but not puréed; stir them into the chili as directed.

1 pound ground beef

1 large onion, minced

2 ribs celery, minced

2 tablespoons butter or meat drippings

2 cans (15-ounce size) kidney beans

1 can (15 ounces) stewed tomatoes

3 tablespoons chili powder (or more to taste)

3 tablespoons water

1 tablespoon flour

1 teaspoon salt

Brown ground beef, onions, and celery in butter or meat drippings. Add kidney beans with their juices and stewed tomatoes. Bring mixture to a simmer over medium heat. Combine the chili powder, water, flour, and salt. Stir into the chili mixture. Cook over low heat, stirring frequently, for 30 to 40 minutes. Serve hot, with corn bread. Makes 6 to 8 servings.

Winona County cooks

Pancakes, meatloaf, and chili were stretched to the limit in restaurant kitchens. Chili parlors offered inexpensive and nourishing meals for millions of Americans: some said that chili saved more lives than the Red Cross.

Savoring cake and tea, 1925

Warner's Restaurant, Winona, 1950s

Who could miss "EAT" in enormous rooftop letters? Families looking for value found flavorful, inexpensive food in these roadside houses-turned-restaurants.

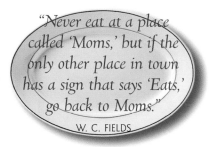

"Never eat at a place called 'Moms,' but if the only other place in town has a sign that says 'Eats,' go back to Moms."
W. C. FIELDS

COUNTRY ARCHITECTURE

Madison Inn, Sandstone, 1920s

Country-style architecture and inexpensive meals appealed to diners looking for made-from-scratch cooking.

Hazel's Steak House, Albert Lea, 1940s

A farmhouse style suggested visits to grandma's for comfort food: chicken sizzling in the frying pan, aromatic breads and pies baking in the oven.

Rustic Inn, Two Harbors, 1930s

Midwesterners loved going to the cabin, even if it was just for dinner. Rustic log buildings with breezy porches made a soup-and-sandwich meal special.

FOOD RATIONING

Government rationing during World War II affected the availability of many foods. Americans were restricted to twenty-eight ounces of meat per week (which now seems like a lot) and limited amounts of sugar, butter, milk, eggs, and coffee. To stay profitable, restaurant owners became more involved by greeting customers, watching over meals coming from the kitchen, and keeping their dining rooms interesting and up-to-date. They provided personal attention and friendly service, and patrons became repeat customers.

When Minnesotan James T. Williams introduced the world to quick-cooking macaroni in 1912, his "macaroni magic" was ready in a speedy seven minutes compared to the standard thirty minutes. For decades, his Minneapolis Creamette plant produced timesaving, tender, delicious, elbow-shaped macaroni for the entire nation.

"As a child my family's menu consisted of two choices: take it or leave it."
BUDDY HACKETT

The Parker House, Mendota, 1940s

Alice and Bill Parker opened the Parker House in 1927 when a new bridge over the Minnesota River linked Mendota and the Twin Cities. Soldiers walked across from Fort Snelling, and regulars played dice games and stuffed their nickels into slot machines in the festive dining room with its bright chair covers, zigzag tile floor, and chrome bar stools. New owners continue to serve visitors in this historic Mendota location today.

A worker wheels a cart into the Kraft Cheese Company caves, where the cheeses join other varieties curing on long racks extending deep into the old sandstone caves. The University of Minnesota used the cavernous spaces for ripening blue cheese, but for nearly one hundred years, beginning in the 1880s, mushrooms grew in most of them, and the gorge near downtown St. Paul was known as "Mushroom Valley."

MAGNIFICENT MACARONI AND CHEESE

Say cheese! Although rationed, cheese was a main ingredient in many restaurant dishes—it made salads snappy, blanketed burgers, and sat browned and crusty atop many a Minnesota "hot dish." Tastiest versions of macaroni and cheese depend not only on Cheddar but also on the assertiveness of mustard. A blend of cheeses makes the dish more interesting; if you prefer more heat, include some pepper cheese in the mix.

1 1/2 cups (6 ounces) elbow macaroni

3 tablespoons butter

4 tablespoons flour

1/2 teaspoon dry mustard (or more to taste)

1/2 teaspoon salt

1/4 to 1/2 teaspoon freshly ground pepper

3 cups milk

3/4 teaspoon Worcestershire sauce

1 small onion, minced

1 to 2 cloves garlic, minced

8 ounces cheese (sharp Cheddar, or a mixture of cheeses with Cheddar predominating)

1/3 cup bread crumbs

3 tablespoons melted butter

Cook macaroni according to package directions in boiling salted water. Drain; set aside. Meanwhile, in a saucepan, melt butter; blend in flour, mustard, salt, and pepper. Add milk gradually and cook until thickened, stirring constantly. Add Worcestershire sauce, onion, garlic, and cheese; stir until cheese begins to melt. Place half of macaroni in greased casserole. Pour on half of cheese sauce. Repeat layers. Combine bread crumbs with melted butter; sprinkle atop casserole. Bake in a 375-degree oven for 30 to 45 minutes or until mixture bubbles and crumbs are browned. Makes 4 to 6 servings.

The Silver Latch

The Silver Latch, 81 South Tenth Street, Minneapolis, 1940s

Earl W. and Inez H. Norton ran the Silver Latch, and their names on the door guaranteed a warm welcome. At the popular downtown tearoom, fresh walleye pike and Russian salad were dependable crowd-pleasers, and sweets lovers could top off lunch with southern pecan pie.

The Stage Coach
Largest Collection Of Historic Arms In The Midwest
On Highway 101 - Midway Between
Shakopee And Savage, Minnesota
STAGE COACH

*The Stage Coach, Highway 101,
midway between Savage and Shakopee, 1950s*

This frontier-style restaurant occupied the site of an early stagecoach stop on the dusty road south from Fort Snelling. Inside was an authentic opera house, and the restaurant showcased historic collections of firearms, antiques, nickelodeons, and coaches. Western hospitality and pioneer food could be found here, fifteen ridin' miles from the Cities.

Ranchburgers and checkered oilcloth pleased friends in 1950

The RANCH HOUSE
Food & Environment Dedicated To You
79th & Lyndale
So. on U. S. Highway 65
MINNEAPOLIS, MINNESOTA
Ranch House

The Ranch House, Seventy-ninth and Lyndale, Minneapolis, 1950s

Surrounded by down-home ranch-house architecture, would-be cowboys chowed down in western-style rooms of post-and-beam construction. This long-occupied building took on many faces over the decades but always remained true to its western heritage.

𝓕ood rationing ended after the war, and populations and incomes grew nationwide. Steaks and chops were back on the menu, and barbecued ribs were featured in "real western atmospheres." Customers sought amusement and entertainment while they ate, and come-and-get-it dining galloped across Minnesota.

THE BUCKHORN

LONG LAKE

The Buckhorn endeared itself to children and adults alike. Its popular pioneer style attracted customers from all over the state. Built in 1931 on the site of owner Kip Hale's grandmother's barn, it was an all-western place. Bowling alleys were added in the 1940s and the impressive collection of trophy heads and prized guns grew steadily as the Buckhorn's fame spread throughout the Midwest.

The Buckhorn, 1940s

REG. U.S. PAT. OFF.

The specialty of the house, "Chicken in the Rough" was one of the earliest restaurant franchises. The proprietary method of cooking chicken, and its irresistible aroma, lured fans back to the Buckhorn again and again.

Chicken-in-the Rough
(Copyrighted)
Served without Silverware
Salad
One-Half Fried Chicken
Gobs of Shoe String Potatoes
or Hash Brown Potatoes
Buttered Hot Rolls — Beverage
Jug-O-Honey
$1.50

THE COVERED WAGON

320 WABASHA STREET, ST. PAUL
110 SOUTH FOURTH STREET, MINNEAPOLIS

The interiors of the Covered Wagon restaurants in St. Paul and Minneapolis were like a wagon train heading for the Oregon Trail. Diners could teeter at a table with a Conestoga cover, tap their toes to the Cow Hands Band, and chow down on prairieland delicacies—mallard duck, ring-necked pheasant, or partridge. Cowpokes from diverse industries, including newspapermen, telephone operators, General Mills office workers, servicemen, shoppers, policemen, and city hall staffers, packed the dining rooms from breakfast until the wee hours.

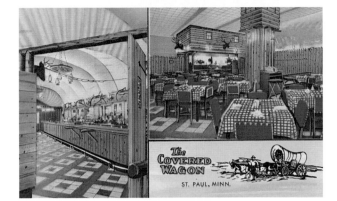

Waitresses in pioneer uniforms on closing day, 1957

Covered Wagon, Minneapolis, 1930s

Steaks ruled the ranch on this menu, but those with adventurous appetites could also find genuine Mexican chili con carne, Welsh rarebit, French onion soup, Maine lobster, Louisiana jumbo shrimp, New York oysters—and Betty Crocker Soups. The amazing chuckwagon menu featured two hundred items.

For thirsty ranch hands, the drink menu listed hundreds of cocktails, fancy drinks, collinses, rickeys, fizzes, sours, flips, eggnogs, hot toddies, wines, champagnes, beers, ales, stouts, cordials, and liqueurs.

FOOD MENU

PROPERLY AGED

WHEN YOU THINK OF GOOD STEAKS GET IN THE COVERED WAGON

Soup Tomato Cocktail Sea Food Cocktail Chicken Livers
Assorted Relish
Covered Wagon Porterhouse Steak
Idaho French Fried, Shoestring or Baked Potatoes
Assorted Breads   Salad
Sherbet or Ice Cream
Coffee
$4.25

Soup Tomato Cocktail Sea Food Cocktail Chicken Livers
Assorted Relish
Covered Wagon T-Bone Steak
Idaho French Fried, Shoestring or Baked Potatoes
Assorted Breads   Salad
Sherbet or Ice Cream
Coffee
$4.00

Special French Fried Bermuda Onions **50c**

Tomato Cocktail Sea Food Cocktail Soup Chicken Livers
Assorted Relish
Covered Wagon Filet Mignon Steak
(Beef Tenderloin)
Idaho French Fried, Shoestring or Baked Potatoes
Assorted Breads   Salad
Sherbet or Ice Cream
Coffee
$3.00

Fresh Mushrooms With Steak Orders **75c**

Tomato Cocktail Sea Food Cocktail Chicken Livers
Assorted Relish
Covered Wagon Sirloin Steak
Idaho French Fried, Shoestring or Baked Potatoes
Sherbet or Ice Cream   Salad
Assorted Breads Coffee
$3.00

Special Western Combination Salad **75c**
(with FRENCH or THOUSAND ISLAND DRESSING)

Tomato Cocktail Sea Food Cocktail Soup Chicken Livers
Assorted Relish
Covered Wagon Blue Ribbon Club Steak
Idaho French Fried, Shoestring or Baked Potatoes
Assorted Breads   Salad
Sherbet or Ice Cream Coffee
$2.50

STEAKS and CHUCK WAGON SPECIALS

WHY OUR STEAKS ARE OUTSTANDING

Our steaks are personally selected by our own specialist, who inspects and accepts only the best young corn-fed beef, after which it is carefully and properly aged. All steaks are from government-graded U. S. Choice Beef.

EVERY

15

SAINT PAUL...WHERE...

Lee's... WHERE GOOD FOOD COMBINES WITH GOOD SERVICE

SIXTH AND ST. PETER STS.
ST. PAUL, MINN.

RECOMMENDED
AAA

Tales from

HOT FISH SHOP
In the shadow of Sugar Loaf Hill
WINONA, MINN.

SALMON

WALL EYED PIKE

LOB

KE TROUT

BROOK TROUT   HALIBUT

Mother's Day dinner
with Dons family
Sun. May 8, 1960

W hile diners waited for their meals, advertising
and promotions appeared on paper place mats
right under their noses. Quotes from owners, customer
endorsements, logos, slogans, and artworks covered
table tents and place mats. From cornball to elegant,
eye-catching illustrations leapt from papers of all
colors, shapes, and sizes surrounded by decorative
borders and curvy edges. Advertising gimmicks aside,
smart mothers turned the place mats over and handed
crayons to the kids.

Criterion
NATIONALLY FAMOUS
RESTAURANT

EDGEWOOD CAFE
and
Motel
"SEVEN MILES SOUTH OF CANNON FALLS"

the grand cafe

Stillwater, Minnesota

FOR RESERVATIONS
CALL STILLWATER, NUMBER 1

Ivan Stigen's
RANCH HOUSE AIR CONDITIONED
Fergus Falls, Minn.
FIVE DINING ROOMS
Special Attention Given To Parties and Banquets

Weber's
SNELLING & LAR

The BUCKHORN
America's Most Unique Cafe
and Amusement Center
Chicken IN THE ROUGH
Kipp Hale - Owner

MARVELOUS
Minne
LAND OF 10

FINEST FOODS
French Pastry Shop
FANCY CAKES
René's Restaurant
ST. PAUL, MINN.

CONVENIENTLY
LOCATED AT
DALE and SELBY
Dale 9601

...TIES, Baked Fresh Shrimp -

REGARDING SPECIAL PARTIES,
LUNCHEONS OR DINNERS
Phone WE 9-8448

Chapma
FINE FO

Edward B. Chapman, Owner
ON HIGHWAY 5 (78th St.) 1 BLOCK WEST OF NORM

BULGING BUFFETS

By the 1950s, a huge boom in the restaurant industry was under way. Interiors were designed for amusement, and food was themed to match. Belt-busting feasts lured diners to smorgasbords, bulging buffets, eye-popping brunches, and juicy carving stations. And, lest we forget, the salad bar was born. This cornucopia was possible because of a major change in restaurant cooking—prepared, prepackaged, and frozen foods. Sauces came ready to heat and potatoes pre-cut, chicken divan popped from freezer to oven to plate, desserts could be whipped up in no time—and it all looked delicious. Buffets held icy bowls of salads and relishes; chafing dishes steamed with beef stroganoff, saucy meatballs, and chicken in mushroom sauce. And customers groaned at the thought of dessert!

Mealey's Restaurant, Faribault, 1950s

Robin Hood Room smorgasbord, Hotel Dyckman, Sixth Street, Minneapolis, 1950s

Jolly Troll, Golden Valley

Soder's, Staples

Gunflint Lodge, Grand Marais

The Bellows, Duluth

Eibner's, New Ulm

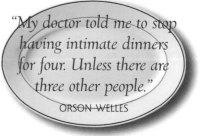

"My doctor told me to stop having intimate dinners for four. Unless there are three other people."
ORSON WELLES

18

R estaurants' popularity and survival during the '50s depended on being contemporary and modern; fickle diners frequently demanded updated designs. Many places offered themed dining experiences, using room-sized graphics and unique elements to attract customers.

Other restaurants hooked their identities to Minnesota waters with names like River's Edge, Edgewater, Lake View, Shore View, Bar Harbor, or Moonlight Bay. If fish was in the name it was certain to appear on the menu.

The Town House, Rochester

Jolly Fisher, Duluth, 1950s

"If it swims, we have it." Fish fanciers needed to look no further for a taste of Lake Superior whitefish or smoked ciscos.

Richard's Roost, Rochester

The Sands, Bemidji, 1950s

While visitors to the Sands took in warm sunny views of Lake Bemidji, larger-than-life murals in the Chalet Room transported diners to a snowy mountain ski scene. Hot soup, anyone?

Fish Fry Lodge, north of Duluth, 1950s

Overlooking rocky Lake Superior, Fish Fry Lodge had easy access to a bounty of Minnesota lake trout, walleye, smelt, smoked pike, catfish, and brook trout.

The President Cafe, 3201 Nicollet Avenue, Minneapolis, 1950s

A central copper fireplace ignited diners' appetites.

FABULOUS FIFTIES

Menu, 620 Club, 620 Hennepin Avenue, Minneapolis

Where "Turkey is King": the 620 Club whipped up meals for legions of fans who clamored for turkey prepared in inspired combinations. Brawny sports figures dined on two-fisted sandwiches next to discerning eaters from the poetry society, and everyone gossiped about recent sightings of popular personalities like Liberace or Phil Silvers.

Menu, Gmitro's, 901 Hennepin Avenue, Minneapolis

Egg dishes were served piping hot in stainless steel sterilized pans—eat them right out of the skillet! Breakfast was crowded, lunch was worse, and dinner could be a long wait at the popular eatery.

"I don't like the turkey, but I like the bread he ate."
ANONYMOUS

DUTRO'S LOBSTER THERMIDOR

Dutro's was well known for its lobster thermidor, a preparation of lobster meat embellished with a sherried cream sauce and tucked back into the shell for broiling.

1 medium to large lobster
(or use 2 lobster tails)

6 mushrooms, diced

4 tablespoons butter

1/2 teaspoon paprika

1/4 cup sherry wine

3 tablespoons white sauce

1 egg yolk

Salt and pepper to taste

3 tablespoons cracker crumbs

2 tablespoons melted butter

Paprika

If using a whole lobster, plunge it into furiously boiling salted water and cook for 20 minutes. Cool in cold water. Clean lobster and remove the meat from the shell, keeping the body shell whole. Dice lobster meat. If using tails, steam or broil the meat until opaque. Remove meat from shells, keeping shells intact. Dice meat.

TO MAKE FILLING: Sauté diced mushrooms in butter. Add lobster meat, paprika, sherry, white sauce, and egg yolk, plus salt and pepper to taste. (To make white sauce, combine 1 tablespoon butter with 1 tablespoon flour in a small saucepan, stirring until flour is thoroughly blended; stir in 1/2 cup milk and cook until the mixture comes to a medium thickness.) Turn mixture in pan until lobster is coated with sauce and the mixture is hot.

TO SERVE: Pile lobster mixture into lobster body or into the two tail shells. Combine cracker crumbs with melted butter; sprinkle over lobster meat. Dust with paprika. Place in a 425-degree oven and heat through. Briefly place under broiler until crumbs are browned. Serves 2.

Earl Dutro prepares a lobster, Dutro's, 828 Hennepin Avenue, Minneapolis, 1935

Dutro's was a Minneapolis hangout for business lunches and a popular spot for dinner, possibly because of the chef's purist approach to fish. The owners considered it a crime to fry fish, preferring to broil or sauté it. Steaming was another palatable option, but never boiling.

The Colonial Inn, St. Louis Park, 1950s

COLONIAL INN PECAN PIE

The Colonial Inn was famous for steaks with onion rings, chicken potpies, and baked goods including this pecan pie produced by their master baker.

4 eggs

1 1/4 cups light corn syrup

1/2 cup sugar

4 tablespoons melted butter

1/4 teaspoon salt

3/4 cup pecan halves

Unbaked 9-inch pastry shell

Beat eggs until light. Stir in corn syrup, sugar, butter, and salt, continuing to beat until well blended. Mix in pecans. Pour mixture into the pie shell. Bake in a 450-degree oven for 10 minutes, then turn heat down to 325 degrees; continue baking for 40 minutes or until firm. Makes 8 servings.

When the Smiths opened their restaurant in 1935, an admiring reviewer wrote that there were no steam tables and all the cooks were women. It was an antique fancier's dream, with a treasure-trove of fine china and silver and collections of old fans, dolls, and Dresden figurines. The French salad dressing was so popular that it was bottled and sold in grocery stores. Though that recipe has since been lost, the building has not: it was moved west on Excelsior Boulevard to become a private house on Long Lake.

McCarthy's, Golden Valley, 1956

LUNCHEONS

Cream of Fresh Asparagus Soup	.15
Fresh Oyster Stew, Half and Half	.90
Blue Point Oysters on Half Shell	.95

Roast Prime Top Round au Jus, Yorkshire Pudding	1.25
Potato Pancakes and Brookfield Sausages, Apple Sauce	1.25
Breaded Veal Cutlet, Creole Sauce	1.25
Broiled Hickory Smoked Pork Chop, Barbecue Sauce	1.35
Calf's Liver Fried in Butter, Bacon or Onions	1.35
Broiled Ham Steak, Glaced Pineapple	1.40
Special Luncheon Steak, Fresh Mushroom Sauce	1.60
Chef's Famous Ground Steak, Grilled Onions	1.00
Broiled Mushrooms and Canadian Bacon	1.50
Roast Prime Ribs of Beef au Jus	1.65
Disjointed Fried Spring Chicken on Toast	1.50
Fried Silver Smelts, Tartar Sauce	1.25
Fried New York Count Oysters, Tartar Sauce	1.50
Fried Wisconsin Frog Legs, Tartar Sauce	1.50
Fresh Brook Trout, Saute Meuniere	1.50
Fried Deep Sea Scallops, Tartar Sauce	1.25
Broiled Swordfish Steak, Lemon Parsley Butter	1.50
Breaded Filet of Sole, Tartar Sauce	1.25
French Fried Jumbo Gulf Shrimps, Tartar Sauce	1.50
Broiled Fresh Chinook Salmon Steak, Parsley Butter	1.50
Filet of Wall-eyed Pike, Fried in Butter, Tartar Sauce	1.00
Casserole of Fresh Lobster and Shrimp a la Newburg	1.00
Steamed Finnan Haddie, Drawn Butter	1.25
Broiled Salt Mackerel, Parsley Butter	
Superior Trout, Parsley Butter	

Whipped Potatoes

Fresh Vegetable

McCarthy's was destination dining in a solid stone building on "beautiful Wayzata Boulevard." Vast lunchtime offerings included prime rib with Yorkshire pudding, fried silver smelts, Chinook salmon steak, broiled salt mackerel, fried Wisconsin frog legs, or steamed finnan haddie. This list was surpassed by the even more voluminous dinner menu. Extra-large martinis and Manhattans teased appetites as customers contemplated the worldly cuisine and listened to soothing music in clubby wrap-around booths.

21

Jax Cafe, 1928 University Avenue Northeast, Minneapolis, 1930s

In 1910, Stanley Kozlak's new store sold hardware, furniture, and funeral services. During the depression years only the funeral service and the second-floor dance hall survived. After Prohibition's end, son Joseph and business partner Jack Dusenka decided to open a bar and restaurant in the building. The sign painter thought a unique spelling would attract customers and suggested the name "Jax." The Grain Belt Brewery down the street offered a "loan" to help launch the business in exchange for advertising on the building—a common arrangement after the days of Prohibition. The area's Polish, Russian, and Slovak immigrants were regular customers from the start; now everyone receives a welcome from Joseph's grandson, Bill Kozlak Jr.

Michael's, Golden Valley, 1960s

Michael's provided the ultimate experience in theme dining. Patrons were seated in the Golden Forest Room, the American Room, or the Caribbean Lounge while trained staff offered guided tours of the sculpture and art collection displayed in the dining rooms. The menu cover featured a full-color reproduction of a woodland painting by Roger Preuss, a nationally known Minnesota wildlife artist.
The table-sized menu boasted of talented chefs and expert kitchen personnel, and diners deliberated over seventy-five entrées and specials. Hunters could bring in their own game or fish for preparation in the restaurant kitchen using Michael's heritage recipes.

JAX BOSTON CLAM CHOWDER

Proprietor Bill Kozlak sampled this clam chowder in Boston and instantly knew that there was nothing like it in Minneapolis. When Jax customers tasted it, they were addicted. "Our restaurant was in a Catholic community and when we started serving Boston clam chowder on Fridays, it was an immediate 'Wow!'" Bill remembers. It is now served daily, a benchmark of their business. Invite a lot of friends over for this restaurant-sized batch.

1/2 pound unsalted butter

4 medium yellow onions, diced

1 stalk (entire head) celery, diced

3 green peppers, diced

3 quarts clam juice

1 pound clam base (available in restaurant supply houses)

2 gallons water

1 tablespoon dried thyme

10 pounds potatoes, cooked and diced

10 pounds frozen chopped clams

2 quarts heavy whipping cream

In a heavy-bottomed stockpot, melt the butter. Add onions, celery, and green peppers; sauté until onions become translucent. Add clam juice, clam base, water, and thyme; bring to a boil. Thicken chowder using a roux (a mixture of 1 cup butter and 1 cup flour cooked together until a golden color). When chowder has thickened, add diced potatoes and clams; simmer for 15 minutes. Heat the cream to a simmer and add it to the chowder. Add more thyme or clam base as needed. Serve hot. Makes 40 servings.

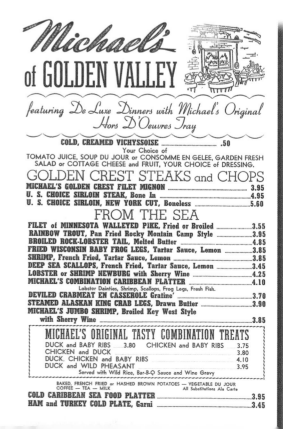

Michael's
of GOLDEN VALLEY

featuring De Luxe Dinners with Michael's Original Hors D'Oeuvres Tray

COLD, CREAMED VICHYSSOISE .... .50
Your Choice of
TOMATO JUICE, SOUP DU JOUR or CONSOMME EN GELEE, GARDEN FRESH
SALAD or COTTAGE CHEESE and FRUIT, YOUR CHOICE of DRESSING.

GOLDEN CREST STEAKS and CHOPS
MICHAEL'S GOLDEN CREST FILET MIGNON 3.95
U. S. CHOICE SIRLOIN STEAK, Bone In 4.95
U. S. CHOICE SIRLOIN, NEW YORK CUT, Boneless 5.60
FROM THE SEA
FILET of MINNESOTA WALLEYED PIKE, Fried or Broiled 3.55
RAINBOW TROUT, Pan Fried Rocky Montain Camp Style 3.95
BROILED ROCK-LOBSTER TAIL, Melted Butter 4.85
FRIED WISCONSIN BABY FROG LEGS, Tartar Sauce, Lemon 3.85
SHRIMP, French Fried, Tartar Sauce, Lemon 4.25
DEEP SEA SCALLOPS, French Fried, Tartar Sauce, Lemon 3.45
LOBSTER or SHRIMP NEWBURG with Sherry Wine 4.10
MICHAEL'S COMBINATION CARIBBEAN PLATTER 4.10
    Lobster Dainties, Shrimp, Scallops, Frog Legs, Fresh Fish.
DEVILED CRABMEAT EN CASSEROLE Gratine' 3.70
STEAMED ALASKAN KING CRAB LEGS, Drawn Butter 3.90
MICHAEL'S JUMBO SHRIMP, Broiled Key West Style
    with Sherry Wine 3.85

MICHAEL'S ORIGINAL TASTY COMBINATION TREATS
DUCK and BABY RIBS   3.80   CHICKEN and BABY RIBS   3.75
CHICKEN and DUCK 3.80
DUCK, CHICKEN and BABY RIBS 4.10
DUCK and WILD PHEASANT 3.95
    Served with Wild Rice, Bar-B-Q Sauce and Wine Gravy

BAKED, FRENCH FRIED or HASHED BROWN POTATOES — VEGETABLE DU JOUR
COFFEE — TEA — MILK   All Substitutions Ala Carte

COLD CARIBBEAN SEA FOOD PLATTER 3.95
HAM and TURKEY COLD PLATE, Garni 3.45

THE FLAME
DULUTH

THE FLAME, 14TH AT LONDON ROAD, DULUTH, MINNESOTA

The SS *Flame* excursion boat, 1960s

On the 1930s a small barbecue stand in Duluth attracted customers with chicken and ribs roasting over an open rotisserie fire in a fanciful glass gazebo. Diners couldn't resist. The Flame grew in size every few years, finally moving in 1946 to the shore of Lake Superior, where it specialized in chicken served on flaming swords. The thoroughly modern building housed stylish dining rooms complete with live dinner music, while the Magic Rooster Bar and Chick Room offered dancing and entertainment. During pleasant weather, the excursion boat SS *Flame* toured the Duluth-Superior harbor so that passengers could view ships from around the world. Restaurant reviewer Duncan Hines listed the Flame in his book *Adventures in Good Eating*, recommending the Lake Superior whitefish, chicken, and ribs.

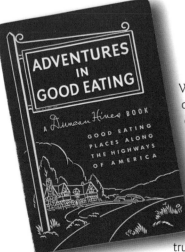

Well-traveled salesman Duncan Hines compiled his list of favorite places to eat in the United States and sent it to friends as his 1935 Christmas card. A year later he published *Adventures in Good Eating*, and by 1939 he was selling 200,000 copies a year in an expanded version. Never accepting free meals or exposing his identity, Hines was trusted by Americans for his honesty and good taste. In 1959 he allowed Procter & Gamble to put the Duncan Hines name on its cake mixes. Other dining guides to regional eateries followed his, including Mobil and Holiday Guides and publications by the American Automobile Association and Diners Club International.

THE FLAME'S BARBECUE SAUCE FOR RIBS

Jimmy Oreck, who ignited the Flame's popularity in Duluth and beyond, was famous for his barbecued ribs. This is the secret family recipe, cut down from the original (which made gallons).

Baby back ribs, the end (or flip) cut off

1 cup Heinz ketchup (or any quality brand)

1/2 cup chopped onion

Generous teaspoon of ground allspice

Tabasco sauce to taste

1 cup water

2 to 3 cloves garlic, minced

1/4 to 1/2 cup apple juice or cider

3 tablespoons brown sugar

1 tablespoon apple cider vinegar

Combine ketchup, onion, allspice, Tabasco, water, garlic, apple juice or cider, brown sugar, and apple vinegar (if barbecuing chicken, substitute Worcestershire sauce for vinegar). Cook over low heat, stirring frequently, until the sauce is thickened. Makes about 2 1/2 cups sauce. Brush sauce on ribs that have been peppered. Barbecue slowly.

OLD ST. PAUL AND DOWNRIVER

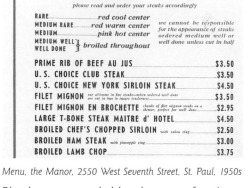

West Seventh Street was a popular destination for dining in St. Paul during the '50s and '60s. Starting at the Mississippi River downtown and ending at the Minnesota River bluffs, it was entertainment central for dining, drinking, and amusement. New bistros, brewhouses, and cafés now nestle among surviving oldies along the eccentric street.

Dinner
CORN FED STEER STEAKS

ALL ITEMS ARE BROILED OVER OUR OPEN HICKORY CHARCOAL FIRE
AND PERSONALLY SELECTED BY THE MANOR CHEF

please read and order your steaks accordingly

RARE	red cool center	we cannot be responsible
MEDIUM RARE	red warm center	for the appearance of steaks
MEDIUM	pink hot center	ordered medium well or
MEDIUM WELL	broiled throughout	well done unless cut in half
WELL DONE		

PRIME RIB OF BEEF AU JUS	$3.50
U. S. CHOICE CLUB STEAK	$3.50
U. S. CHOICE NEW YORK SIRLOIN STEAK	$4.50
FILET MIGNON *our ultimate in fine steaks—when ordered well done are cut in two to insure tenderness*	$3.50
FILET MIGNON EN BROCHETTE *chunks of filet mignon steak on a skewer, perfect for well done*	$2.95
LARGE T-BONE STEAK MAITRE d' HOTEL	$4.50
BROILED CHEF'S CHOPPED SIRLOIN *with onion ring*	$2.50
BROILED HAM STEAK *with pineapple ring*	$3.00
BROILED LAMB CHOP	$3.75

Menu, the Manor, 2550 West Seventh Street, St. Paul, 1950s

Blend-your-own salad bowls were a favorite on the Manor's menu, providing a flavorful complement to seared steaks and chops. The Manor's steaks were "crème de cocoa"—the cattle buyers' term for the finest in beef. These corn-fed steer steaks were cooked to order over hickory charcoal grills.

Mancini's Char House, 531 West Seventh Street, St. Paul, 1940s

Originally a 3.2 beer tavern, Mancini's was remodeled and expanded into a sprawling restaurant and lounge under the guidance of owner Nick Mancini. The menu remains limited to grilled steak, lobster, chicken, and walleye. Those who crowd the place nightly know the selections by heart and are confident that the simplest choice will be dependably good. Others enjoy sipping a martini or a Manhattan while seated in one of the bar's nearly room-sized red vinyl booths.

Gannon's
GREAT STEAKS
COCKTAILS

Located where West Seventh ends at the river bluffs, Gannon's was a long-time favorite dining spot famous for liver steak smothered in onions.

The Mississippi Belle
Hastings, Minnesota

AUDREY'S MISSISSIPPI BELLE ORANGE ROLLS

Audrey Reissner was a proponent of "eat dessert first." Her book Dining on the Plush *collected favorite recipes from the Mississippi Belle. The first 118 pages were devoted to Reissner's famous pies, giving short shrift to the Belle's seafood favorites and quirky recipes such as Dill Pickle Soup and Peanut Butter Soup. Once on board, diners appreciated the riverboat décor and probably gobbled several of Audrey's simple-to-make orange rolls.*

1 box of hot roll mix prepared according to package directions, or a favorite recipe for sweet-roll dough

Melted butter

3/4 cup sugar

Grated rind of two oranges

1 cup powdered sugar

1/4 cup fresh orange juice

When the dough is ready to form into rolls, pat out to 1/4-inch thickness. Spread dough with melted butter and sprinkle with a mixture of sugar and grated orange rind. Roll up as for jellyroll. Cut into 1-inch slices. Place cut side down in greased muffin pans. Cover and let rise until dough is doubled. Bake in a 350-degree oven for about 20 minutes or until golden brown. Meanwhile, make a syrup of powdered sugar and orange juice, heating briefly until sugar melts. Remove rolls from oven and pour orange syrup over them. Serve warm. Makes 12 to 15 rolls.

The Mississippi Belle, Hastings, 1950s

The interior of the Mississippi Belle restaurant set diners cruising aboard a riverboat. Leaded glass windows and gaslights in the lounge put the river theme in motion.

The Lexington, 1096 Grand Avenue, St. Paul, 1940s

THE LEXINGTON'S WALLEYE ALMONDINE

The Lexington menu remains full of stalwart midwestern favorites—steaks, prime rib, broiled Atlantic salmon—with occasional forays into more exotic Cajun and Szechuan flavors. But everyone's favorite there is walleye almondine featuring Canadian walleye flown in fresh.

8-ounce fresh walleye fillet

Salt and pepper

Egg wash (whole egg mixed with 2 tablespoons milk)

Japanese bread crumbs (or other fine dry unseasoned bread crumbs)

Melted butter

2 tablespoons slivered almonds

Season walleye fillet on both sides with salt and pepper. Dip in the egg wash until coated. Dip in crumbs, patting to adhere a light coating. Brush one side with melted butter; place fillet buttered side down on a well-oiled baking pan. Brush the top side with more melted butter. Bake in a 425-degree oven for 12 minutes or until fish is flaky and crust is golden. Meanwhile, toast slivered almonds in the oven or in a pan until they are light brown. Sprinkle almonds on walleye as it is plated. Makes 1 serving.

n 1935, Pat and Veronica McLean flipped a coin to name their newly purchased neighborhood pub located at the corner of Lexington and Grand, and it became the Lexington instead of the Grand. Locals loved the original pub cuisine: hamburgers, peanuts, and pretzels. For nearly seventy years, families from St. Paul's Hill District have celebrated happy events, held ladies' luncheons and card parties, and consoled themselves after wakes with libations at "the Lex." And for most of that time they were greeted by Don Ryan, an ex-Marine who managed the restaurant during his entire civilian career.

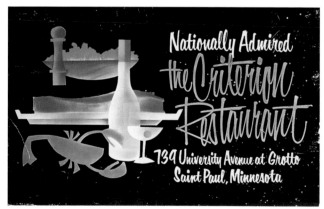

The Criterion, 739 University Avenue, St. Paul, 1950s

A predecessor to the well-known Criterion Restaurant was Stoika's Cafe, which opened in 1920. When Stoika's became the more elegant Criterion, it featured a lobster tank from which diners could select their own crustaceans. All-you-can-eat crab leg feasts—another crowd pleaser—were served in the red-draped dining room. Long considered one of the Twin Cities' fine dining spots, the Criterion on University succumbed to a huge blaze in 1978 and reopened in Bloomington, where it eventually served its last lobster tail.

DINING MODERNE

Restaurant design provided the most stunning evidence that the Midwest was moving into a new age. Proprietors were demolishing dowdy, old-fashioned, and occasionally historic structures while building "modern" inside and out. Streamline Moderne Style, a later version of Art Deco, was a popular look in America after the 1930s. Streamlining was applied to objects and surfaces never intended for speed: rooms were designed with ribbons of horizontal lines, rounded edges, and shiny finishes. Furniture and stylized decorations appeared futuristic and dynamic. Everyday items like toasters, clocks, and radios looked as though they might fly.

Vic's Theatre Lounge, 507 Hennepin Avenue, Minneapolis, 1955

Tufted vinyl and checkered floors welcomed theatergoers before or after the show.

The vertical orientation, curved bar, and smooth surfaces in the Grand Cafe are similar to early Art Deco or Moderne designs from the 1920s. The furnishings—curvy aluminum chairs, geometric patterns, and burgundy and green walls—were classic deco style. Patrons could choose the exotic Paradise Room, the Zebra Room, or the Spanish Room and be assured of a thoroughly modern dining experience.

The Grand Cafe, Stillwater, 1950s

Michael's, Rochester, 1951

Michael's in Rochester has offered fine dining under the guidance of Pappas family members since 1915. A photo parade of famous faces lines the entry walls, including accolades from Mitzi Gaynor, Mantovani, Rich Little, Dudley Moore, Liberace, Kenny Rogers, Eddie Albert, Sean Connery, Joe Garagiola, Victor Borge, Louis Rukeyser, Chet Huntley, Warren Burger, Abigail Van Buren, Ed Sullivan, and Danny Kaye. For an updated list, visit Michael's today.

STOUFFER'S

89 SOUTH SEVENTH STREET, MINNEAPOLIS

Although sleek and modern on the outside, Stouffer's welcomed diners into Colonial surroundings to be served by "friendly Stouffer girl" waitresses. Lunchtime shoppers and office workers rubbed elbows over unique sandwiches, bubbly casseroles, and sweet confections.

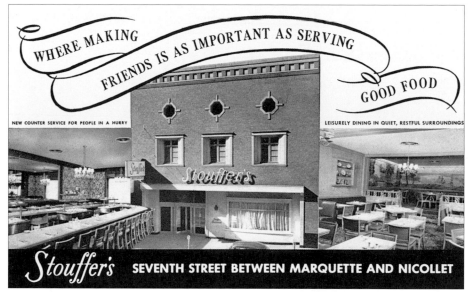

WHERE MAKING FRIENDS IS AS IMPORTANT AS SERVING GOOD FOOD

NEW COUNTER SERVICE FOR PEOPLE IN A HURRY   LEISURELY DINING IN QUIET, RESTFUL SURROUNDINGS

Stouffer's   SEVENTH STREET BETWEEN MARQUETTE AND NICOLLET

Stouffer's, 1950s
Waitresses at Stouffer's on opening day, 1946

Twin Citians loved Stouffer's, but it was not exclusively theirs: Stouffer's was a national chain long before the concept of franchising unified American dining. The company eventually closed its restaurants, but a line of frozen foods carried on the name.

RIVALING THE FLOWERS

"Where do you find such attractive girls?" our guests frequently ask. "They're so neat, so charmingly natural, such *nice* girls—it's a joy to meet them!"

They *are* nice girls and we're proud of them! So proud that we take pains to make sure their appearance does them credit at all times. Fresh, becoming uniforms and suggestions about a hair-do, makeup and nail polish all help. Even more important is the girls' own pride in the Stouffer Girl tradition of attractive appearance. Before every meal period they get together to give each other "the once-over." It's this friendly co-operation for harmonious detail that makes such a pleasant over-all picture!

STOUFFER'S SHRIMP CREOLE

Stouffer's pioneered the standardized recipe, testing dishes in its Cleveland kitchens and streamlining for taste and presentation, even purchasing ingredients for their menus across the country. Dietitians gave menu items their stamp of approval, and dining room managers gathered opinions from the final critics—the customers. New Orleans–style shrimp creole went through that Stouffer's fine-tuning to become a favorite everywhere, including in Minnesota.

1 pound shrimp, cleaned and cooked

1/4 pound mushrooms, diced in 1/2-inch pieces

1 tablespoon finely chopped onion

3 tablespoons butter

1/4 cup green pepper, cut in 1/4-inch pieces

2 tablespoons cornstarch

1 tablespoon flour

3 cups canned tomatoes

1/3 cup chili sauce

1 tablespoon vinegar

2 teaspoons sugar

1 1/2 teaspoons salt (or to taste)

1 teaspoon Worcestershire sauce

Cut cooked shrimp in half. Sauté mushrooms and onion in butter until tender. Add green pepper. Cook 1 to 2 minutes. Stir in corn-starch and flour. Cook thoroughly for 3 to 5 minutes. Add tomatoes, chili sauce, vinegar, sugar, salt, and Worcestershire sauce. Bring to a boil. Add shrimp to sauce and heat through. If desired, spoon over cooked rice. Serves 8.

MURRAY'S

26 SOUTH SIXTH STREET, MINNEAPOLIS

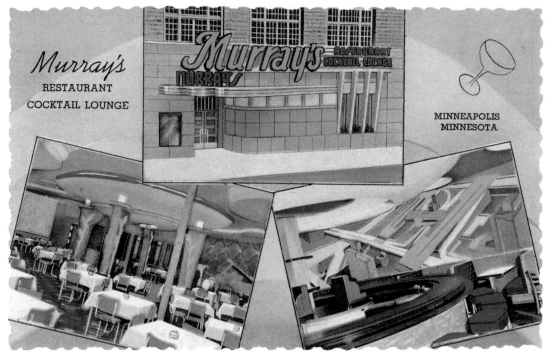

Murray's, 1950s

Diners who tasted Murray's Silver Butter Knife Steak would be back for more, guaranteed! Famous for steaks, crunchy garlic toast, and dinner-hour violinists, this enduring restaurant has served generations of true-blue customers. The walls are now dressed in mirrors and pink satin, but the irresistible sizzle of tender steaks brought tableside by on-their-toes waitresses remains the same.

Murray's Restaurant and Cocktail Lounge presents...

The *Cocktail* LUNCHEON $1

2 'til 5 daily except sunday

Imagine: cocktails and luncheon for one dollar, and the cocktail was a Manhattan or a martini. Anyone out for a day on the town could take advantage of this bargain, but only between 2 and 5 P.M.

MENU

Cocktails, choice of:

OLD FASHIONED

MARTINI BACARDI

HATTAN DAIQUIRI GIBSON DUBONNET

Single Plate Service, choice of:

Creamed Turkey a la King en Pattie Shell with fresh frozen peas, salad, hot rolls, coffee or tea.

California Fruit Plate served on crisp lettuce, honey dressing, toasted nut bread, coffee or tea.

Club House Sandwich, single deck, with pickle, olive, salad, coffee or tea.

Fresh Lobster Salad, sliced tomato and hard boiled egg, hot buttered roll, coffee or tea.

New England Deep Sea Scallops, fried with Saratoga chips, salad, hot roll, coffee or tea.

Large Crisp Combination Salad en bowl, dressing, rye crisp, coffee or tea.

Tenderloin of Beef Chips on Mushroom sauce on toasted triangles, salad, hot buttered roll, coffee or tea.

Desserts:

Ice Cream 20

Murray's DeLuxe Ice Box Pie 25   Chocolate Sundae 30

Pecan Pie 25   Home-made Cake 20

Fresh Apple Pie 20

Dancing Nightly From Nine O'clock

Free parking for our customers in the Plymouth Building Garage, 6 P.M. to 1 A.M.

MURRAY'S HICKORY-SMOKED SHRIMP

According to host-owner Pat Murray, this simple appetizer remains a frequently served favorite of his customers.

Jumbo shrimp (10–12 to the pound)

Thick, tangy red French dressing (bottled or homemade)

Bacon

Cocktail sauce

Marinate shrimp in French dressing for about 6 hours. Wrap each shrimp in a half-piece of bacon and secure with a toothpick. Broil shrimp until bacon is crisp, brushing with additional cocktail sauce and turning once. Allow four shrimp to a serving. Serve with cocktail sauce.

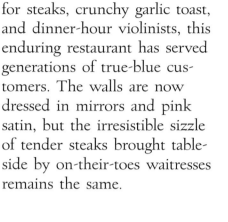

PUSH FOR SERVICE

Need a waitress? Just "push for service" and, like magic, one will appear. Inventor and restaurant owner Art Murray also developed sizzling steak platters, insulated beverage servers, and other restaurant products that are now marketed nationwide.

Garrison Keillor

The Age of Elegance

Agnes and Gladys and pink drapes and Deep Purple

THESE PERFECT FALL DAYS MAKE ME SAD, AND THERE have been so many of them lately in Minnesota. My cure for sadness is, first, to clean off my glasses and, second, to take a fast ride on a bicycle. If that doesn't work, I go to Murray's. The next step is to join the Men in Their 50s Coping with Melancholy group, and I've never had to do that.

Murray's is a restaurant in downtown Minneapolis that's been around longer than I have. In my childhood, there were the Big Three, Charlie's, Harry's and Murray's, and only Murray's survives. It is the sort of grand old joint you find in any big city, restaurants with pink drapes and a 70-year-old coat-check girl and a pianist who plays *Deep Purple* and the waitresses have names like Agnes and Gladys and the menu harks back to the Age of Steak; a place where a fiftyish couple can enjoy a Manhattan and tuck into a chunk of cow and au gratin potato. Murray's serves the Silver Butter Knife Steak for Two. That's the special, and it's been around since I was learning to read—I saw it advertised on billboards around town. I'd form the words MURRAY'S and SILVER BUTTER KNIFE STEAK phonetically, and say them aloud as we passed, and the mystery and elegance of them stuck with me.

My parents never went to restaurants. We ate at home or at the homes of relatives—we were sensible people, not spendthrifts or dreamers. Once a year we went to the state fair and had Pronto Pups. That was it. Every Sunday morning, however, my father drove us to church, and the route took us past Murray's, and I would glance up from my Bible and the verse I was memorizing for Sunday school, and there was Murray's big marquee and the name written out in orange block letters and, above, a sign that said COCKTAILS/DANCING, and over the years, memorizing one verse after another, you build up an intense interest in a place like that. You imagine walking in and finding yourself in a movie—the maître d' takes your coat and hat and nods toward a corner banquette, and there sits Fred MacMurray, your boss at Acme, stubbing out a Lucky, grinning, and you realize it's all true—you're assistant manager now, you got the big raise, you and Sue and Becky and Little Buddy can move out to Sunny Acres.

I saved up Murray's for years, and then, when I turned 21, I couldn't go there because I was under the terrible burden of being hip—it took years for that to wear off, during which I ate what hip people were eating in Minneapolis then, ethnic food, most of it awful. I thought of Murray's as a den of Republicans: steaks became (in my mind) politicized. And then, on the very last day of my misspent years in graduate school, my role model and hero Arnie Goldman said, "School's out—what do you say, let's go to Murray's," and so it was cool. We put on our corduroy sportscoats with the leather elbow patches and had dinner, and he ordered us martinis, and the gin made me as witty as Robert Benchley. We swapped timeless repartee for a couple hours and ate liberal Democratic steaks and felt the glow of scholarly brotherhood.

I have gone back about once every three or four years, and the magic seems never to wear off, the sight of the pink drapes, the mirrors, the candelabrum sconces, the red plush chairs, the candles flickering on the white linen—it still elates me, the Silver Butter Knife feels like a bright sword in my hand. And last year I returned with four old friends and my wife Jenny. It was one of the happiest nights I can remember, everyone yakking and laughing, eating steak, drinking a big booming red wine, feeling flush and lovable. And then I went back one night last week with Jenny and my son and his girlfriend. We strolled in, and I saw the pink drapes, and I felt the old euphoria rise in my heart, and it dawned on me that I had invented Murray's: as a child, reading the words SILVER BUTTER KNIFE STEAK FOR TWO off billboards, meditating on them, I had created a kingdom of elegance more durable than any restaurant where an immaculate young waiter introduces himself and tells you about the broiled marlin served in fennel mustard sauce on a bed of basmati rice and topped with shredded asiago cheese and lightly toasted pine nuts. I would never take out-of-towners to Murray's. Nobody whom I wanted to impress. Only my dearest friends. Only old Minnesota pals who grew up with Murrayism and know it as a symbol of all we hold dear.

On a beautiful fall day, when I recall what was grand and exalted and now is gone forever—the Burlington *Zephyr* and the *North Coast Limited*, the *New Yorker* of my youth, Memorial Stadium where we spent Saturday afternoons cheering for the Golden Gophers, the Earle Brown farm that was turned into a mall and a subdivision—I think of the SILVER BUTTER KNIFE STEAK FOR TWO, looming above me on a billboard, our car stopped at a red light on Lyndale Avenue in 1952, the Bible on my lap open to *Ecclesiastes*, my head anointed with Wildroot hair oil, and I feel restored. Some glories remain. You for sure, and me, perhaps, and, absolutely, Murray's. ∎

STEPHEN ALCORN FOR TIME

Garrison Keillor reflected on life at Murray's restaurant in Time magazine, 1997.

HARRY'S CAFE

ELEVENTH AT NICOLLET, MINNEAPOLIS

ℋarry's was dining at its best—like being in New York! Diners entered through impressive front doors and took a long, skinny elevator for a slow ride to the dining rooms on the upper floors. Art Deco zigzag designs, faceted mirrors, and indirect lighting enveloped culinary aficionados who knew just what to order to use all those forks, knives, and spoons on the tables. Harry's dished up flavorful soups and salads, formidable entrées were cooked to order, sauce-making was an art, desserts were decadent, and the chopped liver appetizer wasn't just chopped liver.

DINNERS

(Served from 5:00 to 11:00 P. M.)
FRIDAY

HARRY'S FAMOUS SEAFOOD TRAY $1.50 PER PERSON
SPECIAL SHRIMP COCKTAIL $1.25—DINNER SIZE 65c.

★

Choice of
Coney Island Clam Chowder,   Consommme Clear,   Vichyssoise with Chives,   Jellied Consomme,
Chopped Chicken Livers,   Bismark Herring,   Tomato Juice or   Grapefruit Juice

★

HALF BRAISED PHEASANT SUPREME, Mushrooms, Kumquats, Cherries, Wild Rice 4.00
HARRY'S FAMOUS FRIED SPRING CHICKEN, Disjointed 3.50
BOILED FANCY OX TONGUE, New Spinach 3.00
ROAST LONG ISLAND DUCKLING, Apple Sauce, Dressing, Wild Rice 4.00
U. S. PRIME N. Y. CUT SIRLOIN STEAK 5.25
ROAST RIBS of U. S. PRIME BEEF AU JUS 4.25
U. S. CHOICE T-BONE, Natural 5.50
U. S. PRIME STEER TENDERLOIN STEAK . . . . 3.
CHICKEN a la KING in CASSEROLE, All White Meat
SIRLOIN TIPS SAUTED in Butter, Mushrooms or Onions
BROILED SPRING LAMB CHOPS, Mint Jelly
SCALLOPINI of VEAL, Bordelaise Sauce, Under Bell
BROILED COMBINATION VEAL CHOPS, Kidney, Bacon and Mushrooms
BROILED PORK CHOPS, Apple Sauce
FRESH CHICKEN LIVERS SAUTED in BUTTER, Onions or Mushrooms
CALF'S LIVER, Sauted, Bacon, Onions or Mushrooms
HARRY'S FAMOUS GROUND STEAK, Grilled Onions or Mushrooms
BROILED SWEETBREADS and Mushrooms on Toast
LOBSTER THERMIDOR with FRESH LOBSTER
GRILLED CHINOOK SALMON, Lemon Butter
BROILED FRESH LAKE SUPERIOR TROUT
BROILED FRESH COD STEAK, Lemon Butter
FRESH MAINE LOBSTER a la Newburg . . . . 4.
FILED FANCY LOBSTER TAILS, Drawn Butter 3.50
FILET of SOLE, Marguerite, en Casserole 3.60
DEEP SEA SCALLOPS, Tartar Sauce 3.25
MAINE LOBSTER Au Gratin en Casserole 4.50
FILET of WALL-EYED PIKE, Fried in Butter, Tartar Sauce 4.00
FRIED FRESH JUMBO SHRIMPS, Tartar or Chili Sauce 3.00
FRESH WISCONSIN BROOK TROUT (3), Saute Mouniere 3.50
BROILED SWORDFISH STEAK, Anchovy Butter 4.50
BREADED FILET of SOLE, Tarta
FRIED WISCONSIN

FREDDIE'S CAFE

605 SECOND AVENUE SOUTH, MINNEAPOLIS

Menu, Freddie's Café, 1950s

In the heart of downtown Minneapolis, Freddie's was the place for a lively business luncheon or a romantic dinner date. But late at night Freddie's began swingin' as jazz sauntered in the door with the likes of Ella Fitzgerald, George Shearing, and Count Basie—in person. Crowds jammed the room to hear the smooth jazz piano, soaring voices, and wailing trumpets. Freddie's became famous throughout the Upper Midwest for glamorous entertainment and urbane dining.

GALLANT DINING

Camelot, Bloomington, 1960s

A watery moat surrounded the castle, and diners crossed a drawbridge to enter the magical world of Camelot. The medieval experience began with libations in the Ale House and continued with feasting in moody dining rooms rich with dark wood, tapestries, oil paintings, suits of armor, and swords. King Arthur would have cheered the lively entertainment in the Jester Lounge.

BLUE HORSE HOUSE SALAD

The house salad and chilled Dungeness crab were favorites, as were osso buco, veal cutlet cordon bleu, and Chicken Wandzel, named for the Horse's first chef, George Wandzel.

SAUCE VINAIGRETTE:

1/4 teaspoon salt

1/4 teaspoon freshly ground pepper

1/4 teaspoon dry mustard

6 tablespoons olive oil

2 tablespoons wine vinegar

Juice of 1/2 lemon

Dash of Worcestershire sauce

SALAD INGREDIENTS:

1/2 cup canned beets, cut in thin julienne strips

Hearts from two heads of romaine lettuce

1 cup meat picked from cooked and chilled Dungeness crab legs (or 1 cup canned crabmeat)

1 hard-cooked egg

Combine the ingredients for the vinaigrette in a bowl, beating with a wire whisk until emulsified. Add the julienne beet strips and allow to rest for a few minutes, then lift beets out of the dressing and set aside. Meanwhile, remove the tender inner leaves of romaine, leaving them whole. Toss the romaine hearts with the dressing mixture. Lift romaine from dressing and place on 4 plates. Add the crab to the dressing remaining in the bowl, stir briefly, then place crab and dressing on romaine and sprinkle the beets over the romaine and crabmeat. Grate hard-cooked egg over top of salads. Serves 4.

Napoleon's, 1355 University Avenue, St. Paul, 1950s

In the early 1960s, with Cliff and Jeanie Warling holding the reins, the former Napoleon's on University Avenue became the Blue Horse, soon a consistent winner in the race for diners' loyalty. Legislators lunched there, and dinner guests knew it was the place to be seen. At Christmas, the famous Blue Horse Holiday Feasts were both a tradition and a terrific deal: seven courses of impeccable fare for only around twenty dollars, the Warlings' annual gift to their customers.

Napoleon was his name, and his restaurant catered to legions of fans who craved his sumptuous French cuisine.

Highball glass from the Blue Horse

CHARLIE'S CAFE EXCEPTIONALE
701 FOURTH AVENUE SOUTH, MINNEAPOLIS

Charlie's Cafe Exceptionale, 1950s

This landmark restaurant was renowned for exceptionally beautiful dining rooms and equally exceptional American cuisine. It all added up to Charlie's Cafe Exceptionale. One of the most beloved restaurants in the Upper Midwest, Charlie's regularly filled its dining rooms and lounges with enthusiastic crowds of celebrities, loyal customers, and visiting culinary experts—all fans of the sophisticated menu. Advertisements promised, "You'll savor the exotic dishes prepared by world-renowned chefs and served in an extraordinary atmosphere. And the drinks are man-sized and expertly mixed." It was all true.

Flaming Desserts a la Exceptionale

Cherries Jubilee — with **Charlie's** vanilla ice cream and a bing cherry sauce . . . flamed with brandy . . . . $1.95 per person

Crêpes Suzettes — with a sauce of butter, orange and lemon flamed with Grand Marnier, Cointreau, and Cognac . . . . $3.00 per person

Bananas Foster — bananas with brown sugar, crème de banana, rum and ice cream . . $2.25 per person

Crêpes Elaine — **Charlie's** crêpes filled with vanilla ice cream . . . topped with fudge sauce . . . flamed with rum and crème de cacao . . . $3.00 per person

(minimum two orders)

In addition to the standout menu of appetizers and specialty entrées, the 1960s dessert menu was uniquely Charlie's.

Minnesota restaurants have provided meals from down-home nourishing to up-scale decadent for over 150 years. Many chefs shared their recipes, others kept them secret, but midwestern diners have been the lucky beneficiaries of talented and inspired cooks creating bountiful and imaginative menus.

CEDRIC ADAMS SANDWICH

Named for the famous Minneapolis Star columnist and WCCO radio broadcaster, this sandwich is a classic from Charlie's menu. Rich and robust—like its namesake, who provided the best in Minnesota news, events, and gossip throughout his forty-year career.

1/4 cup butter

3 tablespoons flour

2 cups half-and-half

2 tablespoons white wine

1 cup sliced mushrooms (fresh preferred), sautéed briefly

2 slices of firm white bread

2 generous slices of roasted turkey breast

1/4 cup freshly grated Parmesan cheese

1/4 cup grated Cheddar cheese

TO MAKE SAUCE: Melt butter in a small saucepan over medium heat; stir in flour plus salt and pepper to taste. Stir until flour is blended with butter. Slowly stir in half-and-half. Increase heat slightly and continue stirring until sauce thickens. Stir in white wine and sautéed mushrooms; continue stirring until sauce is medium-thick. For a richer hue, add a couple of drops of yellow food coloring.
TO MAKE SANDWICH: Toast bread and place a slice in each of two small casseroles or ramekins. Layer with turkey breast. Divide sauce between sandwiches. Sprinkle with

cheeses. Place casseroles under broiler until cheese is browned. Serve hot. Makes 2 servings.

Chefs in the kitchen at Charlie's

Nankin Cafe, 17 South Seventh Street,
Minneapolis, early 1900s

Partygoers loved to linger
at the original Nankin Cafe.

CHAPTER TWO

Melting Pot

New England Yankees and recent arrivals from Scandinavia, Germany, and Britain were the first settlers to the territory of Minnesota in the mid-1800s. Soon Minnesota had more Finns, Swedes, Danes, and Norwegians than any other state in the union. Germans were the largest group of immigrants until the turn of the century, when immigration to Minnesota was at an all-time high and the Swedes took over first place.

Midwestern pioneers were a diverse group: farmers, lumber speculators, homesteaders, businessmen, politicians, and land developers. Many new citizens opened restaurants and brewhouses to revive nostalgic memories of meals back home. Italians and Greeks set up cafés, Chinese became small business owners, and Eastern Europeans opened markets.

Old-world flavors became new midwestern standards as international foods found table space together. Swedish meatballs vied for popularity with Czech goulash, German sausage with Italian spaghetti, Irish stew with Chinese chow mein. Meals were complemented by the appropriate liquor: German food demanded hearty beer, Irish pubs poured velvety whiskey, Scandinavians sent home for icy aquavit, Chinese opened bottles of rice wines, Italians brought in Chianti, Frenchmen uncorked Burgundy, and tequila and rum traveled up the Mississippi River by steamboat.

At the 1939 New York World's Fair, food was the main attraction, and entirely new flavors were showcased from all over the world. Unusual seasonings competed with American standbys, and Minnesotans began tasting Russian borscht, Indian curry, Greek salads, and Jewish matzo balls.

Creative architecture outside advertised the food served inside. Restaurant buildings sported pagoda roofs, Mexican hats, and Viking ships. Inside were re-creations of Oriental gardens, Spanish courtyards, Italian kitchens, and German beer halls. Many early restaurants survived for decades under the care of next-generation family members, who proudly preserved and honored recipes and traditions from the "old country."

Curiously, many immigrants opened restaurants and cafés that did not specialize in their native dishes. Greek families owned and operated numerous popular and successful eateries throughout the Midwest that offered only "American" menus. At the other extreme, the Chinese outdid everyone by establishing countless cafés that served only Asian creations, and "going out for Chinese" became a frequent dinner ritual for thousands of families.

For 150 years, Midwesterners have preserved homeland recipes, developed tastes for previously untried flavors, and welcomed a host of new worldly dishes as each wave of immigrants has brought vitality and excitement to the region's restaurant tables.

VIKING VITTLES

Whole towns in Minnesota grew up in looks-just-like-Scandinavia pine forests or along rocky shorelines reminiscent of the North Countries. Old-fashioned flavors were just around the corner at Taste O'Sweden, A Bit of Norway, and House of Sweden. Platters of picture-pretty open-faced sandwiches, buttery pastries, plump fruit pies, and stocky soups rested on place mats with rosemaling or on handwoven tablecloths. Scandinavian smorgasbord became a popular cooking style, and individual dishes could be very imaginative. Swedish cuisine, Norwegian gourmet, Danish gastronomy— are these phrases in your vocabulary?

— SCANDIA SPECIALTIES —

Svenske Kjöttboller . . . . . . (Swedish Meatballs)	2.25
Fersk Kjöff med Lök Saûs . . . (Select Boiled Beef with Onion Sauce)	3.25
Frikadeller . . . . (Veal Patties Served in Traditional Way)	3.00
Dansk Hakke Böf . . . . . (Chopped Sirloin Fried in Butter, with Onion Sauce)	2.75
Barbecued Rib Dinner . . . . (Our Own Special Recipe)	3.00

AQUAVIT SERVED ICE COLD WITH BEER

Tuborg *(Denmark)*	.75	Heineken's *(Holland)*	.75
Ringes *(Norway)*	.75	Lowenbrau *(Germany)*	.75
Three Towns *(Sweden)*	.75	Aqua Vit/Beer *(Imported)*	1.25
Carlsberg *(Denmark)*	.75	Aqua Vit/Beer *(Domestic)*	.80

Menu, Scandia Kitchen, Crystal, 1950s

Anyone who claims that Scandinavian food is boring never tasted iced Norwegian aquavit with savory Swedish meatballs, perhaps topped off with sweet Danish rum cake.

savarin
SCANDIA KITCHEN

Place mat, Scandia Kitchen

TASTE O'SWEDEN STUFFED CABBAGE ROLLS

Given Minnesota's demographics, it's surprising how few Scandinavian restaurants existed; that ethnic group preferred to dine at home. One enduring eatery was Minneapolis's Taste O'Sweden, operated by native Swede Rolf Nordahl. A description of the restaurant recommended the "lush" homemade sausages and meatballs. Also on the menu were fried potato dumplings with lingonberries, Swedish fruit soup, open-faced sandwiches, lutefisk at holidays, and smorgasbord year-round. A popular daily dish was Kaldolmar, also known as stuffed cabbage rolls.

1 medium cabbage

1/4 cup rice

1/2 cup water

1/2 cup milk

3/4 pound ground beef

1/4 pound ground veal (or omit veal and use 1 pound ground beef)

1 egg

1 egg yolk

1 cup cream

Salt and pepper to taste

Grated onion, if desired

Butter

1 tablespoon corn syrup

1/4 cup water

Core whole cabbage. Immerse cabbage in boiling salted water. Boil 5 to 6 minutes. Remove cabbage and cool. Cook rice with water and milk until rice is tender. To cooked rice, add ground beef, veal (if using), egg, egg yolk, and cream. Season to taste with salt and pepper. Add grated onion if desired. Mix well. Shape some meat mixture into a roll and wrap in a cabbage leaf removed from the head. Continue until 8 rolls have been formed. Place a dollop of butter and the corn syrup in a frying pan; brown the cabbage rolls. Place rolls in a casserole; add 1/4 cup water to the pan drippings and pour over the rolls. Cover casserole and bake in a 350-degree oven for 1 hour. Makes 4 servings.

A Bit of Sweden

Sawtooth Club, East Bay Hotel, Grand Marais

Grand Marais weather could be cold and gray, but the "red hot" Viking lounge promised wayfarers a toasty haven.

Sunday smorgasbord, Hazelglade resort, Wahkon, 1950s

Thick plank floors leading to a big stone fireplace evoked memories of a cozy Norwegian dining room in a sturdy log cottage.

A Bit of Norway, Beaver Bay, 1940s

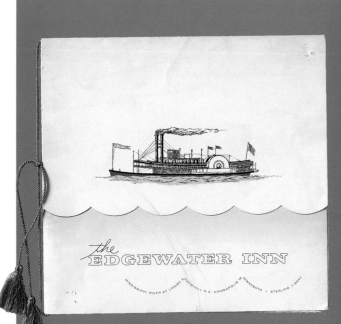

Menu, the Edgewater Inn, Lowry and Marshall Avenue Northeast, Minneapolis

Minnesota's legendary Scandinavian restaurant and hotel personality, Danish-born Jorgen Viltoft, first plied his trade at world-famous hotels, including the Plaza in New York City, the Broadmoor in Colorado, and the Radisson in Minneapolis. Before turning his culinary skills to the Edgewater Inn on the Mississippi River in northeast Minneapolis, he created a namesake peppercorn salad dressing for Marriott hotels that has been emulated nationwide.

The Edgewater Inn menu related a bit of history: "If you had sat down here in 1786, you would have been sitting in the sovereign state of Virginia. In 1787, this spot became part of the Northwest Territory; then, much later, of Indiana and Wisconsin; and after May 11, 1858, the Minnesota we know today."

House of Sweden, Two Harbors, 1950s

DEUTSCHLAND DELIGHTS

*T*his was no place to be on a diet: German food was *wunderbar*, and German restaurants continuously grew in size and number. Dark bock beer arrived at tables in decorated steins, and dinner came with spaetzle, dumplings, red cabbage, or warm potato salad. Wartime anti-German sentiments tainted the popularity of these restaurants, but the hearty food and beer making were so robust that—Prosit!—they survived into the middle of the century and beyond.

Kaiserhof, 242 Nicollet Avenue, Minneapolis, 1900

Really! The Kaiserhof was in Minneapolis, not New York or Munich, and its dining room might have come straight from a palace in Paris. The building façade and interior spaces were designed in the American Beaux-Arts manner, which borrows architectural details from other eras. The Renaissance-style coffered ceiling, molded plaster details with garlands of flowers, and grand window openings were reminiscent of a French chateau or an Italian palazzo. The German food must have been seriously sumptuous to live up to these ornate surroundings. Don't we wish it were still here.

Thauwald's Saloon, 55 West Kellogg, St. Paul, 1886

The Deutsche Bier Halle served up frosty mugs of local brews as friends swapped remembrances of Oktoberfest in beer halls back home.

Zahnen's Affenkasten, 253 Hennepin Avenue, Minneapolis, 1910s

Zahnen's was a drinking man's place—the restaurant played second fiddle to the bar, the cigars, and the spittoons. The dining room was hidden away in the back, and would-be diners wandered down the long aisle in search of food. Located in the heart of the fast-growing metropolitan area, Zahnen's served the working men and builders of the new city. The name *Affenkasten* means "monkey's cage" in German—no doubt an attraction to customers who didn't want life to be all work and no play.

Rathskeller over the Rhine, Moorhead, 1905

This stately building looked more like a Venetian villa on the Grand Canal then a German restaurant, but it held three substantial dining rooms and a very long bar advertising "beverages of every kind served with all kinds of lunches."

"Bier und Brot Macht die Wangen Rot" (Beer and Bread make the Cheeks Red) THE KAISERHOFF RESTAURANT, NEW ULM

JOE'S PICKWICK TAVERN — 508 EAST SUPERIOR STREET, DULUTH, MINN. 6A-H752

Joe's Pickwick Tavern, Duluth, 1930s

Place mat, Heidelberg, Richfield, 1950s

Joseph John Stanley Wisocki left Prussian Poland in 1907 and headed straight for Duluth. Ten years later he bought Pickwick Tavern from the Fitger Brewing Company for two hundred dollars in the midst of Prohibition. Knowing people still had to eat, Joe served solid German and Pennsylvania Dutch food, and the unique tavern full of old wood, antique beer steins, and mounted trophies flourished. Customers have perched on the same stools at the Pickwick bar since 1914, and the dining tables and chairs date from the first Fitger Saloon, open in the late 1880s. Joe's great-grandchildren watch over today's menu and the plentiful helpings of tasty sausages and tangy sauerkraut.

Customers proudly wore this button after devouring a famous Meisterburger.

RESTAURANT EIBNER PRESENTS
GERMAN SPECIALTIES

BRATWURST $1.50
served with German potato salad and sauerkraut

SCHWEINE HAXEN (Pork Hocks) $1.75
served with choice of potatoes and sauerkraut

SAUERBRATEN $2.25
served with spaetzles and red cabbage

RIPPCHEN $1.85
salted, boiled center-cut pork chop with whipped potatoes, sauerkraut

ROULADEN $2.55
bacon, onions, carrots, pickles, rolled in beef and served in its own gravy with spaetzles and red cabbage
These German specialties are served with a roll, coffee, tea or milk

Eibner's store and cafe, New Ulm, 1898

A parcel of land on the Minnesota River was selected in 1855 as the site for a German colony in the Midwest: fittingly, the settlers called it New Ulm. Willibald Eibner opened a bakery there in 1883 with a lot of help from his wife, Mary, and family of eight girls and two boys. Soon it was a bakery with an ice cream parlor, and then a few tables and a delivery truck were added as the family business grew. Restaurant Eibner served German European specialties for nearly one hundred years.

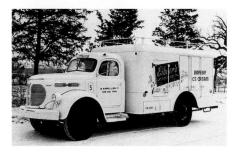

Eibner's delivery truck, 1940s

CARRIE'S CHEESECAKE

No restaurant served tastier desserts than Eibner's. Carrie Bianchi learned many of her baking and pastry-decorating skills at her father's elbow in Eibner's Restaurant and Bakery.

CRUST:

2 cups dry ground bread crumbs

1/2 cup granulated sugar

1/4 teaspoon cinnamon

1/2 cup melted butter

1/2 cup finely chopped nuts

FILLING:

4 eggs

1 cup granulated sugar

1 1/2 pounds dry cottage cheese, finely sieved

1 cup cream

1/2 teaspoon salt

1 teaspoon lemon juice

1 teaspoon lemon rind

1/4 cup flour

1/2 teaspoon vanilla

TO MAKE CRUST: Mix ingredients well and press evenly over the bottom and sides of a well-greased springform pan, reserving some of the crumb mixture for topping.
TO MAKE FILLING: Beat eggs until thick and lemon-colored, gradually adding sugar. Continue beating until light. To the cottage cheese gradually add cream, salt, lemon juice and rind, flour, and vanilla. Add egg mixture to the cheese mixture and mix until smooth. Pour into crumb-lined springform pan, top with reserved crumb mixture, and bake in 325-degree oven for one hour. Leave in oven another hour with heat turned off and oven door slightly ajar. Makes 12 servings.

ITALIAN SPOKEN HERE

Early Italian immigrants to Minnesota came from the south of Rome and opened small family *trattorias*. Italian noodles were curiosities in North America, so Italian American cooks adapted traditional recipes by adding more tomatoes, meat, and fresh vegetables with fewer spices. Dishes were made with rich tomato sauces and noodles or macaroni; upscale pasta came later. Many midwestern Italian restaurants are unique family legacies, with second, third, and fourth generations keeping old recipes alive, often in the same ancestral buildings.

Yarusso family, St. Paul, 1922

Francisco and Dora Yarusso opened their Payne Avenue tavern in 1932 during Prohibition, serving only near beer. They soon expanded their offerings, adding a dining room called the Square Deal Cafe and, for entertainment, a few bocce alleys out back. Over the years, their fourteen children joined the work force to help keep all the customers happy. Second-generation family members eventually changed the name to Yarusso Brothers, and third-generation Yarussos still serve up their grandparents' pizzas, pastas, and sauces, plus a few American dishes that have crept onto the menu. The restaurant remains a neighborhood favorite with its vinyl booths, folksy photographs, and plastic grapes threaded through the latticework.

Menu, Vescio's, 406 Fourteenth Avenue Southeast, Minneapolis, 1960s

"The trouble with eating Italian food is that five or six days later you're hungry again."
GEORGE MILLER

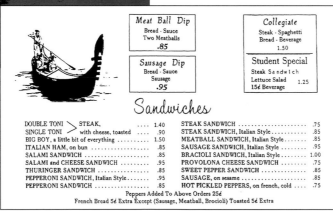

Vescio's has provided pasta brainpower to college students—and other educated diners—for more than fifty years. Frank started the campus restaurant with his mother, Teresa, who re-created the family recipes in the big kitchen. Frank Jr. runs the original Dinkytown restaurant and brother Fred the newer St. Louis Park location, assisted by fourth-generation children and a host of aunts, uncles, and cousins. No melting pot here: it's all old-world southern Italian cooking.

Totino's, 523 Central Avenue, Minneapolis, 1957

Jim and Rose Totino's story began when they met at the Viking Dance Hall in Minneapolis; they soon married and opened an Italian take-out. It was 1951 and customers arrived in bunches. Totino's pizzas became a take-out standard, then a grocery-store favorite. The original restaurant has expanded along Central Avenue under the watch of grandson Steve, and frozen Totino's pizzas are now made and distributed by General Mills.

Venetian Inn, 2814 Rice Street, St. Paul

Geno's Cafe, 670 Payne Avenue, St. Paul, 1960s

Creating an Italian atmosphere was easy with room-sized murals of romantic, watery landscapes, the perfect backdrop for practicing the twist on spaghetti noodles.

The Andrews Sisters were "cutting up" at the Café di Napoli with owner Joe Piazza. The sisters hailed from Minneapolis and were known for recording nearly two thousand songs and selling more than 90 million records, including their hits "Rum and Coca-Cola" and "Don't Sit Under the Apple Tree." From their local start the trio became internationally known, starring in dozens of movies and entertaining adoring troops during World War II.

Café di Napoli's Spaghetti Sauce and Meatballs

Café di Napoli, located amidst Minneapolis's theatrical show houses, welcomed patrons to dine under scenes of Mount Vesuvius and the Bay of Naples. Family recipes flavored the heaping plates of pasta that attracted celebrities and hometown personalities alike. Local sports announcer Halsey Hall once estimated that the café served 2,284 miles of spaghetti each year. It's still 1938 at the Café: the same booths, the same murals, the same Italian spaghetti sauce—a time capsule on Hennepin Avenue run by third-generation Piazzas.

SAUCE:

2 cloves garlic, chopped

1/4 cup salad (vegetable) oil

1 pound coarsely ground beef

1/2 cup chopped onions

2 cans (6 ounces each) tomato paste

5 1/2 cups water

2 teaspoons salt

1 1/2 teaspoons sugar

3 pinches black pepper
(about 1/4 teaspoon)

1 bay leaf

MEATBALLS:

1 pound ground beef

1 egg

1 cup very dry bread

1/4 cup diced onion

1/4 cup bread or cracker crumbs

3 tablespoons grated Italian cheese

2 tablespoons chopped parsley

1/4 teaspoon salt

Pinch of black pepper (several grindings)

TO MAKE SAUCE: Brown garlic in oil for 15 seconds. Add 1 pound ground beef and chopped onions. After beef and onions have browned, add tomato paste, water, salt, sugar, pepper, and bay leaf. Simmer over low heat until thick, about 1 1/4 to 1 1/2 hours, stirring regularly to prevent scorching.

TO MAKE MEATBALLS: Combine remaining ground beef, egg, dry bread which has briefly been soaked in water and squeezed, diced onion, crumbs, cheese, parsley, salt, and pepper. Roll into golf ball–sized balls. Brown in a greased frying pan or in a pan in the oven. Add to sauce during last 20 minutes of cooking. Makes about 12 meatballs.

Café di Napoli, 816 Hennepin Avenue, Minneapolis, 1950s

CHOPSTICKS & CHOP SUEY

Menu, Nankin Cafe, 1956

Many of Minnesota's Chinese immigrants established food-related businesses. The first café-keepers served traditional dishes, but they quickly adjusted their recipes for American tastes, the most obvious examples being chow mein and chop suey. Some may argue that those dishes are not authentically Chinese; however, "chow mein" resembles a Mandarin word for fried noodles with vegetables, and "chop suey" corresponds to a Chinese phrase for "a little of this and a little of that." These recipes, somewhat modified, soon became American food favorites. By 1920, Chinese American restaurants brightened main streets throughout Minnesota.

Nankin Cafe, 17 South Seventh Street, Minneapolis, 1920s

Opened in 1919, the Nankin was one of the most enduring Chinese restaurants in the metro area. The popular spot soon outgrew its dark and cozy dining rooms, moving across the street in the 1950s. The imaginative new space featured a grand staircase up to a picturesque balcony, colorful paper lanterns, and tranquil Asian paintings. Years later, the Nankin moved for a third time, into a huge new space on Hennepin Avenue, equally attractive in décor. The final closing day dismayed thousands of admirers of the Nankin Special Subgum Chicken Chow Mein. That single menu item may have been the most frequently ordered meal anywhere in the Midwest at that time.

Menu, Nankin Cafe, 1933

Advice from this menu: "Chinese foods are famous for their balanced rations. More healthful than the heavy meat dishes that leave one sluggish. For your health and pleasure, eat at least a few Chinese dishes every week."

Nankin Cafe, 15 South Seventh Street, Minneapolis, 1950s

42

Port Arthur Cafe, 413 Robert Street, St. Paul

Port Arthur covered the Twin Cities with its busy and popular eat-in or take-out locations.

The New Shanghai Tea Garden, Sixth and Wabasha, St. Paul

Simpler restaurants suggested their oriental ancestry with lantern lighting and serene Asian artworks, enhanced by irresistible Cantonese aromas wafting through the rooms.

The Mandarin, 25-27 South Fifth Street, Minneapolis

Intricately beautiful interiors were lavish with fretwork and architectural carvings from China, creating an intriguing background for inlaid tables and heavily carved chairs.

Chinese restaurant owners knew the value of marketing. Diners were lured with exotic signage, showy menus, colorful matchbooks, and fanciful Chinese symbols on plates and platters. Take-out traveled home in soon-to-become-classic cartons.

Menu, the White House, Golden Valley, 1950s

Plate, Wong's, Rochester

Established in 1952, Wong's is one of the state's oldest continuously operating, family-run Chinese restaurants.

Take-out cartons, Androy Hotel, Hibbing

Howard Wong's, Bloomington, 1950s

John's Famous Chinese Dishes

FOR YOUR ENJOYMENT OF OUR DELECTABLE CHINESE DISHES, WE SUGGEST
COMBINATIONS OF THESE ITEMS FOR A BALANCED MENU
WE SHALL BE HAPPY TO ASSIST YOU.

APPETIZERS

John's Egg Roll	.90
Barbecued Pork	.75
	Barbecued Spare Ribs
Fried Won Ton Crisps	.60
	Butterfly Shrimps ... 1.00

CHINESE SOUPS

Won Ton — Large	.75	Si-Foon
Small	.40	Chinese Greens
Egg Drop	.30	Sea Weed ... .50
Chicken Noodle Soup	.25	Chicken Rice Soup ... .35
		.50
		.25

JOHN'S SPECIALTIES

PRESSED DUCK (WAR SUE OPP)
Boneless Duckling Molded with Water Chestnut Flour and Fried Crisp
Served with Toasted Almonds and Five Flavored Sauce ... 2.00

SI FOON CHOW YOKE
Chinese Bean Vermicelli with Pork Strips and Green Onions ... 1.50

SWEET AND SOUR WON TON
Won Ton Crisps in a Sweet and Sour Sauce with Pineapple and Peppers ... 1.40

COFFEE OR MILK EXTRA WITH CHINESE ORDERS
No Service Less Than 35¢ Per Person

CHICKEN DISHES

TUNG KOO GUY KOW
Tender Spring Chicken, Chinese Cup Mushrooms and
Crisp Chinese Vegetables, Deliciously Cooked ... 2.50

CHICKEN ALMOND DING
Diced Breast of Chicken Cooked with Diced Vegetables
and Covered with Toasted Almonds ... 1.90

BOR LOR GAI PEN — CHICKEN PINEAPPLE
Thinly Sliced Chicken Cooked with Pineapple and Vegetables ... 2.00

JOW GAI KEW ... 2.25

FRIED CHICKEN — CHINESE STYLE
Tender Chicken Rolled in Egg Batter and Sauted with
Crisp Chinese Vegetables ... 1.65

CURRIED CHICKEN
Crisp Fried in a Delicious Seasoning — Served with Spice Salt ... 1.75

PORK and BEEF DISHES

BEEF, TOMATO AND GREEN PEPPERS
Slices of Tenderloin Beef Cooked with Tomatoes and
Green Peppers, featuring our Chef's Bean Sauce ... 2.00

BEEF OR PORK WITH CHINESE VEGETABLES
Tender Meat Slices Cooked with

BEEF OR PORK WITH BEAN
Bamboo Shoots and

EPPER STEAK
Julienne Mea...

TEAK KEW
Thick Slices of T...

HN'S OWN BEEF RICE
Cubes of Steak with B...

EET AND SOUR SPARE RIBS
Tender Beef and Green...

John's Place / Yuen Faung Low, 28 South Sixth Street, Minneapolis, 1950s

Yuen Faung Low was the formal Chinese name for John's Place, meaning "The Cafe of Exotic Fragrances from Afar." Established in 1883 and surviving almost one hundred years, it was likely the longest-running Chinese American restaurant in Minnesota. Diners climbed to the second floor and entered an intriguing world of gilded camphor wood carvings, richly embroidered silks, and enameled altar pieces, but it was the mother-of-pearl inlaid teak tables with white marble insets that no one could forget. And when those tables were topped with John's famous Chinese meals, patrons wielded their chopsticks in an exotic atmosphere rarely matched in the five-state area.

FOO CHU — Wine List

ZOMBIE
Be Careful!
1.10

WONG'S DELITE
.95
A Must Before Dining!

CHINA SLING
Zest at Its Best!
1.10

LOVING CUP (For 2)
You'll Be Surprised!
2.50
A Delight for Lovers!

PAGODA SPECIAL
You Will Order More!
.95

PLANTER'S PUNCH
A Favorite of Many!
.95

ALMOND EYE
San Francisco Chinatown's Famous After Dinner Drink
.95

FOO CHU Wine List — Thanks and Come Again!
See Other Side for FOO CHU

Menu, Foo Chu Cafe, St. Louis Park, 1950s

Chinese dinners were flavorful at the Foo Chu Cafe, and drinks were deceptively potent: sweethearts beware the Loving Cup (for 2).

Shanghai Low Company, 308 First Avenue South, Minneapolis, 1910s

The Moy family opened the Kwong Tung and Low Company restaurant in St. Paul in the early 1900s, following quickly with the Shanghai Low Company in Minneapolis. The first Chinese New Year celebration at the Shanghai Low Company included dozens of countrymen from surrounding communities, many of whom arrived in native dress with their hair in queues to participate in the evening's splendid feast, fireworks, and live orchestra. Family patriarch Moy Hee was a successful and respected Twin Cities restaurateur and retailer.

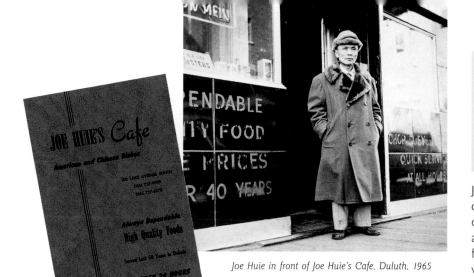

Joe Huie in front of Joe Huie's Cafe, Duluth, 1965

YETCA MEIN and WAR MEIN

Yetca Mein with Egg	1.25
Chicken Yetca Mein	1.45
Plain War Mein	1.55
Chicken War Mein	1.75
Beef War Mein	1.75
Subgum War Mein	1.65
Shrimp War Mein	2.35
Lobster War Mein	2.60

Joe Huie became a Duluth legend with his restaurant offerings of classic Chinese American fare and noodle dishes called yetca mein and war mein. The meins appeared on many early menus and were prepared with fragrant and savory sauces, tender meats, and fresh vegetables. *Yet-Ca Mein* is the Chinese term for a dish of longevity-noodles, in reference to the traditional belief that one who eats the noodles will enjoy a long life.

Located in the heart of the Minneapolis theater district, the melodramatic Kin Chu Cafe was a popular hangout for stagehands and theatergoers alike.

KIN CHU CAFE'S SHRIMP EGG FOO YONG

Kin Chu Cafe opened in 1923 with an all-Chinese staff under the management of Wen Wong, who was in charge for more than thirty years. Dishes ranged from this simple egg patty to the more upscale lobster tail with Chinese green peapods.

BROWN SAUCE:

2 cups boiling water

3 beef bouillon cubes

3 tablespoons butter or margarine

3 tablespoons cornstarch

1 to 2 tablespoons soy sauce, to taste

SHRIMP PATTIES:

6 large shrimp, cooked and diced

2 cups fresh bean sprouts, chopped

2 green onions, chopped fine

3 eggs

Salt and pepper to taste

TO MAKE SAUCE: Pour boiling water over bouillon cubes in a medium bowl; stir until dissolved. Cool to lukewarm. In a saucepan, melt the butter until lightly browned; stir in the cornstarch to make a paste. Slowly add the bouillon mixture, stirring moderately until thickened. Add soy sauce to taste. Keep warm.

TO MAKE PATTIES: Combine ingredients and shape the mixture into four flat rounds. Fry in oil heated to 300 degrees until golden brown. Serve with sauce.

New Kin Chu Cafe, 727 Hennepin Avenue, Minneapolis, 1950s

Asian-style signage informed passers-by that the new Kin Chu Cafe offered Chinese American foods, but the connection ended there, as the design of the storefront was thoroughly American Moderne.

GLOBAL VILLAGE

Many early Minnesota restaurants reflected the owner's cooking expertise and heritage. Neighborhoods of Jewish, Irish, Japanese, Mexican, African American, and other diverse populations supported nostalgic pubs, cafés, delicatessens, and barbecues that preserved culinary cultural traditions.

O'Gara's Bar and Grill, 164 North Snelling Avenue, St. Paul, 1950s

Tex-Mex and Mexican American flavors slowly made their way northward. Margaritas, guacamole, salsa, and tacos finally put Mexican dining on the Minnesota map in the mid-twentieth century. La Casa Coronado was so popular that an occasional busload of students arrived at lunchtime, ready for classes in "Enchilada 101."

Irish and would-be Irish have crowded O'Gara's for more than sixty years to drink and dine under framed photographs, family crests, and a carved shillelagh. Leprechaun cobblers positioned over the bar have brought good luck to O'Gara's: the restaurant has grown through the years to include several dining rooms and most of a city block. Charles Schultz may have dreamed of "Peanuts" as he played in his father's barbershop, located in what is now O'Gara's game room. A nearby wall holds a copy of an original Schultz drawing of Snoopy in the barber chair gazing at merrymakers in the dining room.

Mexican BEFORE DINNER Beverages

AY CARAMBA!	1.50
Tequila Straight Over Crushed Ice	
DIABLO NEGRO	.90
Rum, Vermouth with Ripe Olive	
EL TORO	1.00
Tequila, Grapefruit Juice and Sugar	
EL CLUB KAHLUA	.90
Kahlua, Charged Water	
KAHLUA SOUR	.90
Kahlua, Lemon Juice and Sour	
MARGARITA	.90
Tequila, Cointreau and Lemon Juice.	
MATADOR	.90
Tequila, Pineapple Juice, Lemon Juice	
NIDO DE CUERVO	
Tequila, Vermouth, Lemon Juice	
ORO PALIDO	
Tequila, Orange Juice, Lemon Juice	
TEQUILA COCKTAIL	
Tequila, Sugar, Lemon Juice, Grenadine	
TEQUILA COLLINS	
TEQUILA SOUR	
TEQUILA CUERVO MIST	
Tequila, Beer and Lime Juice.	
TEQUILA STRAIGHT	
with Fresh Lemon Wedge and Salt	
TEQUILA MARTINI	
SENOR WETBACK	
Tequila, Kahlua and Lemon Juice	
SANGRITA	
Tequila and Spicy, Tomato Flavored Orange Ju	

Menu, La Casa Coronado, 154 East Fairfield, St. Paul, 1950s

La Casa Coronado poured a variety of tequila drinks that were not for the faint of heart.

La Casa Coronado Restaurant, 1948

Mama Rose Coronado and members of her family worked at La Casa Coronado, and nephew Alfredo Frias continues the tradition at St. Paul's Boca Chica.

"Laughter is brightest in the place where the food is."
IRISH PROVERB

CECIL'S SWEET AND SOUR CABBAGE BORSCHT

Responding to popular demand, Cecil Glickman opened Cecil's restaurant in 1964 to serve specialties introduced fifteen years earlier when he founded his St. Paul deli. Cecil's daughter, Sheila Leventhal, and her husband, David, have sustained his Jewish kosher cooking style. She gave directions for making their famous sweet and sour cabbage soup—borscht with no beets. The longer it cooks, the better it tastes.

About 2 pounds meaty soup bones

6 cups water

1 small onion, minced

2 ribs celery, including leaves, thinly sliced

2 carrots, peeled and grated

1/2 head of cabbage, thinly sliced, slices cut crosswise into 1- to 2-inch sections

1 can (14.5 ounces) whole or diced tomatoes, including juice

2/3 cup or a 12-ounce can of tomato purée

1 teaspoon sour salt (citric acid, sold in Jewish delis; if not available, use salt and the juice of 1 lemon)

Generous 1/2 cup sugar

Salt and pepper to taste

Use meaty soup bones, koshered beef if available. Place bones in large soup pan; add water. Bring liquid to a simmer. Cover pan and allow liquid and bones to continue simmering until broth has a good beefy taste. Skim off foam or put broth through a strainer, retaining liquid. When bones cool, cut meat off bones and cut into small pieces. Return beef and broth to soup pan; add minced onion, celery, and carrots. Bring to a simmer. Add sliced cabbage, tomatoes, tomato purée, sour salt, and sugar. (If using whole tomatoes, break them apart with a potato masher.) Allow soup to simmer at least 30 minutes, until the cabbage is soft. Taste. Soup should be fairly sweet. Adjust seasonings with salt and pepper, if desired. (Note: Koshered beef is quite salty; if using, taste soup before adding salt.) Serve hot. Makes about 10 servings.

Road Buddy's, St. Paul and Minneapolis

Chet Oden was particular about his barbequed ribs: he smoked them the old-fashioned way—all night long—and credited his sister for her special-recipe sauce. Barbecue lovers from all walks of life, professional to blue-collar, flocked to his restaurants to partake of the best southern cooking available in the Midwest.

Fuji-Ya Restaurant, 420 South First Street, Minneapolis, 1960s

Reiko Weston was determined to build her Japanese restaurant on the Mississippi River, near the lucky signs of a bridge and running water. The 1960s riverfront was dreary and deserted, but Columbia flour mill and Bassett sawmill foundation ruins from the late 1800s remained, and Weston built her restaurant right on top of them. The Teppanyaki Room was surrounded by old stone mill walls, and the first midwestern sushi bar was installed upstairs. The popular new restaurant became an island of tranquility filled with flavorful Japanese cuisine, and Weston received local and national awards for her entrepreneurial talents. Fuji-Ya closed in the late 1980s, but daughter Carol and son-in-law Tom have renewed the tradition at the uptown Fuji-Ya in Minneapolis.

THE LINCOLN DEL'S THOUSAND ISLAND DRESSING

Having resisted numerous inquiries in the past, Danny Berenberg recently shared mom Theresa's secret Lincoln Del recipe for Thousand Island dressing. At the famous St. Louis Park and, later, Bloomington delis, a batch of dressing was four gallons of salad dressing plus a quart of the Del's beet borscht. Canned beet borscht or plain canned diced beets can be substituted. Ingredients are mashed together rather than blended to retain a chunky texture.

1 quart Miracle Whip salad dressing

1/4 cup chili sauce

1/2 teaspoon Worcestershire sauce

1/4 cup beet borscht or canned beets with some juice

3 hard-cooked eggs, sliced

1/2 cup green pepper, finely diced

Combine salad dressing with remaining ingredients. Blend using a potato masher until the dressing is thoroughly mixed. Makes 5 cups.

Abe's Delicatessen, 1902 Plymouth Avenue, Minneapolis, 1948

International dining continues to be a popular choice for Minnesotans. Long-standing Cantonese and Italian restaurants share their borders with new waves of flavors, and together they offer a ticket to worldly dining for armchair epicureans.

Casablanca Victory Bar and Cafe, 408 Hennepin Avenue, Minneapolis, 1945

It's showtime! Dancing, entertainment, and supper, too.

CHAPTER THREE

Supper Clubs

During the late 1800s, saloons offered "free lunches" so that patrons would stay longer and drink more—and the preferred drink was whiskey. They dined little and drank plenty. There were more saloons than cafés on the nation's main streets, and public drunkenness had been a problem since the Civil War. In turn-of-the-century Kansas, an exasperated Carry Nation entered a local saloon armed with her cane, a long iron rod, and large rocks. She demolished all the liquor in sight, destroying a nude painting of Cleopatra in the process. The bleary-eyed early-morning drinkers had their notice, and a temperance movement to ban all forms of alcohol was under way.

Two decades later, on January 17, 1920, Prohibition took effect. Main street saloons vanished overnight, bars turned into lunch counters, local restaurants hung on as best they could, and America's young and hopeful wine industry nearly evaporated. Meanwhile, moonshiners fired up copper stills and poured out gallons of bootleg liquor and bathtub gin. For thirteen years speakeasies flourished behind hidden doors.

When Prohibition ended in 1933, dining out changed drastically. In no time, nearly every midwestern city celebrated newfound freedom by opening snazzy nightclubs, supper clubs, and roadhouses. Inside were glittery stages, theatrical music halls, noisy cabarets, cascading bars, and gigantic dance floors. Couples lindy-hopped to the beat of famous bands—on stage tonight: Les Brown and his Band of Renown—or rubbed elbows with the infamous—was that St. Paul gangster John Dillinger at the corner table?

Urban nightclubs concentrated on drink, dance, and entertainment while serving classy meals: meats in snappy sauces, trendy vegetable soufflés, and to-die-for desserts. Partygoers, a Lucky Strike in hand, sipped on fancy drinks— whiskey sours, Manhattans, martinis, stingers, or pink ladies in glasses dripping with foliage and flowers.

Their country cousins—supper clubs and roadhouses—dished up more casual fare: heartland steaks and chicken, tangy barbecue, potatoes eight ways, and down-home desserts. Beer came in frosty mugs and bourbon in tall glasses. Local bands tempted diners to hit the dance floor for a fox trot or polka.

Going out for dinner became an evening-long event and socializing with friends a priority as newly affluent crowds chattered away, their get-togethers heightened by entertainment, dancing, and live music. Above all, dining out in Minnesota's nightclubs, supper clubs, and roadhouses would be fun, fun, fun!

WHISKEY, WINE, AND BEER

Whiskey and wine arrived with the earliest settlers, and local importers added variety to the storehouse. Old-world favorites and new American blends cured in barrels alongside the essential rye, gin, whiskey, scotch, bourbon, vodka, and brandy. By the end of the nineteenth century, successful breweries could be found in nearly every small town in Minnesota.

Then came Prohibition, and bars and brewers struggled to stay afloat. The new law permitted beer with a .5 percent alcohol content, but many brewhouses could not stay in business with such limited production. After Prohibition, the surviving Minnesota brew makers saw their production grow by leaps and bounds, their lagers, ales, stouts, and malts once again in great demand by the parched local citizenry.

Minneapolis Brewing Company, Delano, late 1800s

Trucks loaded with cases of beer wait to leave Gluek's Brewery immediately after the repeal of Prohibition.

Gluek's Brewery, 2021 Marshall Street, Minneapolis, 1933

A. M. Smith's, 249 Hennepin Avenue, Minneapolis, 1891

Boasting one of the area's largest and finest stocks of wines and liquors, A. M. Smith Company also accepted orders by mail. The wine depot assured quick sales and small profits, charging by the gallon $1.50 for wine, $2.75 for alcohol pure and strongest, $3.00 for cognac, brandy, and Swedish punch, and $4.00 for bourbon and whiskey.

White Star, 47 South Washington Avenue, Minneapolis

The story of the White Star bar is a classic tale of how establishments survived before, during, and after Prohibition. Mr. Anderson and Mr. Sandberg opened the White Star on Washington Avenue in 1902. They had eighteen successful years before Prohibition hit; in response, they converted the bar into a lunch counter and barely survived by selling soups, sandwiches, ice cream, and sodas. The partners were ecstatic when the first delivery of post-Prohibition beer arrived, followed the next day by crowds of merrymakers who packed the room wall to wall.

This celebration at the White Star on April 8, 1933, marked the first Saturday after Prohibition was lifted.

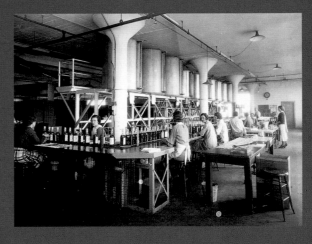

Benz laboratory, bottling department, and delivery trucks, 367 Grove Street, St. Paul, 1937

George Benz and Sons operated a large liquor supply business in St. Paul. From distillery to bottler to delivery, they had the Twin Cities covered in spirits.

WHITE STAR - "NUFF SAID" - 47 SO. WASHINGTON AVE. - MINNEAPOLIS, MINN.

Bartenders and their wives posed for this promotional photograph of the popular bar in 1948. The White Star closed in 1961, a victim of urban renewal.

By 1935, dining with mixed drinks and the proper wine was almost a requirement to be socially in vogue. Pressings from East and West Coast wineries and European vintners began pouring into the state. Liquor importing, bottling, and distribution expanded rapidly, garnering fortunes for enterprising opportunists. Nightclubs and supper clubs competed to offer the biggest and best selection of newfound libations to enhance their up-scale dinners. Some booze menus were as large as a book.

"Wine is sure proof that God loves us and wants us to be happy."
BENJAMIN FRANKLIN

ST. PAUL'S GANGSTER HANGOUTS

𝒯uxedos, evening gowns, exotic cuisine, fine liquor, big bands, high-stakes gambling, and gangsters added up to a roaring nightlife in St. Paul during the '20s and '30s. Grand dining rooms with endless bars catered to Twin City cosmopolitans and the infamous Ma Barker, Babyface Nelson, Machine Gun Kelly, Creepy Karpis, Dapper Dan Hogan, and the Kissing Bandit. Fan dancer Sally Rand performed at the Mystic Caverns, and shoot-outs, murders, bootlegging, looting, fencing, and money laundering went on right under the noses of the St. Paul police.

"Next to jazz music, there is nothing that lifts the spirit and strengthens the soul more than a good bowl of chili."
BANDLEADER HARRY JAMES

Castle Royal, 6 West Channel Street (215 South Wabasha), St. Paul, 1935

After a lavish make-over to the Mississippi River bluffs' rough-hewn, damp, and moldy mushroom caves, Josie and William Lehmann opened Castle Royal in 1933. Featuring marble fountains, Italian chandeliers, cut crystal goblets, oriental rugs, and gracefully domed spaces, the classy club could serve three hundred patrons in tasteful front-of-the-house dining rooms and cater to even more in secret back gambling halls. The posh, offbeat cave was nationally known for sophisticated food and for attracting musical talents like Harry James and Cab Calloway. For years, Castle Royal was a favorite watering hole for those above and below the law, and it survives today, despite a well-documented ghost sighting.

Castle Royal Orchestra

The Plantation Night Club's menu promoted culinary inspirations prepared by the former chef of the White Bear Yacht Club. Dinner was served in a vast space hung with vines supported by tree-trunk columns. The center dance floor provided jitterbug entertainment during an evening of drinks, dinner, and more drinks. But even this grand room played second fiddle to the gambling hall, which held nearly every kind of gambling device as well as a roulette wheel. According to F.B.I. reports, gangsters relaxed their vigilance and indulged in riotous nightlife in White Bear Lake, and the party was usually at the Plantation Night Club.

Plantation Night Club, White Bear Lake, 1930

The Green Lantern, St. Paul

St. Paul's gangsters gathered at the notorious Green Lantern for hot dogs, hard-boiled eggs, and hard-boiled lessons on bootlegging and money laundering.

The Boulevards of Paris, later named Vanity Fair, 1100 West University Avenue, St. Paul, 1934

Coliseum Roller Rink Band, 1927

Hands down, the biggest, the best, the most outrageous places to party in the Upper Midwest were the Boulevards of Paris and the mammoth Coliseum Pavilion. Glamorous patrons sipped their martinis in a full-scale reproduction of the American Bar in Paris, after which they entered the modern, "pretend we're in Hollywood" dining room. Chefs boasted about their "European cuisine of old world origins," appealing to the cultivated tastes of patrons dressed in black ties and slinky gowns. Skimpily dressed cigarette girls roamed the room, and jazz whined into the wee hours with musical giants like Fats Waller, Benny Goodman, and Louis Armstrong, who roused the crowds.

The Coliseum Pavilion, 449 North Lexington Parkway, St. Paul, 1927

If sitting toe to toe with St. Paul gangsters at the Boulevard wasn't exciting enough, dancing side by side with them in the Coliseum Pavilion would really make for a memorable night. Clusters of cars crowded around the huge skating rink–turned–dance palace. The owners claimed that the 100x250-foot dance floor was the largest in the world. Swinging the night away to the fabulously debonair Wally Erickson's Coliseum Orchestra or the funky Roller Rink Band demanded lots of drinks and a few morsels of food to keep energy up and toes tapping.

Wally Erickson's Coliseum Orchestra, 1928

CLUB THEATRICS

For decades, the corner of Sixteenth and Nicollet was party central. Although the name changed from the original Happy Hour to Club Carnival to the Flame Cafe, Twin Citians knew that the address meant a stage crowded with lively performers, Broadway acts, or big bands.

Flame Theatre Cafe, Sixteenth and Nicollet, Minneapolis, 1955

Club Carnival, Sixteenth and Nicollet, Minneapolis, 1949

Jazz musicians at the Happy Hour Bar and Cafe, 1950s

Happy Hour Bar and Cafe, Sixteenth and Nicollet, Minneapolis, 1950s

The Flame offered menu choices that didn't stretch the pocketbook or the belt—how about Norwegian sardines for dinner? Double martinis or Manhattans were strongly recommended, and the complimentary dessert was maple frango ice cream—all for under two dollars, no cover charge or minimum order. And for fun, a guy could have his picture taken with his "flame."

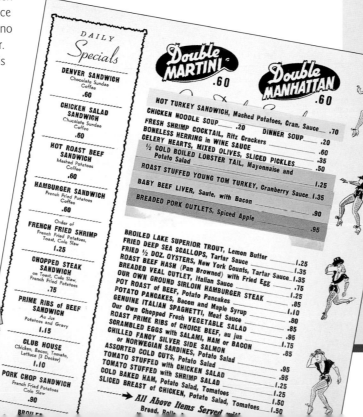

ROAST BEEF HASH WITH FRIED EGG

The Flame likely used prime rib for its hash, making it a doubly-good eating experience. For twice the protein, customers could order their hash with a fried egg on top.

2 tablespoons butter

2 cups cooked prime rib, finely cut

1 cup cooked, peeled potatoes, diced

1/4 cup onion, finely cut

1/4 cup beef broth

Salt and pepper to taste

2 eggs

Melt butter in a skillet. Add prime rib, potatoes, onion, and beef broth; fry mixture, turning occasionally, until crisp. Season to taste with salt and pepper as it cooks. Meanwhile, in another skillet, fry two eggs in butter, seasoning as desired. When the hash is crisp, portion it on two plates, making a slight depression on each plateful. Slide a fried egg onto each portion. Makes 2 servings.

Five O'Clock Club, 34 South Fifth Street, Minneapolis, 1950s

A reliable source remembers newspapermen and businessmen meeting at the Five O'Clock Club to wind down from a long day. In an early example of inter-city rail commuting, one reporter started there with lunch and drinks, took the train from the Milwaukee Depot to St. Paul to finish the afternoon edition, and returned on the train for dinner and more refreshments. No need for entertainment—the customers amused each other.

"When I read about the evils of drinking, I gave up reading."
HENNY YOUNGMAN

Conga line on a Minnesota dance floor, 1953

The **Riviera**
Shakopee's New Glamour Spot
NOW OPEN

Grand Opening
WED., MAY 11

Dining--Dancing
Bar

MUSIC BY CARL GRAY
No Cover Charge or Minimum

The Riviera, Shakopee, 1950s

The St. Paul House, Shakopee, 1950s

NEW St. Paul House SINCE 1854

SHAKOPEE, MINNESOTA
BR. 445 • Shakopee 800-1-2-3

EXTENDS TO
Jac Coller
CREDIT COURTESY
FOR 1954 - 1955
This credit card assures you every courtesy, preferred table location and special services.

N° 8500

Two well-known roadhouses were at journey's end in Shakopee. The St. Paul House, built in 1854 as a railroad hotel, was updated frequently, sometimes lavishly, and for more than one hundred years customers enjoyed frosty drinks and charcoal-broiled steaks. Just down the road, partygoers at the Riviera ascended a grand staircase plush in carpet and polished chrome to reach the second-floor dining rooms and dance floor. The first-floor bar occasionally served up more than scotch and water: rainy weather brought in knee-deep floodwaters from the Minnesota River flats.

WISH YOU WERE HERE

Resort-area supper clubs provided vacationers and locals with night-time amusement on a grand scale. Boaters, campers, and cabinfolk may have arrived at these bucolic clubs with country cooking in mind, but long-lost friends and fast-moving gossip kept people roaming the room before settling in for a night of music and dancing. Let the entertainment begin!

Grand View Nite Club, Dakota, 1940s

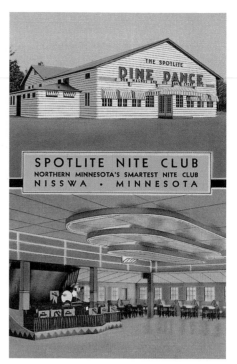

Spotlite Nite Club, Nisswa, 1950s

Bar Harbor on Gull Lake, Nisswa, 1950s

With big bands, a long bar, and a huge dance floor, Bar Harbor attracted locals as well as vacationers and celebrities from nearby resorts. Clark Gable and his movie-star friends were frequent patrons: they fished all day, arrived fashionably late for dinner, and danced the night away. Slot machines and high-stakes gambling were popular pastimes until Minnesota governor Luther Youngdahl decided the "wild life" up north was too wild and stepped up enforcement of anti-gambling laws.

Rumor has it that the slot machines now rest in peace at the bottom of Gull Lake.

Bar Harbor waitress Lee M. Nelson in nautical uniform, 1930s

Bar Harbor's Au Gratin Potatoes

May Fuhrer, who cooked for ten years at Bar Harbor Supper Club, is credited with introducing au gratin potatoes to the menu there. From the first moment these ultra-rich potatoes were served to Bar Harbor diners in the 1960s, they became a house classic.

2 tablespoons butter

3 tablespoons flour

1/4 teaspoon salt

Pinch of white pepper

1 1/2 cups warm milk

1 can Cheddar cheese soup (Campbell's preferred)

3 heaping cups of cold shredded baked potatoes

About 6 ounces shredded sharp Cheddar cheese

Grated Parmesan cheese

Paprika

Melt butter in a heavy saucepan. Add flour a little at a time, mixing well. Let mixture come to the bubble stage, being careful that it doesn't burn. Add salt and white pepper. Turn burner to low and add warm milk slowly, whisking so mixture is creamy and has no lumps. Add Cheddar cheese soup. Let mixture come to the bubbling stage again, then immediately remove from heat. Cool. Fold cold shredded potatoes into cheese mixture. Place potato mixture into a greased 8x8-inch baking dish. Cover with shredded Cheddar cheese. Sprinkle with Parmesan cheese, then lightly with paprika. Bake in a 400-degree oven until cheese is melted and golden brown. Makes 6 servings.

The Oaks stage could hold big bands and musical acts like this group of singers.

The Oaks Night Club, Minnesota City

An 1864 hotel, saloon, and brewery was transformed into the fashionable Oaks Night Club in the 1930s. Headlining food, liquor, and fine orchestra music, the dining room held six hundred while the overflow crowded in along the cocktail lounge's eighty-seven-foot bar. Onstage appearances by Lawrence Welk and Wayne King caused traffic jams clear out to the highway.

The Terrace, Lake City

Tiered seating provided everyone with a good view of the dance floor, and on Saturday night the room came alive with energized voices and rousing music.

𝒯hroughout the Minnesota countryside, thoughts of dining and dancing seduced mortals out of their cozy homes. Nightclubs with glittery stages and shiny dance floors held crowds as large as the nearest town's population. Streamline Moderne designs of sweeping horizontal lines, glowing ceiling recesses, indirect lighting, shiny vinyl surfaces, and glinting stages called to mind show time in Vegas. All-American meals of roast beef and potatoes managed to stay hot on the long trek from the kitchen to the tables of famished dancers seeking rejuvenation during a band break.

Palms Ballroom Band, 1929

No need for cash when tokens could do the trick.

Diamond Jim's guests claimed it was the greatest show place between New York and Las Vegas. Customers joined the semi-private club at the door and then watched costumed "girls" flying overhead on velvet-roped swings, electrifying diners at the tables below. Namesake Diamond Jim Brady was an East Coast financier famous for his voracious appetite and collection of jewelry worth a million dollars. The gourmet buffets and huge servings of steaks, chops, and seafood would have made him feel right at home.

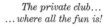

The private club...
...where all the fun is!

Diamond Jim's Supper Club and Club House,
801 Sibley Memorial Highway, St. Paul, 1960s

"Do not allow children to mix drinks. It is unseemly—and they use too much vermouth."
STEVE ALLEN

Prom Ballroom, 1190 University Avenue, St. Paul, 1950s

PROM BALLROOM'S POTATO CHIP CHICKEN

Olive Hobelsberger, who was catering manager at the Prom for nearly her entire long life, came up with this idea for roasted chicken, a concept that predated commercial shake-and-bake products. She poked a couple of small holes in a potato chip bag and beat the contents with a rolling pin. The flavorful roasted chicken was served with mashed potatoes and homemade gravy.

1 large chicken, quartered, then washed thoroughly

About 2 cups crushed potato chips

1/2 teaspoon onion salt

1/2 teaspoon paprika

1/4 teaspoon white pepper

Vegetable oil

Combine potato chips with onion salt, paprika, and white pepper. Dredge damp chicken quarters in the potato chip mixture or shake them in a bag with the chips. Place chicken on an oiled baking pan. Drizzle or brush pieces with a small amount of additional oil. Bake in a 400-degree oven for about an hour, until chicken is thoroughly cooked and the crust is crispy. Makes 4 servings.

Anticipation grew during the long walk to the ticket booth past rows of couches and excited customers at the Prom Ballroom. Would-be dancers searched for the perfect booth, then settled in and ordered the first round. Pandemonium reigned on this gigantic dance floor: gals in crinoline skirts and off-the-shoulder blouses twirled on the arms of fellas in pink shirts, charcoal pants, and white bucks. There wasn't a song the band couldn't play, and the ballroom filled with the beat of the Charleston, swing, twist, cakewalk, polka, cha-cha, lindy, fox trot, or jitterbug. People of all ages loved the Prom: they crowded it to the walls year after year and now remember it fondly.

One frequent Prom-goer describes what he saw inside:

The first thing probably was the bar. You headed there, but first you had to pass a bunch of girls sitting in the round booths in the middle, all staring at you when you came in. You know, they'd just size you up like a farmer would go to an auction sale looking at a main herd of cattle—on that order.

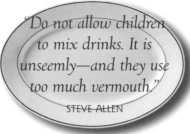

Coat check tags from the Prom and Marigold Ballrooms

idwestern nightclubs from the '30s to the '60s replicated East and West Coast images of glamorous entertainment and dining. Designers created eye-catching architecture and interiors that followed the latest trends: elegant Art Deco in the '30s, glittery stars and lights in the '40s, sleek modern elements in the '50s, chunky stone and glowing neon in the '60s. Landmarks in their communities, these clubs offered social festivities for all comers.

To no one's surprise, big supper clubs, nightclubs, and dance halls eventually saw fickle customers traipse across the street to the newest disco or cabaret. However, today's fans of the old supper-club style are sure to find one along a busy highway or down a quaint country road.

The Casablanca Victory Bar and Cafe, 408 Hennepin Avenue, Minneapolis, 1940s

Dunvilla, Pelican Rapids, 1940

State senator Roy Dunn built Dunvilla as an upscale resort and supper club. The water wheel shown here actually provided power.

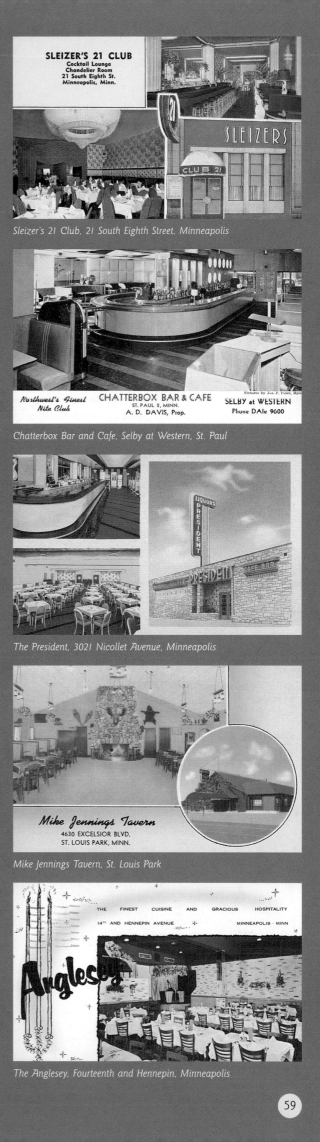

Sleizer's 21 Club, 21 South Eighth Street, Minneapolis

Chatterbox Bar and Cafe, Selby at Western, St. Paul

The President, 3021 Nicollet Avenue, Minneapolis

Mike Jennings Tavern, St. Louis Park

The Anglesey, Fourteenth and Hennepin, Minneapolis

Dan Marsh Cafe, St. Cloud, 1946

Diners perch elbow to elbow,
mid-American-café style.

CHAPTER FOUR

Cafés

While "café" is a familiar French word, not everyone knows that the first cafés got their start in France hundreds of years ago. To be called "cafés," these establishments could sell only beverages: coffees, teas, and waters. Controversy surfaced when a few Parisian cafés began serving light snacks and lunches along with their drinks—could they still be called cafés? A passionate debate developed, and when finally resolved, French onion soup and crusty breads became standard café fare. To encourage conversation, cafés provided customers with newspapers and other reading materials. Patrons, mostly educated and upper-class, belonged to a "café society" that thrived as a focus for spirited debate on current affairs. Cafés became meeting places, a metaphorical public square.

When American diners sought a place where lively conversation was accompanied by a home-cooked meal, they probably found a café—and it was similar in many ways to the old French cafés. Small and unpretentious, Minnesota cafés evolved on main streets where they were supported by local customers or sat on roadsides where weary motorists found reviving food and friendly chat. A hot roast beef sandwich with a mountain of mashed potatoes drenched in gravy was standard café fare, and most midwestern menu boards did not venture far beyond soups and chops. Décor was dictated by regional style or by the personal collections of local mom-and-pop owners.

But cafés' most endearing aspect was their pivotal role in the community. They thrived on local patronage—businessmen meeting over breakfast, family and friends gathering for lunch, students hanging out after school. Customers often knew the waitress—maybe even the cook—and they could depend on good service and eager conversation with every visit. Old-fashioned home cooking was as important as the friendly camaraderie. And when the occasional out-of-town visitor opened the door, everyone in the place turned around to see if it was someone they knew.

Cafés in Minnesota have adapted to changes in their communities, but their unpretentious charm has not been compromised by changing food trends and fluctuating populations. Many now offer expanded menus in modern café-style interiors, but the pot of coffee is always hot, and those seeking a friendly place, easy conversation, and home cooking will probably still wind up at their local café.

WHAT'S FOR LUNCH?

Gohl's Place, St. Cloud, 1935

Many of the earliest cafés were simple lunchrooms, a common sight in small towns and big cities alike. Cooking and serving were studies in cost-effectiveness. To make ends meet, cafés remained small and efficient, turning over customers quickly by offering a limited menu. Lunchrooms provided the local citizenry with plain-talking company in matter-of-fact environments.

Axel's Lunch Room, 1910s

Palmerlee's Place, Dodge Center, 1910s

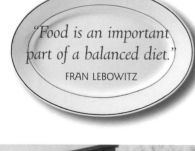

"Food is an important part of a balanced diet."
FRAN LEBOWITZ

The Palm Restaurant and Hotel, Elbow Lake, 1906

Lunch at the Palm cost thirty-five cents and a room upstairs was three dollars per week. Local lore recounts that on cold winter nights guests shared beds to keep warm.

Albert Anderson's, Barrett, 1900s

Customers who arrived by horse found hitching posts at the front door. Sturdy bread crates offered boardwalk seating for people watchers as they puffed away on their Anna Held cigars.

62

Garfield Cafe, Garfield, 1920s

afés offered more than good food and conversation. Many items were displayed for sale at the cash register and behind the counters—candies filled glass jars of all sizes and shapes, and tobacco products, including snuff and cigars, were kept in airtight tins and wooden boxes. And if these options didn't satisfy the last-minute impulse, cafés connected to ice cream parlors, candy shops, or grocery stores could meet customers' every need.

White Front Cafe, Windom, 1910

John Christofferson's Store and Restaurant, Cokato, 1905

Bananas, melons, and other fruits arriving in cylindrical wooden crates supplied both the store and the café. Some of the fruit was destined for homemade ice cream to celebrate the Fourth of July. Flags and skyrockets are barely visible in the store window.

The Royal Cafe, Slayton, 1910s

The Ideal Cafe occupied a back corner of the local Woolworth store. Shelves along the wall held restaurant dishes, confectionery supplies, and tobacco products. Swivel stools anchored to the floor gave customers little elbowroom, and overhead fans kept the air moving.

The Ideal Cafe, Albert Lea, 1930s

Gano's, Pipestone, 1920s

Quality Lunch, St. Cloud, 1926

B. & J. LUNCH

123 SOUTH WASHINGTON AVENUE

HOME COOKED FOOD

SANDWICHES

Egg Salad	.20	Hamburger	.15
Tuna Fish Salad	.25	Cheese Burger	.20
Cheese Sandwich	.15	Vegetable Hamburger	.25
Egg Sandwich	.30	Hot Beef Sandwich	.20
Bacon and Tomato	.30	With Potatoes and Gravy	.40
Denver	.30	Potatoes and Gravy served	
Hot Dog	.10	at dinner and supper only	

SHORT ORDERS

T-Bone Steak	$1.50 & up
Cube Steak	.95
Minute Steak	.75
Pork Chops—1 chop	.40
2 chops	.75
Hamburger Steak	.70
American Fries with Short Orders	.25

BEVERAGES

		Milk	.10
		Grapefruit Juice	.10
Coffee	.05	Orange Juice	.10
Tea	.05	Tomato Juice	.10

PASTRIES

Menu, B. & J. Lunch, Albert Lea, early 1900s

Lunch menus featured "short orders"—meat dishes prepared quickly on the grill—but American fries, bread, and butter were extra. Nary a green vegetable in sight.

STILLWATER AND JOHN RUNK

John Runk had a passion for documenting scenes of Stillwater and the St. Croix Valley, including the region's cafés and restaurants. He started his photography business in 1899, quickly earning the respect and cooperation of the townsfolk, who posed for him in the midst of their activities. The O. A. Anderson Lunch Room, Dubin's Cafe, and Morey's are but a few images from the vast archives of historic John Runk photographs.

O. A. Anderson Lunch Room, Stillwater, 1912

Candy front and center tempted youngsters, but tobacco sat on the back shelves, away from small eyes. This café was well equipped to weigh and wrap those after-lunch purchases.

Morey's, Stillwater

Behind those country curtains, Morey's provided old-fashioned café service and fountain treats.

Dubin's was a model early café with a menu board behind the counter, pressed tin ceiling, and tobacco display. An assortment of tables, chairs, and stools provided places to partake of simple Minnesota fare, and a typewriter on a table waited for a writer.

Dubin's Cafe, Stillwater, 1928

EARLY CAFÉS

By the turn of the century, cafés expanded into more spacious quarters even though many continued to serve only breakfast and lunch. Image became important, and diners looked for attractive table service and well-designed interior spaces along with advertised "wholesome food" served by an army of workers. Many cafés catered primarily to office workers, salesmen, and travelers who simply wanted a quick lunch.

Elgin Lunch, 434 Second Avenue South, Minneapolis, 1925

New Palace Cafe, 413 Hennepin Avenue, Minneapolis

The New Palace Cafe provided meals to travelers and locals alike. With seating available for dozens of people, this café required the attention of fast-on-their-feet waitresses and on-their-toes kitchen staff.

Mitchell Cafe, Mankato, 1910

Ganson's Cafe, 1910

Business meetings were often held in cafés. These men, wearing fashionable white shirts and starched collars, probably discussed the latest business or community news over lunch.

DENVER SANDWICH

Denver sandwiches—which may or may not have been invented in Denver, Colorado—have long been a midwestern café standard. They're ideal for the café customer who missed breakfast and hankers for a midday omelet.

1/4 pound ham, finely diced	1 tablespoon cream
1 small onion, finely chopped	Salt
1/2 green pepper, finely chopped	Freshly ground pepper
Butter	4 slices bread
4 eggs	

In a heated skillet, melt a dab of butter. Sauté ham, onion, and green pepper until browned. Add more butter if the pan seems dry. Beat eggs with about a tablespoon of cream, salt, and pepper. Pour over ham mixture, stirring gently. Let the egg mixture cook into a patty; turn gently and brown the other side. Cut in half and serve between slices of toasted, buttered bread. Makes 2 sandwiches.

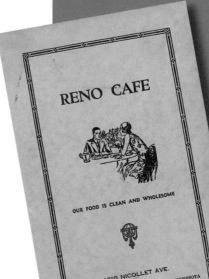

Menu, Reno Cafe, 1310 Nicollet Avenue, Minneapolis, 1930s

The mark of a good café was an eclectic mix of Denver sandwiches, chicken chow mein, and minute steak. The Reno went beyond the basics, offering a total of 158 choices.

LEADING LADIES

Many early cafés were owned and operated by women. The owners cooked meals from scratch, and a variety of waitresses were on hand to serve the customers. Mothers worked the lunch hour, teens helped out in the afternoons, and plenty of extras pitched in during the dinner hour. Freshly baked breads, cakes, and pies always appeared on the menu, and owners often shared their favorite recipes with their customers.

Ann's Cafe, Cokato

Grand Cafe, Rochester

Anna M. Oesterreich advertised grand meals at her Grand Cafe, which she proudly promoted as American owned and operated. Crowds at the popular café could choose seating at the marble soda fountain, in the adjoining dining area, or in a private party room. The interior was beautifully appointed with polished mahogany, lamp lighting, and canvas chair covers. An appropriately grand menu, listing everything from crisp pecan waffles to half a chicken simmering in buttery sauce, invited diners to order almost anything twenty-four hours a day.

Brokerage Coffee Shop,
296 East Fifth Street, St. Paul

Owner Myrtle Schilling taking a break with two of her waitresses and hugging her brother-in-law at the Brokerage Coffee Shop.

Rose Marie Cafe, 617 Selby Avenue, St. Paul, 1928

"Vegetables are a must on a diet. I suggest carrot cake, zucchini bread, and pumpkin pie."
GARFIELD, CARTOONIST JIM DAVIS

Cokato Pantry, Cokato, 1930s

Emma May owned the Cokato Pantry, and her smiling staff would surely agree that home cooking made this small café a hub for town activity.

THE PANTRY'S BANANA BREAD

Delicious breads, cakes, and pies were another measure of a good café. This banana bread recipe is a favorite from the Cokato Pantry.

1 1/2 cups sugar

1/2 cup shortening

1 egg

1/4 cup buttermilk mixed with 1 teaspoon baking soda

3 ripe bananas, mashed

4 cups flour

1 teaspoon salt

Cream sugar and shortening. Add egg, then buttermilk with soda, bananas, flour, and salt. Mix well. Pour into a greased loaf pan. Bake in a 350-degree oven for 40 minutes. Makes 1 loaf.

A FAMILY AFFAIR

afés could be profitable family businesses. Many husband-and-wife owners called on the help of children and friends, who joined them in putting in long hours. Cafés were fun places to work. Through the door came all the town gossip and details about current scandals and politicians on the campaign trail. Counters held a jumble of signage, racks of cellophane-wrapped candies, cards of sunglasses, and displays of pipes and tobacco.

Olympia Cafe and fruit store, Osseo, 1920s

Delano Cafe, Delano, 1920s

Wendell Cafe, Wendell, 1920s

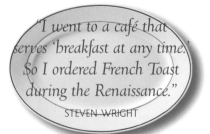

"I went to a café that serves 'breakfast at any time.' So I ordered French Toast during the Renaissance."
STEVEN WRIGHT

Canary Cottage, Osseo, 1920s

Sunlight Bakery and Cafe, St. Cloud, 1930s

Felix and Mary Kamrowski opened the Sunlight Bakery in 1918, and the original bakery with its coal-fired ovens soon grew into a busy café. Eight children and a few extra hands baked, displayed, served, and sold to throngs of customers.

Helen Kamrowski, Felix and Mary's daughter, documented the rhythm of a typical day in a small-town café:

8–9 A.M.	Businessmen sat at the counter and didn't do much talking, just read newspapers while they ate breakfast.
10–11 A.M.	Clerks on break stopped for a quick cup of coffee and donuts or a cinnamon roll.
12–2 P.M.	Families, shoppers, farmers, and office workers created the busy lunch hour.
2–4 P.M.	Coffee breakers stopped in for coffee, pie, and pastries.
5 P.M.	Clerks and secretaries picked up bakery goods to take home.
6–8 P.M.	Single men occupied most of the tables for supper: bachelors, men whose wives were away, salesmen, and businessmen.
8–10:30 P.M.	Crowds swarmed in after the movies for sundaes, malts, sodas, and banana splits. Actors and late-night workers came in for sandwiches at the very end of the evening.

Finney's Cafe, later the Wadena Cafe, Wadena, 1930s

Finney's Cafe opened in the 1920s with whirling fans mounted on a tin ceiling and oversized scenic pictures on the walls. The café had more than its share of famous visitors. In the 1930s, Clark Gable was looking forward to an uneventful lunch at this small-town café when crowds of gaping fans gathered round. He agreed to sign autographs if they would wait until he finished eating. They waited and were all late for school. Waitress Marie Schertler told the local newspaper that she was so nervous she had to try three separate times to get a cup of coffee to Gable without spilling it. A decade later, movie star Vera Ellen lunched in a wooden booth and charmed admirers during a visit to her grandmother, who lived in Wadena.

Vera Ellen in a booth at Finney's Cafe, 1940s

During the 1940s, some cafés provided motorists and neighborhood workers with simple Minnesota fare in the most basic of buildings. Diners didn't care. The steaks were midwestern grown and the food home cooked.

Café, Isabella, 1940s

Frank's, Aldrich, 1950s

Dickey's Stockyards Cafe and Steak House, Rice Street, St. Paul, 1940s

Armed with forks and knives, patrons knew that the huge, juicy steaks coming out of this kitchen would satisfy big appetites. No frills here: the lighting was fluorescent, the floors scrubbed clean, and the furnishings utilitarian—just the sort of place "where men who know meat, meet to eat."

69

GOLDEN GLOW BEAUTY SHOPPE

Elsie Wentzel, Prop. *Assisted by Hildegard Wentzel*

OUR BEAUTY WORK
Makes You Appear Youthful

Open Evenings
by Appointment

3002 27th Avenue South
JUST OFF LAKE STREET

Residence: Dupont 4614 Shoppe: Drexel 9657

Second Cup of Coffee Free with all Lunch orders of 25c or more. Ask for it.

SHORT ORDERS

Bread, Butter or Toast, Potatoes, Coffee, Milk or Tea Included with Short Orders

Special Grilled Porterhouse Steak.	.65	Ham Omelet	.40
Grilled T-Bone Steak	.50	Plain Omelet	.35
Grilled Pork Chops	.45	Cheese Omelet	.40
Ham and Eggs	.45	Special Small Steak	.40
Fried Premium Ham	.40	Hamburger Steak	.35
Fried Premium Bacon	.40	Bacon and Eggs	.45

2 Eggs [any style] .35

SANDWICHES
No Extra Charge for Toasted Sandwiches

Cold Roast Beef	.15	Swiss Cheese	.15
Cold Roast Pork	.20	Denver	.25
Premium Ham	.15	Sliced Chicken	.30
Plain Ham	.10	Lettuce, Tomato	.20
Fried Ham	.15	Peanut Butter	.10
Fried Ham and Egg	.20	Egg Salad	.15
Fried Pork Chop	.20	Olive Salad	.15
Fried Egg	.10	Nut Salad	.15
Smoked Goose Liver	.15	Chicken Salad	.20
Hamburger	.10	Salmon Salad	.15
American Cheese	.10	Toasted Marmalade	.20

SPECIAL TOASTED 3-DECKER SANDWICHES
With Lettuce and Mayonnaise Dressing

Ham and Tomato	.25	Chicken Salad and Bacon	.35
Ham and Cheese	.25	Peanut Butter and Cheese	.20
Bacon and Cheese	.30	Special Club House	.45
Bacon and Tomato	.30	Egg Salad and Tomato	.30
Sliced Chicken and Bacon	.40	Chicken Salad and Tomato	.35

BEVERAGES

Coffee	.05	Green Tea, Pot	.10
Milk	.05	Hot Chocolate	.10
Half and Half	.10	Iced Tea	.05
Orange Pekoe Tea, Pot	.10	Butter Milk, large glass	.05

We Put Up Lunches to Take Out

PASTRY
We Make Our Own

Pie, per cut	.10	Doughnuts, 3	.10
Cake, per cut	.10	Cookies	.05
Pie or Cake a la Mode or with Whipped Cream	.15	Wafers	.05
Pie with Cheese	.15	Sweet Roll and Butter	.05

Pies and Cakes made to order to take out

If there is anything not listed on menu that you would like, ask for it. We will be glad to make it for you.
Protect yourself—all dishes and silverware thoroughly steralized by electricity

---

We Serve MEATS of the Finest Quality from the

Val Ness
QUALITY
MARKETS

2714 East Lake St.
Dupont 2353-2354

4157 Minnehaha Ave.
Drexel 2870

For Good Food that Satisfies

BETTER FOOD

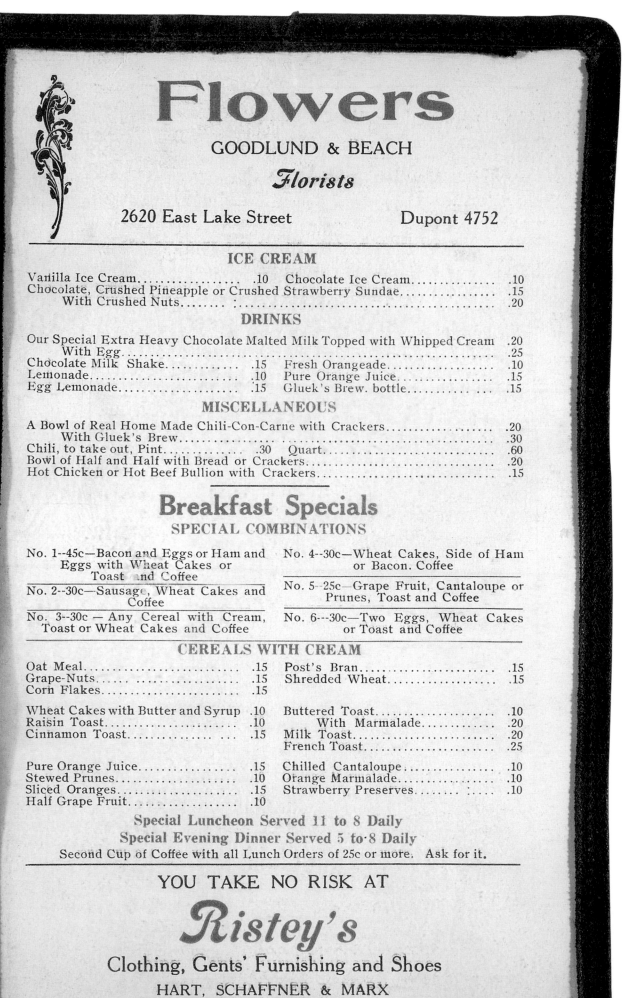

Flowers

GOODLUND & BEACH
Florists

2620 East Lake Street   Dupont 4752

ICE CREAM

Vanilla Ice Cream................. .10   Chocolate Ice Cream............. .10
Chocolate, Crushed Pineapple or Crushed Strawberry Sundae................ .15
    With Crushed Nuts........ :.. .20

DRINKS

Our Special Extra Heavy Chocolate Malted Milk Topped with Whipped Cream .20
    With Egg.. .25
Chocolate Milk Shake............. .15   Fresh Orangeade............... .10
Lemonade...................... .10   Pure Orange Juice............. .15
Egg Lemonade................... .15   Gluek's Brew. bottle............ .15

MISCELLANEOUS

A Bowl of Real Home Made Chili-Con-Carne with Crackers................... .20
    With Gluek's Brew.. .30
Chili, to take out, Pint............. .30   Quart.......................... .60
Bowl of Half and Half with Bread or Crackers............................ .20
Hot Chicken or Hot Beef Bullion with Crackers........................... .15

Breakfast Specials
SPECIAL COMBINATIONS

No. 1--45c—Bacon and Eggs or Ham and   No. 4--30c—Wheat Cakes, Side of Ham
    Eggs with Wheat Cakes or   or Bacon. Coffee
    Toast and Coffee

No. 2--30c—Sausage, Wheat Cakes and   No. 5--25c—Grape Fruit, Cantaloupe or
    Coffee   Prunes, Toast and Coffee

No. 3--30c — Any Cereal with Cream,   No. 6--30c—Two Eggs, Wheat Cakes
    Toast or Wheat Cakes and Coffee   or Toast and Coffee

CEREALS WITH CREAM

Oat Meal.......................... .15   Post's Bran...................... .15
Grape-Nuts...... .... .15   Shredded Wheat.................. .15
Corn Flakes....................... .15

Wheat Cakes with Butter and Syrup .10   Buttered Toast.................... .10
Raisin Toast...................... .10   With Marmalade.............. .20
Cinnamon Toast................ ... .15   Milk Toast....................... .20
                                         French Toast..................... .25

Pure Orange Juice................. .15   Chilled Cantaloupe............... .10
Stewed Prunes.................... .10   Orange Marmalade................ .10
Sliced Oranges.................... .15   Strawberry Preserves........ :.... .10
Half Grape Fruit.................. .10

Special Luncheon Served 11 to 8 Daily
Special Evening Dinner Served 5 to 8 Daily
Second Cup of Coffee with all Lunch Orders of 25c or more. Ask for it.

YOU TAKE NO RISK AT

Ristey's

Clothing, Gents' Furnishing and Shoes

HART, SCHAFFNER & MARX
SUITS and OVERCOATS

3014 27th Avenue South   Just Off Lake Street

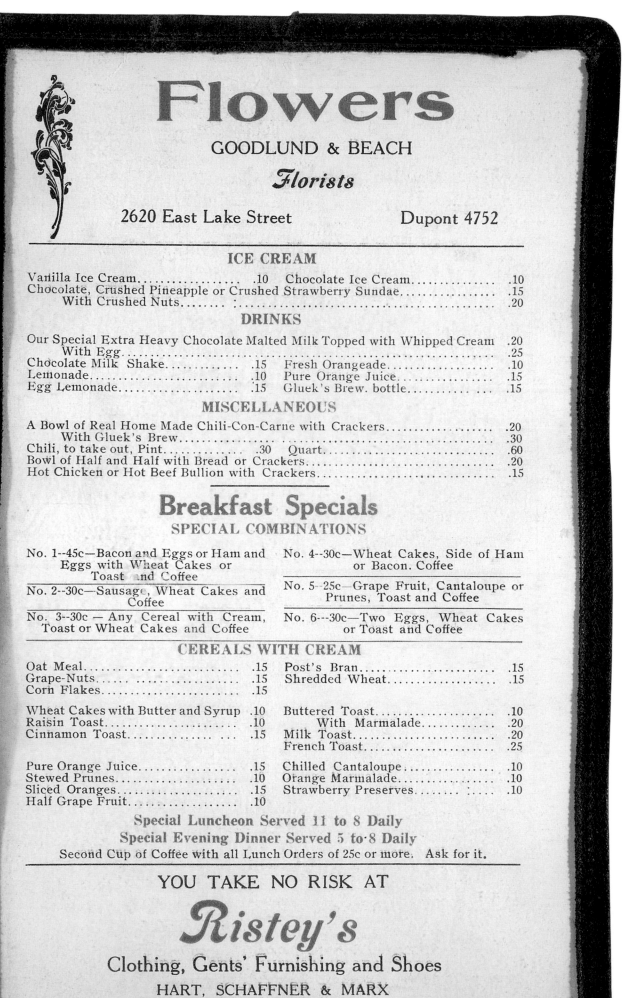

Menu, Carlson's Restaurant and Sandwich Shop, 2940 Twenty-seventh Avenue South, Minneapolis, 1940s

Printed menus came into use around the mid-1800s. In their earliest form they offered simple menu information, promotions of the café's cleanliness, warnings to watch one's belongings, and advertisements for cigars and candy.

It didn't take long for Minnesota merchants to realize they could buy advertising space on menus. Company logos and typographic elements graced the edges of menus wrapped in the latest clear plastic covers. By the 1940s and '50s, oversized menus became elaborate marketing tools, complete with illustrated menu options and graphic touches.

COFFEE, TEA, OR LUNCH

Pan's Cafe, St. Cloud

On a break from work or while visiting the city, many people took their meals in one of the numerous cafés and coffee shops sprinkled throughout downtown areas.

St. Cloud promoter Sam Pandolfo built an automobile empire. When that enterprise failed, he turned to making his next fortune in . . . donuts! The Pan Health Food Company began selling "greaseless do-nuts" in 1927.

Black and White Cafe, Little Falls, 1940s

In 1931, a small-town diner opened on the main street of Little Falls, and today a grown-up café continues the tradition, serving scrumptious hamburgers to patrons seated at tables surrounded by photos and memorabilia, local artwork, and stacks of bargain books.

"One of these do-nuts every morning for each of your family will keep the doctor away and put iron in your blood and clean the digestive tract of all foul, decayed matter and will brighten up the eye, clear the skin and put more life in your step. If every family in St. Cloud will use these wonderful health do-nuts daily, in two months I will have a health food factory going here that will put the town on the map. All farmers coming to town should take a dozen or two home. Price 30 cents a dozen." Who could resist a promotion like that?

Coffee shop, 1938

New York Soda and Lunch, 142 East Fourth Street, St. Paul, 1920

MRS. JONES'S APPLE DUMPLINGS WITH BUTTERSCOTCH SAUCE

Long before the IDS Center's Crystal Court made indoor alfresco dining popular, Mrs. Jones Courtyard Restaurant decorated the Baker Arcade in downtown Minneapolis with indoor trees and garden flowers. Among the dishes recommended by Duncan Hines was Mrs. Jones's apple dumplings glistening with butterscotch sauce.

Pie crust (enough for 2 double crusts)

1 1/2 cups sugar

5 tablespoons flour

3 tablespoons butter

1 teaspoon cinnamon

8 medium Jonathan or Winesap apples

BUTTERSCOTCH SAUCE:

2 cups brown sugar

1 cup water

2 tablespoons butter

3 tablespoons cornstarch

3 tablespoons water

TO MAKE CRUST: Roll pie crust and cut into circles large enough to wrap around apples. Mix together sugar, flour, butter, and cinnamon. Peel and core apples. To make dumplings, spread a pastry circle with 1 tablespoon of the sugar mixture. Place an apple in the center of the pastry circle and fill the core with sugar mixture. Brush edges of pastry with water and fold over apples, pinching edges together. Continue until all apples are covered with pastry. Place apples in a buttered baking pan. Bake in a 425-degree oven until the pastry is browned, about 15 minutes, then reduce heat to 350 degrees and continue baking until apples are tender when pierced with a sharp fork, about 1 1/4 hours. For a darker crust, brush pastry with milk before placing in oven. Serve dumplings hot with butterscotch sauce. Makes 8 servings.

TO MAKE BUTTERSCOTCH SAUCE: In a saucepan combine brown sugar, 1 cup water, and butter; boil for 10 minutes. To thicken, stir in a mixture of cornstarch and 3 tablespoons water, blending until sauce is of desired consistency.

The Arts and Crafts movement swept through the Midwest during the first part of the twentieth century. Handcrafted furniture in simple but sturdy designs became popular for home interiors and also appeared in numerous tearooms and coffee shops. Copper vases, earthen-glazed ceramics, handwoven textiles, even carpets and wall coverings were fashioned with artistic designs that respected the simplicity of the materials from which they were made.

Alexander's Cafe, Andrus Building, Fifth and Nicollet, Minneapolis

Lake View Tea Room, 1920s

Handicraft Guild Tea Room
89 SOUTH TENTH STREET :: MINNEAPOLIS

Convenient and Delightful
for Luncheon and Afternoon Tea
Open Daily from 12 to 5 o'clock

Special Arrangements for Suppers, Dinners and Banquets

N. W., M. 3264   T. S., 3952

Handicraft Guild Tea Room, 89 South Tenth Street, Minneapolis, 1910

The Handicraft Guild in Minneapolis was one of the nation's most famous art institutions during the Arts and Crafts period. Students worked in a variety of creative endeavors, and many became certified art instructors. Prairie School artist Grant Wood studied in one of the studios and probably had lunch in the Tea Room with his fellow painters.

Elks' Cafe, Mankato

*Landstrom's Coffee Shop,
61 East Fifth Street, St. Paul, 1921*

DOWN THE MISSISSIPPI

Like many Minnesota towns, Red Wing and Winona had a number of popular cafés. Most of them had bead-board ceilings and patterned tile floors and offered seating in pressed-back chairs or on rows of counter stools.

Little Cafe, Red Wing, 1920s

Corner Cafe, Red Wing, 1930s

Joe's Restaurant, Red Wing, 1930s

Blue Bird Cafe, Red Wing, 1930s

Hot Fish Shop, Winona

Opened in 1931 by fisherman Henry Kowalewski, the Hot Fish Shop became famous for its batter-fried wall-eye pike. The appetizer menu offered a seafood feast: herring, anchovies, scallops, crab and lobster meat, oysters five ways, shrimp four ways, and fried frog legs. Duncan Hines visited Winona to sample his favorite fresh fish and made the Hot Fish Shop #1911 on his list of recommended eateries.

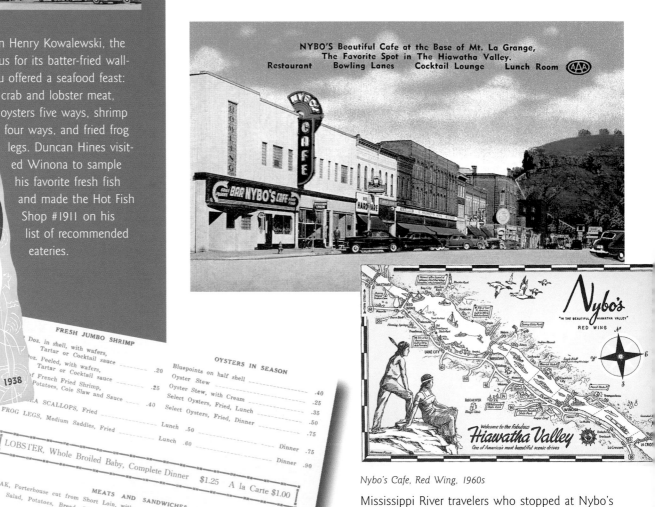
Nybo's Cafe, Red Wing, 1960s

Mississippi River travelers who stopped at Nybo's in Red Wing found that the steaks outnumbered the fish in this river town. Nybo's survived in its original location into the 1980s.

Larsen's Cafe, Fergus Falls

Cozy wooden booths on black-and-white tile floors beckoned customers to this appealing café, and rightly so, as Larsen's provided "the biggest and best meals in town." It was tidy and clean, the candy and cigars were ready by the door, and the soda fountain was a convenient stop for an ice-cream cone on the run.

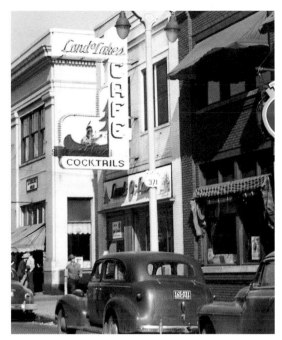

Land o' Lakes Cafe, Brainerd, 1940s

The 1940s were years of expansion for cafés throughout the Midwest. Towns in western and northern Minnesota experienced surges of new citizens and tourists. Blue lakes lured summer vacationers and cabin owners who traveled two-lane highways in search of relaxation and water play, with a hospitable, home-cooked lunch along the way.

Hart's Coffee Shop, Moose Lake

Diners overlooked Moose Lake from Hart's spacious wraparound porches. Opened in 1927, the café quickly attracted local diners and, as the roads improved, Hart's travelers' specials brought in wayfarers from near and far.

TICK TOCK CAFE OLIVE NUT SANDWICH

Olive-and-nut sandwiches were a popular snack in cafés during the '30s and '40s. This recipe is from Klock's Tick Tock Cafe in St. Cloud.

Chopped pimiento-stuffed green olives
Finely chopped walnuts
Homemade mayonnaise

Combine chopped olives and walnuts; moisten with mayonnaise to a good spreading consistency. Start with 2 parts olives to 1 part walnuts, then adjust for taste. The bread can be dark or white, toasted or plain.

CAFÉ SOCIETY

afés were all about people. The surroundings, seating, dishes, even the food were secondary to the companionship found inside these eateries. Customers often knew each other, café staff developed an easy camaraderie, and everyone forged long-lasting friendships.

Cunningham's Steak Shop, Winona, 1947

Danielson Cafe, Buffalo, 1946

Sheper's Cafe, St. Cloud, 1940s

Sweet Shop, Cokato, 1940s

Spudnut Shop, Willmar, 1950s

Short-order lunch counter, 1950s

Chicken Shack, 629 Sixth Avenue North, Minneapolis, 1930s

Waitresses behind counter, 1940s

Dan Marsh Cafe, St. Cloud, 1950s

Busy lunch counter, 1950s

Three girls in a wooden café booth, 1945

Men at short-order counter, 1945

Lunch in a cozy booth, 1949

LAKE MINNETONKA

An easy day trip from the Twin Cities, Lake Minnetonka was a favorite destination. As cars became commonplace, a Sunday drive around the lake after a leisurely lunch was an inviting way to spend an afternoon.

Hardy's Cafe, Excelsior, 1920s

On the south side of Lake Minnetonka, Hardy's Cafe provided homemade meals for Excelsior residents and a refreshing stop for travelers in their Model Ts. The unusual live palm tree reminded diners that they were near the water, even if it wasn't the tropics.

Anchor Inn, Excelsior, 1950s

Facing the Excelsior waterfront, the Anchor Inn was a harbor stop for skippers and boat admirers alike.

Hart's Cafe, Wayzata, 1930s

Hart Du Prey opened his café in Wayzata in 1927, remodeling a two-story clothing store into the one-story Hart's Cafe, which included a six-lane bowling alley. It became a stopping point for those seeking directions around the lake and a destination for streetcar and tour bus passengers in need of refreshment. In the 1950s, Hart's was again remodeled, into a modern glass and stone building that survived until 1983. Sunsets Restaurant occupies the site today.

Deephaven's Chowen's Corners was a main intersection for the growing permanent lake population on the eastern shore. Early residents and workers in the up-and-coming area found refreshment in early cottage and cabin architecture.

Log Cabin Inn, Deephaven, 1950s

Log Cabin Cafe, Deephaven, 1957

Nolan's, Edina, 1940s

Friends who wanted to be hip met at Nolan's perfectly modern café.

Hasty Tasty, 3601 Lyndale Avenue South, Minneapolis, 1953

Among the most charming cafés in Minneapolis during the '40s and '50s, the Hasty Tasty offered a vast sandwich listing, "from A to Z." The Lake Street location with its famous glass staircase and a third location next to the Edina Theater were the main attractions for family fun and popular with students cruising for a prom date.

Peter's Grill Chocolate Fudge Cake

The original owner of Peter's Grill, Peter E. Atcas, believed there was no substitute for quality. He encouraged customers to visit his restaurant's kitchen, which he called "a homemaker's dream." Minneapolis diners might not have always accepted his invitation, but they seldom turned down a slice of chocolate fudge cake when it was offered.

CAKE:

2 cups boiling black coffee

1 cup cocoa

1 teaspoon soda

2/3 cup hot black coffee

1 cup shortening

3 cups sugar

1/2 teaspoon salt

4 eggs

4 cups sifted cake flour

2 teaspoons baking powder

2 teaspoons vanilla

FROSTING:

1/3 cup milk

2 tablespoons granulated sugar

3 1/2 cups powdered sugar

4 tablespoons butter, melted

5 squares chocolate
(semi-sweet or dark), melted

2 teaspoons vanilla

1/4 teaspoon salt

TO MAKE CAKE: Stir cocoa into 2 cups boiling coffee. Cool. Add soda to remaining hot coffee. Cream shortening, sugar, and salt. Beat in eggs one at a time. Sift together flour and baking powder. Add to the creamed mixture alternately with the cocoa mixture. Beat in the coffee-soda mixture and vanilla. Grease either a 9x13-inch pan or two 9-inch square pans. Pour batter into prepared pan or pans. Bake in a 350-degree oven for 1 hour.

TO MAKE FROSTING: Bring milk and granulated sugar to a boil. Pour the hot milk over the powdered sugar, stirring until smooth. Beat in melted butter and chocolate. Add vanilla and salt, stirring until smooth. Spread on cooled cake.

Peter's Grill, 85 South Ninth Street, Minneapolis, 1957

Founded in 1914, Peter's Grill has known several locations in downtown Minneapolis. The original wooden booths still embrace customers as seasoned waitresses plunk down heavy plates of Peter's famous hot turkey dinner, complete with dressing and mashed potatoes awash in brown gravy.

The Convention Grill, Edina

Opened in 1941, the Convention Grill became a hangout for students and families, all of whom mobbed the tiny café in their quest for juicy hamburgers, piles of fries, and thick chocolate malts. And if that makes your mouth water, customers are still welcome at the grill in its "authentic" retro style.

Perkins Pancake House, 6023 Nicollet Avenue, Minneapolis, 1950s

Minnesotan Wyman Nelson operated a gas station on Nicollet Avenue, and on a cold winter day he looked across the street at a warm and toasty pancake house and decided to trade his gas pump for a hot griddle. He bought the Perkins Pancake House right then and there! Wyman had a way with pancakes and good, clean restaurant service, and he eventually owned four hundred Perkins restaurants across the country. Today they number more than six hundred and are operated by Holiday Inn. The next time the urge for fluffy pancakes hits, head to the oldest Perkins in America, located at 6023 Nicollet Avenue.

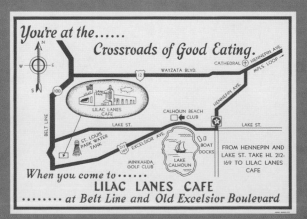

Lilac Lanes Cafe, St. Louis Park, 1950

A destination for St. Louis Park students and for travelers on the belt line was the Lilac Lanes Cafe, which overlooked a bowling alley and evolved into the King's Inn. An afternoon snack included a peek at muscular pinsetters as they dodged the balls crashing into the pins.

Rainbow Café, Hennepin and Lake Streets, Minneapolis

Modern in every sense of the word, the Rainbow Café featured a spectrum of shiny surfaces, plastic coverings, and bright colors. Opened in 1919 at the busy intersection of Lake and Hennepin, the café served 750,000 patrons annually, and they came to take pleasure in the ever-changing shows arranged for local artists by the Legeros family. The Rainbow served under sunny skies for more than half a century.

Rainbow Café Strawberry Cream Pie

Food at the Rainbow was prepared and served by a staff of one hundred, and one of the classics was strawberry cream pie.

1 pint strawberries, washed, hulled, and sliced

1 cup sugar, divided

4 1/2 tablespoons cornstarch, divided

1/2 teaspoon salt

3 eggs, slightly beaten

2 cups milk, scalded

Baked 9-inch pie shell

Whipped cream

To sliced strawberries add 1/2 cup sugar. Let stand 2 hours. Drain off juice, saving liquid. To the strawberry juice add 2 tablespoons cornstarch. Cook over low heat until thickened, stirring constantly. Fold in strawberries. Combine remaining 1/2 cup sugar with remaining 2 1/2 tablespoons cornstarch and salt. Add the three eggs to the sugar mixture, mixing thoroughly. Add scalded milk. Cook in a double boiler until thick, stirring constantly. Pour mixture into the baked pie shell. Cool. Pour strawberry mixture over top of pie. Refrigerate. Cut into wedges and garnish with whipped cream.

Makes 6 to 8 servings.

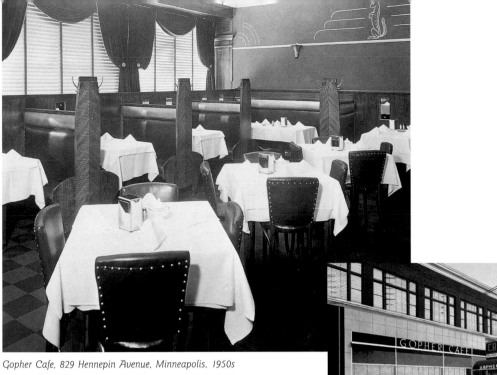

Gopher Cafe, 829 Hennepin Avenue, Minneapolis, 1950s

Located in the heart of the theater and business district and beloved for its modern, informal, clublike aura, the Gopher Cafe was busy night and day. The café offered several dining options: service in a cozy little booth, at the counter in a swivel chair, or in the back room with cushioned seating and white tablecloths.

"Not good lookin', just good cookin'"

SERLIN'S CAFE

Serlin's Cafe, 1124 Payne Avenue, St. Paul

Irvin Serlin worked hard to make his café the best in the neighborhood. He was so successful that politicians, housewives, legislators, teenagers, and locals packed the old painted booths toe to toe. Frank Sinatra once sent his chauffeur to sneak through the back alley and pick up cheeseburgers and pie. There's still a little elbowroom there today, as customers are watched over by Irv's wife, Doris, and her sons.

THE GOPHER CAFE'S CHICKEN SAUTÉ

The Gopher Cafe's customers savored menu favorites such as chicken sautéed with vegetables. Advice to cooks from the kitchen staff: white meat cooks more quickly than dark meat, so remove it from the pan and keep it warm while the dark meat continues cooking to tenderness.

2 tender young chickens
(2 1/2 pounds each)

Lemon juice

Salt and pepper

1/4 cup butter

8 small green onions, finely chopped

2 green peppers, diced

1 cup sliced mushrooms (caps only)

4 tablespoons chopped parsley

Disjoint chickens. Rub the skin with lemon juice and season with salt and pepper. In a large frying pan, melt butter; brown chicken in butter until golden. Add green onions, peppers, and mushrooms. Cook for 2 to 3 minutes, adding more butter if necessary. Cover and cook slowly until chicken is tender when pierced with a fork, about 30 to 45 minutes. Remove chicken. To the drippings and vegetables, add chopped parsley, stirring until well combined. Pour drippings over chicken. Makes 8 servings.

Former Minnesota governor Wendell Anderson frequented Serlin's Cafe. When he was governor in the 1960s, Anderson would send his driver to Serlin's to bring back cheeseburgers, soup, and pie, enough to feed attendees at a legislative meeting.

He recalled,

When I was a young, single law student living on St. Paul's East Side, I ate breakfast at Serlin's nearly every morning. The food was wonderful and incredibly low-priced even if the booths were very uncomfortable. No matter who came in the door, they were treated the same. . . . Irv Serlin was a Damon Runyonesque character who lived above the restaurant. He gave the mailman and the milkman keys so they could come in to make their own coffee very early in the morning.

CRABTREE'S KITCHEN SWEDISH APPLE PIE

The simple foods served at Crabtree's were reminiscent of the area's Swedish settlers' culinary traditions. This apple pie was everyone's favorite.

PIE:

Generous 2 cups apples, peeled and sliced

2 tablespoons flour

3/4 cup sugar

1 egg

1/8 teaspoon salt

1 teaspoon vanilla

1 cup sour cream

9-inch unbaked pie shell

TOPPING:

1/3 cup sugar

1/3 cup flour

3/4 teaspoon cinnamon

1/4 cup cold butter or margarine

Toss sliced apples with 2 tablespoons flour and 3/4 cup sugar. Stir together egg, salt, vanilla, and sour cream; mix with apples. Pour mixture into unbaked pie shell. Bake in a 450-degree oven for 20 minutes, then reduce heat to 350 degrees and bake 20 minutes more. Meanwhile, make the topping by combining 1/3 cup sugar, 1/3 cup flour, and cinnamon. Cut in cold butter until crumbs form. Remove pie from oven and sprinkle topping over apples. Bake an additional 20 minutes at 350 degrees. Serve warm.

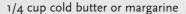

Akre's Dutch Oven, Nisswa

"Known from coast to coast," Akre's cafés were located in the heart of vacationland. The Dutch Ovens served fresh bakery goods and operated old-fashioned delicatessens and refreshing soda fountains.

Blue Goose Inn, Garrison

Fishing was *the* attraction on Mille Lacs Lake, and the Blue Goose served up its specialties fresh from the lake. Cool metal lawn chairs rocked the summer crowds waiting for a table, and if the plan was to celebrate the daily catch, this was the place to do it. Stories of the ones that got away can still be heard in a brand-new Blue Goose Inn.

Crabtree's Kitchen, Marine on St. Croix

This 1854 pioneer building originally held a general store, boat works, gas station, and Prohibition brewery complete with fast women. In 1949 Crabtree's moved in as a side-of-the-road café for those enjoying a scenic drive along the St. Croix River.

Cook, Crabtree's Kitchen, 1950s

Castle Falls Cafe, Anoka

Self-described as the gateway to northwest vacationland, the Castle Falls Cafe had a picturesque waterfall, rustic bridge, and lovely castle. Who could resist a stop at this quirky and photogenic café?

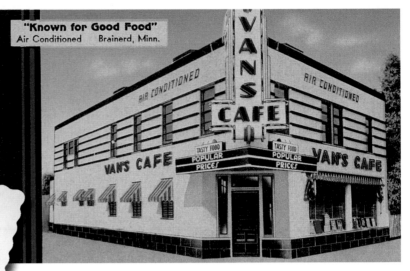

Van's Cafe, Brainerd

Vacationers knew that getting to Brainerd for lunch meant their holiday had begun. One option was Van's Cafe. Originally an 1893 lumber mill office, the building was moved in 1908 to a location across from Brainerd's landmark water tower, where it became a restaurant. The enduring structure, in one remodeled style or another, has offered "good food at popular prices" ever since.

Betty's Chocolate Layer Pie

Sandwiches made with Betty's freshly baked rye bread were served daily beginning in the late 1950s, but tourists flocked to Betty's Pies because of the myriad fruit and fluffy pies. A half-century later, after selling the restaurant and planning to retire, Betty is still baking pies, among them this dreamy chocolate creation that has remained among the top three sellers at her roadside destination.

9-inch baked pie shell

MERINGUE:

2 egg whites

1/2 teaspoon white vinegar

1/2 cup sugar

1/4 teaspoon salt

1/4 teaspoon cinnamon

FILLING:

2 egg yolks, slightly beaten

1/4 cup cold water

1 cup semi-sweet chocolate chips

TOPPING:

1 cup heavy cream, whipped

1/4 cup sugar

1/4 teaspoon cinnamon

TO MAKE MERINGUE: Beat egg whites until frothy. Add vinegar, beating until soft mounds form. Gradually add 1/2 cup sugar, salt, and 1/4 teaspoon cinnamon. Beat until meringue stands in stiff, glossy peaks. Spread on bottom and sides of the baked pie shell. Bake in a 325-degree oven for 20 minutes or until lightly browned. Cool.
TO MAKE FILLING: Combine the egg yolks, water, and chocolate chips; stir over very low heat until chips are melted. Spread 3 tablespoons of chocolate mixture over the cooled meringue. Cool.
TO MAKE TOPPING: Whip the cream until thick; add the remaining sugar and cinnamon. Spread half of whipped cream over the chocolate layer. Combine the remaining whipped cream with the remaining chocolate mixture. Spread over the whipped cream, right to the edges of the pie shell. Chill at least 4 hours before serving.

Betty's Pies, Two Harbors

Betty Lessard sold her pies out of a North Shore fishing shack. When pies crowded out the space for fish, it became known as Betty's Pies. With a spectacular view of Lake Superior, Betty's was, and still is, nationally famous for slices of homemade pie packed with the freshest ingredients.

CAFÉS FOR CAMPERS

For those about to embark on a wilderness trek, cafés in Grand Marais and Ely offered a final opportunity for a civilized meal. When the weather turned stormy, adventurers gathered at these warm sanctuaries to hear the latest weather reports, news, and gossip and to trade stories of their hair-raising adventures.

Campers Home Cafe, Two Harbors

When the campfire went out, outdoorsmen headed for the rustic Campers Home Cafe.

Le Sage's Cafe, Grand Marais, 1933

Campers geared up for long trails with short orders at Le Sage's Cafe.

Edgewater Inn, Tofte, 1930s

DuNord Cafe, Grand Marais

Tony's Eat, Grand Marais, 1940s

SHORT ORDERS

Sizzling T-Bone Steak	95c	Veal Chops	50c
Sirloin Steak	60c (with onions 10c extra)	Liver and Bacon or Onions	50c
Lake Superior Trout	50c	Lamb Chops	65c
Fillet of Herring	50c	Ham or Bacon and Eggs	50c
Cubed Steak	50c	Home Baked Beans and Ham Sandwich	35c
Pork Chops	50c	Asparagus Tips on Toast	35c
Breaded Pork Tenderloin	50c	Cold Meats and Potato Salad	40c
Hamburger Steak	45c	Stuffed Tomato and Egg Salad Sandwich	35c

Chili Con Carnie and Crackers 20c

Potatoes, Bread, Butter and Beverage Included With Above Orders

Log Cabin Inn, International Falls, 1935

CHICAGO CAFE - International Falls, Minnesota

Chicago Cafe, International Falls, 1940s

Depending on their mood, diners could lunch at the rustic Log Cabin Inn, loaded with a zoo's worth of heads and pelts, or slide into the sleek and modern Chicago Cafe. International Falls was the last stop before Canada, and travelers from both sides of the border experienced their first or last taste of American home cooking here.

"I've been on a diet for two weeks and all I've lost is two weeks."
TOTIE FIELDS

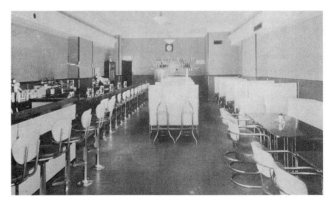

Vertin's Cafe, Ely

Café-Style Meatloaf

Cafés served what is now called comfort food, and nothing was more comforting than a thick slice of meatloaf sharing a plate with mashed potatoes, gravy, and peas. This classic meatloaf can also fill sandwiches.

1 1/2 pounds lean ground beef

1/2 pound ground pork

2 eggs, beaten

4 large soda crackers, crushed, or 1/2 cup dry bread crumbs

2 tablespoons minced celery

1/4 cup minced onion

1/2 teaspoon poultry seasoning

1 teaspoon salt (less if using salty crackers)

1/2 teaspoon freshly ground pepper

Beef stock or bouillon

2 tablespoons flour

Combine ground beef with pork. In a bowl, combine meats with beaten eggs, crushed crumbs, celery, onion, and seasonings. Mix well. Pack into an ungreased bread pan. Bake in a 400-degree oven for 45 minutes. Pour off liquid, saving it to make gravy. Return meatloaf to oven and continue baking for about 15 minutes or until browned. Serve sliced meatloaf with mashed potatoes, gravy, and vegetable. Serves 6 to 8.

TO MAKE GRAVY: Skim fat from drippings. Add beef stock or bouillon to drippings to make 1 cup liquid. Bring liquid to a boil and stir in about 2 tablespoons flour; whisk until smooth. Season to taste with salt and pepper. If it is too thick, add more beef stock.

TO MAKE MEATLOAF SANDWICHES: Cut warm meatloaf into thick slices. Place between slices of white or whole-wheat bread. Serve sandwiches with ketchup, chips, and pickle.

The Broiler, 627 Hennepin Avenue, Minneapolis, 1950s

Austin's, Rochester

Huson's, Grand Rapids

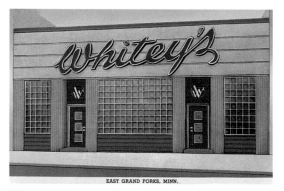

Whitey's Cafe, East Grand Forks

The Connoisseur, 389 Wabasha Street, St. Paul

CAFÉ MODERNE

Design took a giant leap forward in the 1950s as cafés shed the period look and became modern inside and out. Creative type styles allowed for artistic signage that was smartly incorporated into sleek new café exteriors—and no one could miss the name. Interiors were all curves and streamlined shapes. Counters were sweeps of plastic laminate rounded at the corners, and plump vinyl-covered stools and padded booths encouraged customers to stay awhile. Bright colors made rooms lively.

Hotel Holland, Duluth, 1930s

At Erickson's Cafe mirrors and curving lines swept diners into the interior of this polished space. The finishes of chrome, ceramic tile, laminate counters, and etched glass panels completed the nearly perfect picture of modern dining. Music could be ordered from the tabletop jukebox, handbags rested on the shelf under the counter, and dessert lovers asked for Erickson's famous Georgia pecan pie. Everything was up-to-date, and the date was 1950!

Third Street Cafe, Bemidji, 1950s

*Capital Eat Shop,
Rochester, 1950s*

Many Rochester cafés were Streamline Moderne
in design, squeaky clean, and efficient in operation, appealing
to customers coming from the Mayo Clinic, which was also modern in design,
squeaky clean, and efficient in operation. The patterned floor tile, indirect lighting, smooth vinyl seating, and chrome edging epitomized the '50s look found in
cafés throughout Minnesota.

The Royal Cafe, Lake City, 1950s

afés, coffee shops,
tearooms, and lunch-
rooms remain a permanent
part of midwestern cities,
small towns, and rural routes.
These enduring eateries will
always be found tucked in
the heart of the city or along
a country road. They may
change in design and adapt
to food styles, but corner
cafés, with their charm
and companionship, will
captivate diners for
generations to come.

Gold's Grill, Albert Lea, 1950s

Snack Shop, Rochester, 1949

Erickson's Cafe, Sixth and Hennepin, Minneapolis, 1950s

Soo Chu Cafe, 3003 Hennepin Avenue, Minneapolis, 1940s

Richards Treat Cafeteria, 114 South Sixth Street, Minneapolis, 1944

Lenore Richards and Nola Treat admire a full complement of sweet confections at their bakery counter.

CHAPTER FIVE

Cafeterias

From their first appearance in the late 1800s, cafeterias provided an inexpensive alternative to sit-down menu service and an efficient way to dish up meals to large numbers of customers. They offered communities a unique eating situation—dining rooms could be unpretentious, service was straightforward, and large quantities of stored food supplies were not required.

For customers, an instant meal on the tray wasn't the only advantage. Diners could view all the options at once, decide what appealed to them at that moment, and carry it to their table within minutes. Cafeterias provided vital nourishment to a hungry population, especially during lean times or when students and workers sought economical meals. Unfortunately, steam-table food, though plentiful, was not always palatable. Main dishes were overheated, vegetables were soggy, desserts hovered on the stale side. But cafeterias grew in popularity, and customers continued to come in, optimistic that the food and facilities would eventually improve.

In the work place, lunchrooms were originally tucked in dark unused areas, spaces that did little to refresh those on their noon break. When the cafeteria concept finally came to office and industrial environments, employees enthusiastically embraced the cheerful and attractive lunch areas and serving lines.

By the 1920s, cafeteria cooks finally overcame the boring steam-table image by developing recipes with staying power. Advancements came in the form of foods whose taste improves with time, like hearty soups, chilis, and stews, plus fresh made-to-order entrées and sandwiches. Food presentation became an art form as eye-catching pastries, bountiful main courses, and fresh bakery aromas kept customers coming in the door and traveling down the line. And prices remained reasonable.

To attract customers' attention, exterior architecture was animated and exciting. Some buildings became landmarks in their communities, their interiors appropriately designed to match the outside style. Seating areas were fashionably furnished and the ambiance enriched with art and antiques, as if to say that efficient dining could also be fine dining.

Today's cafeterias, with their modern gourmet style, are hardly recognizable as such. They offer the latest food preparations, exotic coffees, and the philosophy of "life is short, take dessert first." Others introduce variation with stations of specialty food—salads here, hot entrées there, beverages near the checkout. In these festive eateries, few seem to notice that they are carrying their tray of food to a table, "cafeteria style."

LINEAR TEMPTATIONS

Minnesota State Capitol Rathskeller, St. Paul, 1913

Carling's cafeteria was a spectacular assemblage of beautiful wood, rich patterns, and warm lighting. The unusually attractive food line appealed to modern diners in St. Paul and beyond.

Carling's, 349 Robert Street, St. Paul, 1960s

A hungry group of boys filled Carling's cavernous dining room in 1957.

One of the most beautiful cafeterias in the Midwest was built within the cellars of the Minnesota State Capitol. In 1905, German American immigrants stencilled the rathskeller's walls and ceiling with fanciful patterns and whimsical mottoes, but their work was painted over in 1917 when anti-German sentiment ran high. Thanks to a sensitive restoration in the 1990s, the present room retains a historic and stately character, with reproductions of the original stencil paintings, traditional wall colors, and restored floor tiles. Politicians and citizens have dined here for one hundred years, and the Rathskeller continues to serve politically correct cafeteria lunches today.

"One more for that dismal weather."
RATHSKELLER INSCRIPTION, 1913

Duluth's Arrowhead Cafeteria offered a wide variety of items, including thirty sandwich specialties, dozens of breakfast selections, and numerous chop suey, egg foo yong, and rice combinations. The eclectic choices were an ambitious undertaking for a cafeteria of that era.

Arrowhead Cafeteria, Duluth, 1915

ARROWHEAD CAFETERIA
219 West Superior Street
DULUTH — MINN.

We Serve Meals 8 A. M. to 4 A. M.

MAY 9th, 1944

ICE CREAM SUNDAES

Vanilla Ice Cream	.10	
Orange Sherbet	.10	Strawberry Sundae
Chocolate Nut Sundae	.25	Raspberry Sundae .15
Marshmallow Sundae		Cherry Sundae .15
Peach Sundae		.15
Pineapple Sundae		.15
Chocolate Sundae		.15
Caramel Cream Sundae	.15	Hot .15
Butterscotch Sundae	.15	Hot :20
...le Sundae	.15	Hot .20
...an Nut Sundae	.15	Hot .20
...d Almond Sundae		.20
... Salad Sundae		.15
... Salad		
...a Split		
... Thought		
...and White Sundae		.30

PARFAITS

Chocolate Parfait		
Strawberry Parfait	.25	Caramel Cream Parfait .25
Raspberry Parfait	.25	Butterscotch Parfait .25
Cherry Parfait	.25	Maple Parfait .25
Peach Parfait	.25	Fruit Salad...

Grandma Miller's,
20 South Seventh Street, Minneapolis, circa 1890

Miller's Cafeteria, 20 South Seventh Street, Minneapolis, 1931

O n 1876, Grandma Miller served thirty-six diners in her little boarding house with its grass front lawn—on the corner of Seventh and Hennepin. Her food was good, and hordes of customers soon outgrew the quaint building. An Art Deco vision emerged on the site, eventually seating four hundred and serving more than five thousand meals daily. For a time, there were Miller Cafeterias in Duluth, Rochester, and sixteen other locations in Minnesota and Wisconsin. Modern building exteriors complemented streamlined interiors, successfully projecting an image of sophisticated style and modern food service.

Waitresses, Miller's Cafeteria, Duluth, 1933

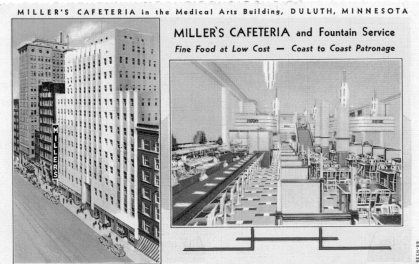

MILLER'S CAFETERIA in the Medical Arts Building, DULUTH, MINNESOTA

MILLER'S CAFETERIA and Fountain Service
Fine Food at Low Cost — Coast to Coast Patronage

320 West Superior Street, DULUTH, MINN. -- 20 So. 7th Street, MINNEAPOLIS, MINN.

Miller's Cafeteria, Duluth, 1950s

The caption for this postcard boasts that Chef Chris has worked at Miller's for forty-eight years, supervising more than 50 million meals.

Miller's Cafeteria, 924 Nicollet Avenue, Minneapolis, 1964

When Miller's Cafeteria closed after eighty-eight years in business, the final cups of coffee were served by waitress Ethel Durgin.

RICHARDS TREAT

114 SOUTH SIXTH STREET, MINNEAPOLIS

Plenty of people and a mountain of trays were on hand to serve the waves of customers arriving in the 1950s for the famous chicken potpie, baked ham, roast beef, and apple pie.

Richards Treat Cafeteria and Food Shop was created in 1924 by Lenore Richards and Nola Treat, two former University of Minnesota home economics instructors who believed that variety was the spice of the food business. Food writer Duncan Hines called it "Educated food for educated people," and in 1944 the partners were elected to the American Restaurant Hall of Fame. The menu was varied, carefully prepared, and served in a setting decorated with antiques collected during the owners' travels. In the Colonial dining room, murals graced the walls, tables held candles and fresh flowers, and it felt "just like home." Diners thought so, too—they crowded the bakery counters, jammed the serving line, packed the dining rooms, and relished the first-rate food for more than thirty years.

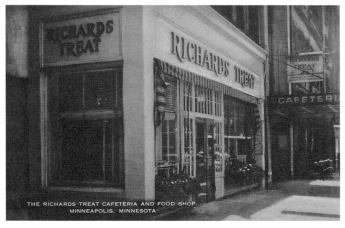

Richards Treat, 1950s

A handwritten note on the door announced the opening of Richards Treat in 1924. On that first day, twenty-two guests paid a total of $10.41, a successful beginning for the new restaurant.

RICHARDS TREAT CHICKEN POTPIE

CRUST:

2 cups all-purpose flour

1 1/2 teaspoons baking powder

1/2 teaspoon salt

1/2 cup fat (lard, shortening, or butter)

Cold water

FILLING:

2 chicken breasts, roasted or boiled, meat cut into cubes

1/2 cup chicken fat or butter

1/4 cup minced onion

3/4 cup flour

1/2 teaspoon celery salt

2 1/4 cups chicken stock, heated to boiling

1 1/2 cups hot milk

1 egg yolk

TO MAKE CRUST: Sift the flour, baking powder, and salt together into a large bowl. Work in the fat with a pastry cutter or fingertips. Add water a little at a time, distributing evenly throughout the mixture. Mix until blended. Add water as needed but avoid making the dough too wet. Chill dough. Roll about 2/3 of dough to about 1/4-inch thickness. Cut to fit six shallow 8-ounce casserole dishes. Press dough rounds into casseroles. Keep remaining dough and any rolled scraps chilled until needed.

TO MAKE FILLING: Melt the fat in a saucepan. Add the onion and cook until golden brown.

Stir in the flour and celery salt, blending well. Stir in the boiling chicken stock, mixing rapidly with a wire whip. Cook over medium heat for 7 to 10 minutes. Mix the egg yolk into the hot milk, then stir into the hot stock mixture. Cook until thickened.

TO FINISH POTPIES: Divide cubed chicken among the six casseroles. Add 3/4 cup hot gravy to each casserole (it is important that the gravy be hot so the bottom crusts don't become soggy when baked). Roll out remaining crust into six rounds and place atop the casseroles, cutting slits or crescents in the top crust to allow steam to escape. Crimp edges to seal. If desired, for a golden crust, brush with an egg beaten with 1 tablespoon milk. Bake in a 375-degree oven for 20 to 25 minutes, or until the top crust is golden brown. Makes 6 potpies. (Note: For more colorful, nutritious potpies, add chopped carrot and peas or broccoli to the casseroles before pouring hot gravy over the chicken.)

THE FORUM

36 SOUTH SEVENTH STREET, MINNEAPOLIS

The Forum Cafeteria, 1930s

On 1930 the grand old Strand Theater closed and the seats were ushered out. Within its shell rose the dazzling Forum Cafeteria. The interior shimmered with classic Art Deco zigzag patterns, angular shapes, green etched-glass partitions, and cascading frosted-glass chandeliers. Columns were clad with silvery mirrors and walls featured hand-painted scenes of Twin Cities lakes and neighborhoods. The extravagant style was unusual and a bit flashy for the Midwest, but countless diners lined up for a meal and sat down to admire the surroundings for more than forty years.

The Strand's nineteenth-century theater façade supported the new Forum Cafeteria sign. The exterior was dismantled and placed in storage in 1972.

The stunning interior, now listed on the National Register of Historic Places, remains an exceptional example of Art Deco design. Other restaurants that have called this building home are Scotty's on Seventh and Goodfellow's.

Menu, The Forum, 1950s

Chicken pie was a signature Forum meal offered daily at lunchtime. Dinner choices were the good old standbys of the era, today's comfort foods.

Classic Cafeteria Swiss Steak

Every cafeteria offered a steam pan brimming with Swiss steak in glistening tomato sauce. Cooked to total tenderness, its gravy studded with bits of onion and celery, this hearty meat was best served atop mashed potatoes.

3 pounds thick-cut round steak, cut into pieces

2/3 cup flour

1 teaspoon salt

1/4 teaspoon pepper

Oil for browning

1 large onion, diced

2 ribs of celery, diced

3 cups canned tomatoes, plain or stewed

With a meat mallet, pound a mixture of flour, salt, and pepper into the meat on both sides, flattening steak in the process. In large heavy skillet, heat oil, mixed with butter if desired. Brown meat pieces on both sides, setting finished ones aside until all meat is browned. Remove all meat from skillet. Briefly brown onion and celery in skillet. Return meat to pan. Pour tomatoes with their juice over the meat and vegetables. Cover. Cook over low heat for 2 hours. Uncover and cook an additional 1/2 hour to thicken the sauce. Serve hot with mashed potatoes. Serves 6 or more.

Clayton, Jeanne, and Tim Sonmore in Becky's Cafeteria, 1934 Hennepin, Minneapolis, 1960s

Opened in 1924, Becky's Cafeteria was named after the Beck sisters, but it earned national renown after engineer Clayton Sonmore bought it in 1949 and added antiques and decorative allure. In a *Minneapolis Star* article from 1966, Barbara Flanagan wrote that Becky's was where actors from the Guthrie Theater liked to relax: "Those New Yorkers love that prune-whip and homemade meatloaf atmosphere." Becky's owners were known to pepper the restaurant with their stock of Bibles, believing that spiritual and emotional fulfillment came from both the Good Book and good food. Customers mourned when Becky's closed its doors after sixty years in business.

Becky's Cafeteria Sour Cream Cookies

Becky's specialties included tapioca pudding made from a recipe by friend and restaurant critic Duncan Hines, who frequently praised Becky's in print. A long-time favorite were these rich cookies, solid enough for dessert.

1 cup lard (or shortening)	1/2 cup sour cream
1 cup sugar	1/2 cup buttermilk
1 cup brown sugar	3 3/4 cups sifted all-purpose flour
2 eggs	1 1/2 teaspoons soda
1 teaspoon vanilla	1 1/2 teaspoons baking powder
1 teaspoon lemon extract	1/4 teaspoon salt

Cream lard or shortening with sugars and eggs. Add vanilla and lemon extract. Combine sour cream and buttermilk; add to creamed mixture. Sift together dry ingredients and stir into creamed mixture. Refrigerate dough overnight.
TO MAKE COOKIES: Roll dough 1/4-inch thick on heavily floured cloth-covered board, using a pastry sleeve on the rolling pin. Cut dough with a floured 2-inch cookie cutter. Sprinkle rounds with sugar. Bake in a 400-degree oven until browned, 8 to 10 minutes. Makes 2 1/2 dozen large cookies.

touch of the **good old days**
now in its 40th year
the one and only
Becky's Cafeteria
1934 HENNEPIN AVE.

NOW! AMPLE FREE PARKING

HOLLAND'S NICKEL and DIME Savers for the Week

	IN BOTH CAFETERIAS			IN OUR BAKERY	
— MONDAY, JULY 30, 1956 —					
BEEF TIPS OVER		Save	CHOCOLATE NUT-TOPPED		Save
HOT BISCUIT	45c	10c	CAKE DOUGHNUTS	Doz. 50c	10c
— TUESDAY, JULY 31, 1956 —					
CHOPPED PRIME		Save	CLOVER LEAF DINNER		Save
ROUND STEAK	35c	10c	ROLL, Tender	Doz. 30c	10c
— WEDNESDAY, AUGUST 1, 1956 —					
BEEF NOODLE		Save	TOLL-HOUSE COOKIES		Save
CASSEROLE	45c	10c	Choc.-Chip Delight	2 Doz. 50c	10c
— THURSDAY, AUGUST 2, 1956 —					
TURKEY A LA KING OVER		Save	SPICE CUP CAKES, Serve		Save
HOT BISCUIT	45c	10c	with Ice Cream	Doz. 50c	10c
— FRIDAY, AUGUST 3, 1956 —					
TUNA FISH LOAF with		Save	FIG FILLED BRAN MUFFINS		Save
Parsley Butter Sauce	45c	10c	Delectable!	Doz. 50c	10c
— SATURDAY, AUGUST 4, 1956 —					
ROAST LOIN OF PORK		Save	CHOCOLATE FUDGE		Save
With Dressing	45c	10c	BROWNIES	Doz. 74c	10c
Enjoy our 99c Family Night Supper Every Wed.—5 to 7 p.m.—Children 69c					

HERE'S **HOLLANDS** OF ROCHESTER, MINN.

This exuberant advertisement complements Holland's funky interiors. Wavy cut-out ceiling openings, modern art, ample seating, and a take-out bakery made this cafeteria a popular destination.

Holland's, Rochester, 1930s

Originally a one-story food market, Holland's later added a second story to accommodate a popular cafeteria, coffee shop, and bakery. The bakery produced a series of whimsical bread sculptures in 1954 called "yeastie beasties"—French bread shaped like crocodiles, turtles, lobster, catfish, even ears of corn. Retailing at two to three dollars, these festive creations were shipped all over the country.

EDUCATED CHOICES

University of Minnesota cafeteria workers, 1912

Starched and serious, this staff knew it had important work to do: hundreds of hungry university students would soon be looking for brain food.

St. Barnabas Hospital,
901 South Sixth Street, Minneapolis

St. Barnabas nurses set up trays for "room service."

Student nurses line up for a healthy lunch—possibly Swedish meatballs.

Swedish Hospital, 914 South Eighth Street, Minneapolis, 1960

Cafeteria at the University of Minnesota, 1940s

Well-dressed and clean-cut university students select hot roast beef sandwiches for their noon meal.

The Auteria automatic cafeteria, 374 South Wabasha Street, St. Paul, 1924

Two businessmen contemplate a model Auteria, invented by Woodland H. Gilbert. The St. Paul Auteria opened in 1924 and lasted only a few years. The Auteria, called an Automat on the East Coast, created a quirky style of cafeteria service. Women in booths at the front door provided nickels that customers inserted into a slot beside the desired item. The glass door unlocked, granting access to a plate of hot or cold food. Customers liked the shiny fittings and thought the service was both fun and sanitary. The most famous Automat, Horn & Hardart in New York City, became an American icon in 1912.

Unidentified cafeteria, 1925

Company cafeterias grew into huge facilities, and crowds of friends engaged in animated conversation made lunchtime lively, noisy, and fun.

WILLING WORKERS

Dreary lunchrooms in the Washburn Mill were replaced with state-of-the-art cafeterias in the 1920s. Hundreds of ecstatic employees joined in a month-long opening celebration that included entertainment by the Girls' Packing Department Trio and the Loading Department Band.

The Washburn A Mill, 703–709 South First Street, Minneapolis, 1859

Munsingwear cafeteria, Lyndale and Glenwood, Minneapolis, 1925

Munsingwear was an educational and entertaining place to work. Employees took advantage of music and theater clubs, recreation rooms, social services, medical departments, a branch of the Minneapolis Public Library, and full cafeteria service.

Munsingwear kitchen and staff, 1920

This kitchen area was renovated in 1985 when the building became International Market Square. Today, diners in the Atrium Restaurant's great courtyard can imagine the clatter of horse and wagon or visualize a smoky freight train of nearly one hundred years ago passing by exactly where they sit.

Office cafeteria, General Mills, 400 Second Avenue South, Minneapolis, 1955

General Mills office employees tested products, held meetings, and dined in their elegant downtown cafeteria surrounded by beautiful marble walls under an Italianate vaulted ceiling.

Dining room, Northern States Power, 1925

Shiny glazed tile covered the walls, columns, floor, and ceiling in Northern States Power's employee cafeteria. Coffee from the five large urns behind the counter kept everyone awake all day for sure.

Northwestern National Life Insurance Company, 200 South Washington, Minneapolis, 1965

Lucky employees dined "at the top of the mall." The furnishings reflected architect Minoru Yamasaki's design sensibilities for this graceful structure.

The eagerly awaited noon hour provided a stretch from the desk and the pleasures of socializing and companionship. In-house dining spaces became stylish, with comfortable seating for leisurely lunches and a broad medley of menu choices. Valued for the camaraderie and nourishment they offer, cafeterias are here to stay.

Opened in 1949, this lunchroom was designed by University of Minnesota color advisor John Hopkins, who selected a "symphony" of color: red, green, yellow, and gray.

Saint Paul Fire & Marine, 1950s

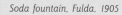

Soda fountain, Fulda, 1905

Soda fountains became popular after the Civil War, and by the 1900s thousands operated throughout America.

CHAPTER SIX

Soda Fountains

oda fountains got their start in the early 1800s when visitors to health resorts asked to take home the fizzy mineral water served at the spas because they thought it made them feel better. Enterprising pharmacists began importing the water as a healing tonic, and it quickly grew in popularity. Because the water was expensive to bottle and transport over long distances from the springs, it wasn't long before artificial mineral water that could be produced locally was developed. Called "soda water," it became the new health drink sought after in drug stores.

To disguise soda water's bitter taste, lemon juice was supposedly added by a perfume dealer around 1830. The simple addition of a "flavor" made the water taste better, and soon various other fruits and roots were gathered for taste testing. Further evolution came when syrupy sugar was added to create the sweet soda—fizz, flavoring, and sweetener—that we know today. These peppy new drinks swept across the nation like wildfire.

Dispensing machines were needed to hold the many flavored syrups now in demand by soda water customers. At first these machines were utilitarian, but they quickly developed into fabulous "fountains," their sweet contents pouring forth from exotic contraptions of gleaming metal and richly colored glass. Customers mobbed the creamy marble counters holding the glamorous new creations.

Much later, around 1870, the first dollop of ice cream was dropped into a glass of soda water, possibly by accident. Customers raved about the refreshing new combination. Fountain choices expanded tenfold, and ice-cream sodas became the next national frenzy.

Soda fountains were so popular, legend has it, that local governments forbade them to serve on Sunday for fear of losing churchgoers. Clever fountain operators got around the restrictions by creating a non-soda concoction of ice cream with syrup drizzled on top. They named it "sundae" to fool the local authorities.

Then the doors flew open to all kinds of creations. Along came a parade of malts, shakes, banana splits, frappés, parfaits, egg drinks, phosphates, and freezes. With great skill and showmanship, "soda jerks" embellished ordinary ice cream with bubbly waters, sweet syrups, mounds of whipped cream, and flourishes of cherries and nuts.

Soda fountains became neighborhood social centers as confectionery counters pushed out medicine displays while tables and chairs came in to hold the growing crowds. Originally quirky and curious, early fountain dispensers were soon designed to be elegant and irresistible. In Minnesota, fashionable ice cream parlors and fabulous fountains rivaled the best in the country.

Midwestern five-and-dimes joined the soda-fountain craze, and menus expanded with selections of sandwiches, soups, and pie. Stores cleared out their aisles to make way for elongated lunch counters next to islands of tables. Customers lined up to claim a swivel chair or crowded into booths with friends. The soda fountain–lunch counter became a cherished and uniquely American dining experience.

WHAT THE DOCTOR ORDERED

Drullard's Drug Store, Seventh and Nicollet, Minneapolis, 1880s

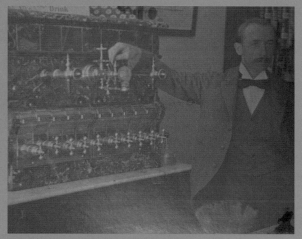

B. F. Carter Soda Fountain, St. Cloud, 1890s

J. C. Arnold Soda Water Fountain, Montevideo, 1900s

The flavors labeled on these spigots include ginger, sarsaparilla, orange, chocolate, pineapple, lemon, and vanilla. Arnold's bragged that it served the purest and most healthful ingredients known to science.

innesota's earliest soda fountains were located at drug store counters, where the pharmacist put soda orders on hold while finishing batches of the latest medicines. Customers waited patiently until the pharmacist finally opened the spigot, poured sticky syrup into a glass, and filled it to the top with bubbling soda water.

A. J. Guernsey Drug Store, Dale and Selby, St. Paul, 1896

n May 1886, Dr. John Stythe Pemberton stirred up a hot syrupy mixture of sugar and flavorings in his Atlanta, Georgia, backyard to improve his "French Wine of Coca," a bitter headache tonic. He shared this new recipe with his partner, bookkeeper Frank Robinson, who loved it at first taste. Robinson sat right down and created the famous flowing script Coca-Cola trademark. Pemberton offered samples at Jacob's Pharmacy, where, supposedly, a squirt of carbonated water accidentally spilled into a glass of the syrup. The fizzy drink was better than the syrup alone, and the winning Coca-Cola formula was born.

Sold as a patent medicine in the late 1800s, Coca-Cola was thought to be a cure for headaches and hangovers. A very good cure indeed, for early formulas contained the narcotic extract of the coca plant—cocaine.

customers soon tired of standing at fountain counters to enjoy their foamy treats. Stools arrived in short order, but more seating was needed, and major remodeling occurred in drug stores throughout the Midwest.

Arthur Hullstrum's restaurant, Marietta, 1915

Rex Cafe, Thief River Falls, 1900s

Lauer and Son Drug Store, Winona, 1908

Edmund J. Fuchs Drug Store, 796 East Seventh Street, St. Paul, 1925

Hagen and Olson's Soda Shop, Hawley, 1912

When underground water flows through pockets of minerals, it becomes mineral water, and when it passes through pockets of carbon dioxide gas, it becomes naturally carbonated. To make artificially carbonated water, or "soda water," a variety of ingredients could be used. One technique was to liberate carbonic gas from marble dust. In New York City, John Mathews produced carbonated water from scrap marble he collected during the construction of St. Patrick's Cathedral in the mid-1800s.

FASCINATING FOUNTAINS

By the turn of the century, soda fountains were moving into prime positions in drug stores. Rows of dusty medicine bottles faded into the background, and shiny marble counters held bowls of fresh fruit and jars of colorful candy for garnish. In a bid for higher visibility, fountain dispensers moved from back shelves to front counters. Enriched with beautiful marble and gleaming brass fittings, they became irresistible attractions. Fascinated customers couldn't put down their nickels and dimes fast enough.

American Beauty Confectionary, 700 Hennepin Avenue, Minneapolis, 1915

Solberg's Store, Elbow Lake, 1920s

Palace of Sweets, Montevideo, 1924

Villa Restaurant, Storden, 1920

Pool hall and soda fountain, Wilder, 1910

Sinclair Lewis described a soda fountain in his classic novel *Main Street*: "A drug store with a soda fountain that was just huge, awful long, and all lovely marble; and on it there was a great big lamp with the biggest shade you ever saw—all different kinds of colored glass stuck together; and the soda spouts, they were silver, and they came right out of the bottom of the lampstand! Behind the fountain there were glass shelves, and bottles of new kinds of soft drinks, that nobody ever heard of. Suppose a fella took you there!"

As flavors were added and fountains grew in popularity, the pharmacist went back to mixing medicines while fountain professionals donned white shirts or jackets to take orders from customers and operate the dispensers. The term "soda jerk" came into use early in the twentieth century. Though an effort was made to change the name to "fountaineer," the term "soda jerk" was here to stay.

Swanson's Bakery, Red Wing, 1893

Pauline's Confectionary, Osseo, 1920

Palace of Sweets, Red Wing, 1920s

In 1885, medical school graduate Charles Alderton put together a unique cluster of ingredients that eventually became the soft drink Dr Pepper. After tinkering with his formula, Alderton asked drug-store owner Wade Morrison to offer tastes of the syrup to local soda fans. News spread in a hurry, and demand overwhelmed the pair's ability to supply soda fountains with the new drink. Originally called "Waco," after the Texas town in which it was first served, the beverage was renamed "Dr Pepper's Phos-Ferrates" in 1891 by a Texas bottler and made its first international appearance at the 1904 St. Louis World's Fair.

Lemon Lime Phosphate

On hot summer days before the blessing of air conditioning, the neighborhood soda fountain and a phosphate drink—over ice—provided a cooling respite. This lemon-lime version is like the original fizzy medicinal drug-store beverage collected from mineral springs.

3/4 cup lemon juice

3 tablespoons lime juice

3/4 teaspoon grated lemon zest

1/2 teaspoon grated lime zest

1/2 cup water

1 1/2 cups sugar

3 quarts chilled seltzer or club soda

Combine all the ingredients except seltzer or club soda in a small saucepan. Bring to a boil, stirring to dissolve sugar. Reduce heat and simmer for 1 minute. Allow to cool to room temperature, then refrigerate, covered, until chilled. Place a squirt (about 4 teaspoons) of syrup in a tall glass. Fill with chilled seltzer or club soda; stir. Garnish with lemon and lime slices. Can also be made, using all of syrup and seltzer, in a large pitcher or punch bowl. Makes 6 large glasses or 24 punch-cup servings.

Entrepreneur Josie Wanous operated a soda fountain and drug store located on the Syndicate Block in Minneapolis. The fountain occupied the front of the store, and wall-to-wall drug shelves dazzled visitors in back.

Wanous Drug Store, 720 Nicollet Avenue, Minneapolis, 1905

Josie Wanous at the soda fountain, Wanous Drug Store

Josie Wanous' Shampoo-Bag production, 1900

Above the Wanous Drug Store was the production room for Josie Wanous' Shampoo-Bag, an herbal mixture in a disposable cloth bag that become internationally known. Today, near the perfume city of Grasse in France, century-old advertising and sales receipts from the Wanous Company are on display in the Fragonard perfume museum.

GREEK SODAS

Soda fountains eventually moved out of drug stores and into their own homes. Unique and appealing, they were unlike any other dining environment. Customers walked in on shiny tile floors, curvy wire chairs clustered around marble-topped tables, and ceiling fans circulated the air. The newly discovered ice-cream soda enticed enthusiasts, and sundae combinations soared to imaginative new heights. Soon gooey and delectable candies joined the menu of sugary delights.

Peter Boosalis Ice Cream and Candy Emporium, Sixth and Hennepin, Minneapolis, 1905

The Olympia, Faribault, 1915

Minneapolis Fruit Store, 301-303 Hennepin Avenue, Minneapolis, 1909

t the turn of the century, many groups of soon-to-be-citizens arrived in Minnesota determined to open food-related businesses. Throughout the state, dozens of Greek families, many of them related to each other, opened fresh fruit and candy stores that quickly grew into soda fountains and cafés.

In Minneapolis, John Lankis began by selling fruit from a cart and eventually opened the Minneapolis Fruit Store, complete with beautiful soda fountain.

Minneapolis Fruit Store and owner John Lankis, 1920s

Ted Boosalis at Avalon Cafe counter, 1934

Down the street and across town, other Boosalis relatives operated charming soda fountains. Many of them evolved into cafés that survived for decades serving lunches and light dinners.

Avalon Cafe, 1605 East Lake Street, Minneapolis, 1934

Theodore N. Boosalis at the Minneapolis Fruit Store, 1920s

After thirty years of bustling business, the Minneapolis Fruit Store's size was reduced by half. The classic spindly ice cream parlor chairs and tables gave way to sturdy, modern wooden booths.

George N. Boosalis and Ruth Hollister after remodeling, Lankis Cafe, 1930s

In the 1930s the Minneapolis Fruit Store was further remodeled into a deco-style café with a smaller soda fountain and even more booths. Through the many changes, one feature remained the same—the intricate tile floor.

HERE'S THE SCOOP

S oda fountain menus stressed purity and freshness, safe ingredients, and healthful tonics—always important considerations. Some menus included subtle statements to remind customers that the store had more to offer than ice cream.

VOEGELI'S Fountain

NEATNESS

Everything about our Fountain, inside and out, is as neat as wax. It's so neat that it makes everything taste better.

DAINTINESS

Our glasses are delicate, tumblers thin and dainty. Being so they add a relish to the Soda.

LIBERALITY

We "spread" ourselves with syrup, crushed fruit, ice cream and everything else that goes to make good Soda. We do it purposely. We have gotten the name of serving the best Soda in town, simply because we serve everything in a neat, dainty, appetizing and liberal manner.

THE VOEGELI BROS. DRUG CO.
PRESCRIPTION DRUGGISTS
WASHINGTON AVENUE, CORNER HENNEPIN
MINNEAPOLIS, MINN.

VOEGELI

GOOD SODA

Comes from good materials skilfully combined. We use the best of everything. Whenever it is possible to improve a drink we do it. The cost doesn't worry us half as much as the quality.

SKILL

Mixing and serving Soda is an art. Perhaps you can't see the use of so many quirks, but if we didn't do it that way you would not like the Soda so well. That fancy manipulation gives Soda the rich flavor. We don't know why it does, but it does.

THE VOEGELI BROS. DRUG
PRESCRIPTION DRUGGISTS
WASHINGTON AVENUE, CORNER H
MINNEAPOLIS, MINN.

Veritable fountains of refreshment, Voegeli's stores grew in downtown Minneapolis on prime pedestrian street corners and in the lobbies of the West and Nicollet Hotels. Tired tourists and townsfolk just couldn't resist these menu treats in the early 1900s.

VOEGELI'S FLAVORS

come from the fruits. What a difference in flavors! Many druggists use those horrible flavoring extracts (imitation fruit juices). We never use such synthetical preparations (chemical compounds).

VOEGELI'S .... FRUIT JUICES

from ripe and perfect fruits, prepared with skill, knowledge and care, compared with others (the imitations), afford a striking contrast between our Soda and that sold elsewhere.

VOEGELI'S ".." CRUSHED FRUITS

Nothing but the choicest and soundest fruits used.

The above are some reasons for the popularity and success of our Fountain.

CORNER WASHINGTON AND HENNEPIN

Voegeli's Popular
5c. Thirst Quenchers

Ice Cold Root Beer
Orange Phosphate
Lemon Cola
Wild Cherry Phosphate
Orange Phosphate
Lime Phosphate
Claret Phosphate
Lemon Phosphate
Grape Phosphate
Pineapple Phosphate
Celery Phosphate
Moxie
Coca Cola

UNTHER'S CHOCOLATES
.... AND ....
BONS BONS

We have them fresh, received direct from headquarters

None Better

Telephone or mail orders promptly filled. Unless you have an account with us or send money with order, we will ship C. O. D. (which costs you 15c. more than if you send the money and let us prepay the express charges).
City delivery free.

THE VOEGELI BROS. DRUG CO.
MINNEAPOLIS, MINNESOTA

THE ONLY OPEN-ALL-NIGHT DRUG STORE IN THE CITY

MENU

Ice Cream 10c

VANILLA   STRAWBERRY   CHOCOLATE

PLAIN ICE CREAM, 5c   ICE CREAM CONES 5c

Ice Cream Sodas and Sundaes

ALL FLAVORS 10c

RASPBERRY   STRAWBERRY   PINEAPPLE

CHOCOLATE   BUTTER SCOTCH   CHOP SUEY

ORANGE   CHERRY   BANANA

MAPLE   CHOCOLATE NUT   MAPLE NUT

CRUSHED RASPBERRY   STRAWBERRY   CHERRY

MARCHINO PINEAPPLE

NUT ICE CREAM SODAS WITH ANY OF
THE ABOVE FLAVORS, 15c

Fancy Sundaes

Marchino Pineapple.....................
Caramel Nut..............................
Fig Sundae ....
Pineapple Special.......................
Banana Special ....

The ice-cream cone was invented by Charles E. Menches when he filled a cone-shaped pastry with two scoops of ice cream. The new treat made its debut at the 1904 St. Louis World's Fair and was a walk-away success.

*Menus, R. E. Shauer & Company, Hoffman, 1916 (top),
St. Croix Drug Company, Stillwater, early 1900s (bottom)*

FOUNTAIN
SERVICE

COURTEOUS SERVICE
TASTY DELICIOUS SANDWICHES

GANO & MUTZ
PIPESTONE, - MINN.

"Age does not diminish the extreme disappointment of having a scoop of ice cream fall from the cone."
JIM FIEBIG

Menu

Specialties

Mexican Sundae	15
Fig Souffle	15
St. Croix Special	20
Chocolate Dream Happy Thot	20
Fruit Salad Happy Thot	20
St. Croix Beauty	25
Combination Happy Thot	20
Chocolate Nut Happy Thot	20
Ladies' Delight	20
"A" Quaintance Sundae	15
New Yap's Special	25
Elks' Delight	25
Two Bit Sundae	15
Maple Mousee	20
Mutt & Jeff Sundae	15
Banana Split	20
Tutti Frutti	20
Fruited Happy Thot	15
Marshmallow Happy Thot	2
St. Croix Special	
Oriental Parfait	
Maple Nut Salad	
York Beauty	

Fancy Mixed Drinks

Siberian Freeze	15
Grape Float	10
Roman Punch	10
Claret Punch	10
Manhattan Punch	10
Fruited Punch	10
Claret Freeze	15
Mint Freeze	10
Lime Freeze	10
Grape Freeze	10
Root Beer Cream Float	10
Chocolate Cream Float	10
Fresh Orangeade	10
Silver Fizz	10
Raspberry Shrub	10
Grape Juice High Ball	15
Stillwater Breeze	15
Coca Cola Freeze	10
No. 19	10
No. 23	20
Fresh Limeade	15
White Grape Juice	10
Orange Julep Freeze	10
Lime Manhattan	15

The "Mondae"—a chocolate soda with a chocolate sundae floating on top—was served in a glass specially designed to hold the doubly rich treat.

CANDY, FRUIT, CIGARS . . . AND JEWELRY?

Growing throngs of soda-fountain customers provided a captive audience for other items, and soon bakery goods, cigars, toiletries, and, in one early store, even jewelry shared space with sodas. As soda fountains left their drug-store incubators, they diversified and promoted their identities as candy kitchens, confectionaries, or simply ice cream parlors.

Bakery, lunch counter, and soda fountain, Elbow Lake, 1921

Elbow Lake customers who took a soda break could also pick up groceries, fresh bakery goods, and a cigar or two.

Morningside Pharmacy, Edina, 1926

Olympia Cafe and ice cream parlor, Osseo, 1920s

CHERRY SODA

Creative soda jerks who added ice cream to flavored bubbly water made an even more popular treat right in front of customers' eyes. Many a pair of sweethearts sipped, through side-by-side straws, a cherry soda or spooned into a pink, frothy cherry ice-cream treat.

3 tablespoons cherry syrup	Soda water

TO MAKE YOUR OWN CHERRY SYRUP: Mix one package cherry flavored drink mix with 1 1/2 cups water and 1/2 cup sugar. Stir until sugar is dissolved.

TO MAKE CHERRY SODA: Add two to three tablespoons of cherry syrup to your favorite glass. Top with soda water and ice. Makes 1 serving.

CHERRY ICE-CREAM SODA

1/2 cup cherry syrup	2 scoops vanilla ice cream
Soda water	

Add half the flavoring and enough soda water to fill half a glass. Add ice cream and the rest of the flavoring. Continue to add soda water until glass is foaming to the top. Serve with a straw and long-handled spoon. Makes 1 serving.

J. Fredell's Confectionary and Jewelry Store, Center City, 1910

Phonograph music accompanied sodas at Fredell's, and with everyone in a good mood, who could resist a fine piece of jewelry?

Soda fountain, Renville, 1930s

Ragtime piano music was a treat for the ears while soda business was conducted at the fountain.

Parlors and fountains serving ice cream had many unusual names, including "dairy bar" and "sweet shop." Friends gathered to watch an expert pull out a shapely glass, squirt in a dollup of syrup, plop in a ragged scoop of ice cream, and finish with a swirl of whipped cream. Lip smacking and finger licking were allowed.

Sjoberg Dairy, Grand Marais, 1930s

Plate, Baltimore Dairy Lunch, 1930s

Tepeetoka Ice Cream Parlor, Winona

Winona had one of the state's more unique ice cream parlors— the Tepeetoka. It was designed like a tepee, with birch bark and Native American accessories surrounding classic ice cream parlor tables and chairs.

Grand opening, Marigold Dairy Bar, Red Wing, 1940s

Beginning in Baltimore and expanding through the Midwest, with locations in Minneapolis and St. Paul, the Baltimore Dairy Lunch operated dozens of soda fountains and lunch counters during the '20s and '30s.

IVEY'S FUDGE SAUCE

Ivey's on Nicollet Avenue in Minneapolis was a favorite of shoppers looking for a light lunch and a heavy dessert. This sauce swathed many an Ivey's hot fudge sundae.

2 squares unsweetened chocolate

1/4 cup butter

3/4 cup sugar

1/4 cup cocoa

1/2 cup cream

In top of double boiler, melt chocolate and butter. Add sugar, cocoa, and cream. Stir until smooth. Cook over low heat for about 10 minutes, stirring occasionally. Spoon over ice cream. Makes about 1 1/2 cups sauce.

Ivey's Chocolate Shop, 927 Nicollet Avenue, Minneapolis, 1926

Ivey's was known for dazzling varieties of ice cream topped by a splendidly rich fudge sauce. Adoring multitudes came through the front door and walked smack into a candy counter filled with Ivey's signature chocolate leaves piled in dizzying stacks. Customers scraped the bottoms of their ice cream dishes while seated in dark mahogany booths set on white tile floors.

CONFECTION CONNECTION

Soda fountains and candy went hand in hand. Sweet treats garnished ice creams while chocolate chunks, chewy caramels, and pulled taffy traveled home in a bag. Candy making was big business; full warehouse floors were devoted to manufacturing, wrapping, and packing confections for delivery. The Paris Factory in Minneapolis distributed candy products to soda fountains, confectionary stores, and cafés around the Midwest.

Paris Factory, National Candy Company, 123 North Second Street, Minneapolis, 1916

Mankato Candy Kitchen, Mankato, 1881

The earliest candy kitchens also sold ice cream and a host of other sweet items to satisfy local residents' every craving.

Maple Delight Creams

Think fudge, but with the earthy flavor of maple.

1 1/2 cups medium brown sugar

1/2 cup milk

3 tablespoons maple syrup

3 tablespoons melted butter

1 teaspoon vanilla

1/2 cup chopped nuts (optional)

Combine brown sugar, milk, maple syrup, and butter in a heavy-bottomed saucepan. Bring to a boil and continue boiling until mixture reaches 230 degrees. Stir so the mixture doesn't scorch. Pour hot mixture onto a marble slab or countertop and knead the candy for 5 minutes (start by using a metal spatula while the mixture is hot, then use hands as it cools). Add vanilla and nuts, if desired. Knead in thoroughly. Pat the mixture into a square and cut into pieces.

Palm Cafe, Donnelly, 1920s

The Palm Cafe advertised its preference for Paris candies on its display case.

The Candy Kitchen, Alexandria, 1919

The Alexandria Candy Kitchen also dished out ice-cream treats from a long fountain, and café tables and dark booths were eventually added for light lunches.

PURE CANDY

THE PURITY OF OUR CANDY IS A HOBBY WITH US.

We buy the best materials we can find and then in our clean candy kitchens we make them into Candy of delightful wholesomeness.

Children and grown folks can eat all they want and enjoy every piece.

Take a box home two or three times a week. It is a pleasant habit to have.

The Candy Kitchen
Alexandria, Minnesota
(2t-33)

andy kitchens and soda fountains often grew up into cafés. Including sandwiches on the menu extended the season, and when hot soups were added, these fledgling cafés were busy all winter long.

Rigby's was a reliable book. It survived many years of candy making in the busy Princess Cafe kitchen.

Princess Confectionary, Rochester, 1920s

Soda fountain workers, Princess Cafe, 1950s

The Princess Confectionary made candy and ice cream from 1921 until 1936, when it was remodeled into the Princess Cafe, a full-service restaurant that dished up ice cream and candy for an additional thirty-five years.

Princess Cafe, 1950s

The sweet old store of the '20s soon disappeared, replaced by a café with checkerboard tile, indirect lighting, and seating for modern people to enjoy up-to-date convenience.

BANANA NUT SUNDAE

Hafner's in Rochester prepared its own toppings for specialty sundaes, including this big batch of banana topping, discovered in its handwritten recipe manual.

1/8 ounce banana extract

3/8 ounce yellow food coloring

5 pounds bananas, peeled and cut into chunks

1/2 pound sugar

1/2 quart (2 cups) nuts, preferably walnuts

In large saucepan, combine banana extract, yellow food coloring, banana pieces, and sugar. Cook over low heat until sugar melts and coats banana pieces. (Note: Adding the juice of half a lemon will keep the bananas from browning during cooking and storage.) Stir in nuts. Refrigerate mixture until needed.
TO MAKE SUNDAE: Spoon banana mixture over 2 scoops of ice cream in a banana split dish. Add dollops of whipped cream and 2 maraschino cherries for garnish.

The banana nut recipe from Hafner's book is covered with spills from countless fountain treats.

World War II soldier Ricky Sorenson at an Anoka soda fountain, 1945

Canelake's Cafe, Hibbing, 1940s

Canelake's menu included a statement about war production and its effect on service during World War II. In the spirit of the times, the café offered patriotic sundaes alongside its regular fountain specials.

Soda fountains and ice cream parlors were affected by food shortages during World War II. When restrictions were finally lifted, joyful customers packed the counters and filled the booths front to back.

CUSTARD ICE CREAM

The epitome of ice creams begins with a rich egg and cream base cooked smooth to a custard before chilling in the freezer. This recipe has true homemade taste and is reminiscent of old-fashioned soda parlor treats.

2/3 cup sugar, divided

1 1/2 tablespoons all-purpose flour

1/8 teaspoon salt

1 cup whole milk, heated to scalding in a double boiler

1 whole egg

2 cups half-and-half

1 cup whole milk

1 cup whipping cream

1 teaspoon vanilla

Mix 1/3 cup sugar with flour and salt; stir slowly into scalded hot milk in a double boiler. Stir and cook until the mixture is thick. Beat egg slightly; add remaining 1/3 cup sugar. Stir egg mixture into hot milk mixture, stirring well. Cook, stirring, for 1 minute. Remove from heat. Cool. Add half-and-half, milk, and whipping cream, then stir in vanilla. Freeze as directed in ice cream machine. Makes 2 quarts.

Special Sundaes

Four Queens	50c
U. S. Bond	50c
Paris Sundae	50c
Wilson's Delight	40c
Uncle Sam Special	45c
Roosevelt's Delight	45c
Pershing's Delight	45
Harding's Delight	4
American Beauty	
Over There	
Liberty Sundae	
Fruited Happy Thought	
Fig Delmonico	
Pecan Nut	
Tally Ho	
Half Moon	
Yankee Special	
Hot Bitter Sweet	
(with almonds)	
Hot Butter Scotch	
(with salted almonds)	
Pecan Sundae	
Maraschino Sundae	
Canelake Special	
Maple Salad	
Nut Salad	
Banana Split	
Delmonico	
Fruit Smash	
Coney Island	
New York Sundae	
Howard Street Girl	
Canelake Sweetheart	30c
Club House	30c
Heart	30c
Ladies' Delight	30c
Elfin Delight	30c
Turkish	30c
Marshmallow Special	30c
Happy Thought	

DEAR PATRON:

Let's be absolutely honest with each other about War Prod and its effect upon service, deliveries, and even our private lives.

Admittedly, this war is too serious a matter for small talk. W all doing our part because it must be done. We haven't had any o choice since Pearl Harbor.

Without a question we are all up against something that is big than any one person, company or any one industry. We are compell to recognize that this stupendous effort has brought about new pro lems in our relationships, both in business and personally.

There can be only one conclusion. We're all in the same predica ment—or to borrow a phrase, "we're all in the same boat. Let's pull to gether and win!"

In short, what we are trying to say is that we desire greatly to please you—but due to the restrictive measures, all businesses are up against, including food processors and individual rationing as applied to food commodities, we are operating under a gross handicap—a handi cap, however, which we are all glad to share, considering its ultimate purpose and the supreme sacrifices being made by others.

If any portion of our service, or the construction of any bill of fare is not entirely satisfying, we heartily solicit your correction and con structive criticism. Our satisfaction, in fact our permanence in bus iness, is dependent upon it. We want to take corrective measures you deem advisable—and which we are capable of meeting.

If you find we can't supply you with an exactitude formerly at our disposal, before we all got into the same boat, we are only hoping you will recognize our position and that we will still pull together,

Thanking you for your patronage, we remain,

Canelake's Cafe

Ice cream trucks tempted pedestrians with their advertising.

Soda fountain, 1946

Ice cream aficionados share a plateful in 1950

Minneapolis mayor Hubert H. Humphrey drinking soda pop at the 1945 Aquatennial

Sign, Eibner's, New Ulm, 1920s
Fan, Eibner's Weneeda Bakery, New Ulm, 1920s

For much of its history, Eibner's manufactured its own ice cream. As demand grew, the hand-powered freezer was replaced with a treadmill powered by sheep. Electric motors eventually retired the sheep.

Eibner's Weneeda Bakery gave away fans so that customers could keep cool while waiting for their frozen fountain orders.

Village Pantry, Marine on St. Croix, 1950s

A SHORT LUNCH AT A LONG COUNTER

By the '40s and '50s, in-store dining returned to the Midwest in the form of full-service lunch counters. Customers lined up from morning to night: readers pored over a paper or a book, couples on a date giggled while sharing a malt, mothers and children split sandwiches and sodas, uncles and aunts came in for coffee and pie. Lunch counters were streamlined and modern, busy and popular.

Bridgeman's interior, 621 Hennepin Avenue, Minneapolis, 1937

Bridgeman's began selling ice-cream cones in drug stores in 1936. Decades later, "meet me at Bridgeman's" was a call to indulge in contests to see who could eat the biggest sundae. A Twin Cities mainstay, Bridgeman's became famous for serving an ice-cream extravaganza called the Lalapalooza.

Clancy's Drug Store, Edina, 1951

Clancy's Drug Store was famous beyond its Edina borders. Students, families, and shoppers stopped for lunch or a soda at this corner landmark in the high-rent district.

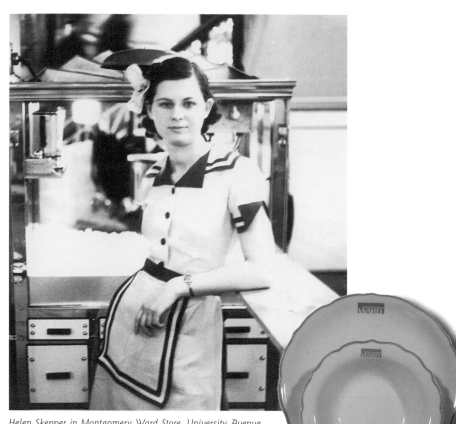

Helen Skepper in Montgomery Ward Store, University Avenue, St. Paul, 1930s

Waitress Skepper joked with friends that she worked at "Monkey Wards." Counter serving was a terrific job for young women because there were plenty of interesting customers and lots of activity.

The Cloverleaf, Donaldson's, Seventh and Nicollet, Minneapolis, 1960

NORTON AND PEEL

Many stores devoted space to a lunch counter. From small and cluttered village five-and-dimes to big-city retailers, rows of stools kept step with stretches of counters, and shoppers stopped long enough for the guilty pleasure of a strawberry frappé.

Minneapolis photography firm Norton and Peel documented lunch counters and other businesses in an amazing collection of pictures taken from the 1920s to the 1960s. Often hired by shopkeepers, Norton and Peel captured the architecture, interiors, and working environments of Twin Cities retailers and eateries. Many images show scenes in restaurants and cafés, some include people, and others simply record the style and furnishings of the period. The fabulous soda fountains of the '40s and '50s have disappeared, but these photographs preserve priceless views of bygone dining fun.

Soda fountain, 1949

Borgstrom Drug, St. Paul, 1950

Soda fountain, 1949

F. W. Woolworth, St. Paul, 1956

Soda fountain, 1949

FIVE-AND-DIMES

Dime stores, later called variety stores, occupied prime corners in most midwestern towns and stocked just about anything a person needed. When lunch-counter cooks heated up the grills and started frying onions, customers at the far end of the store couldn't resist a quick lunch or light snack. Those counter stools filled up fast.

S. S. Kresge, 415 Nicollet Avenue, Minneapolis, 1936

Kresge, St. Paul, 1950s

Kresge, Rochester, 1940s

A barrage of advertising faced patrons seated on chrome and vinyl seats, and when they turned around another batch of signs waved from merchandise tables nearby. The S. S. Kresge Company opened its first five-and-dime in 1910. Sixty years later, the business had evolved into Kmart Corporation.

Ben Franklin, Thief River Falls

Lunch counters started out as long, straight lines, but later U-shaped sections were added, allowing people more elbowroom, a chance to talk to each other, and the opportunity to watch the counter activity. More diners could be seated in less space, and the waitress could chat with everyone at once.

W. T. Grant Store, Seventh and Minnesota, St. Paul, 1950s

F. W. WOOLWORTH

Touting "amazing buying opportunities for your nickels and dimes," the first F. W. Woolworth Company store opened in 1879. For nearly one hundred years lunch customers were sandwiched between long aisles of merchandise, and even today eating and shopping go hand in hand. The early soda fountains and, later, lunch counters were important features of Woolworth stores and became lighthearted spots for friends and neighbors to talk while rotating on swivel chairs. Maybe they'd give in to an impulse purchase on their way out.

F. W. Woolworth Company, 309 East Hennepin Avenue, Minneapolis, 1924

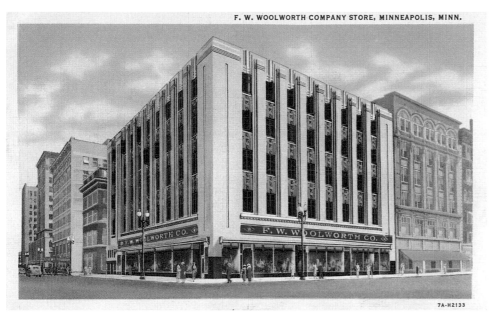

F. W. Woolworth, Seventh and Nicollet, Minneapolis, 1950s

Woolworth's lunch counter, Duluth, 1940s

Woolworth's waitress, Thief River Falls

Woolworth's, Austin, 1950s

Woolworth's lunch counter, Thief River Falls

Mushel Drugs, Walgreen Agency, Little Falls, 1952

Walgreen's, 531 Hennepin Avenue, Minneapolis, 1950

Walgreen's, One Washington Avenue South, Minneapolis, 1949

WALGREEN'S

Founded in Chicago by Charles R. Walgreen in 1901, these drug-store soda fountains and luncheonettes were huge—the largest of their kind anywhere. Perpetually filled with customers slurping sodas, nibbling on salads, or chomping on sandwiches, they were noisy, clattery places. The fountain's aroma filled the store and proved irresistible to shoppers or office workers coming in for supplies.

According to Walgreen's, the ice-cream malted milk was invented by Ivar "Pop" Coulson in 1922 using Walgreen's extra-rich ice cream. It was an instant sensation, attracting thousands of admirers and causing traffic jams at the counters.

Walgreen's, Ninth and Nicollet, Minneapolis, 1937

Walgreen's Fountain Delicacies

SUNDAES
Mild Bittersweet Chocolate 15
Chocolate Walnut 15
Crushed Fruit 20
Caramel 20
Butterscotch 20
Marshmallow 15

SODAS
Mild Bittersweet Chocolate 15
Crushed Fruit 15

MALTED MILK AND MILK DRINKS
Walgreen's Double Rich Chocolate Malted Milk
with Whipped Cream and Wafers 20
Malted Milk with Egg 25
Egg Chocolate 20
Chocolate Milk Shake 15
Hot Ovaltine 15
Cold Ovaltine 20

DELICIOUS ICE CREAM
Vanilla 10   Orange Ice . . . 10   Chocolate 10

REFRESHING DRINKS
Fresh Orangeade 15
Fresh Lemonade 10
Fresh Limeade 10
Hires Root Beer 10

For Sunday dinner or any special occasion, there
is nothing to beat a brick of WALGREEN'S
delicious Ice Cream.   We Deliver.

WALGREEN'S FAMOUS MALTED MILKS
—so rich, creamy and delicious
—owe their popularity to the
goodness of our own ice cream
with which they are made

You're Always Welcome at Walgreen's

Menu, Walgreen's, Moorhead

Soda fountains and lunch counters provided quick meals in friendly atmospheres and were seductive attractions for decades of shoppers. As fast-food franchises grew, drug-store dining declined and lunch counters made way for more merchandise. By the late 1970s the sleek and streamlined counters had nearly disappeared. Dates with a sundae or meetings with a malted would never be the same.

WALGREEN'S CHOCOLATE MALT

Adding malt powder to a rich ice cream milk shake was a Roaring Twenties soda-fountain revolution, introduced first to Walgreen's customers in Chicago. The idea quickly traveled to Minnesota drug stores. This recipe is adapted from Walgreen's web site.

1/2 ounce chocolate syrup

3 large scoops vanilla ice cream

5 1/2 ounces cold milk

1 heaping tablespoon malt powder

Whipped cream

Place all ingredients except whipped cream in a frosted malt can and position on mixer only until mixed. Do not overmix. Pour malted milk in glass until approximately 2/3 full. Top with a dollop of whipped cream. Serve remainder of malted in can along with the glass, plus straws and package of fountain treat cookies.

Picture Panorama of the Store

7th OFFICES · CREDIT DEPARTMENT · ADJUSTMENTS

5th NORTHWEST'S BIG ONE-FLOOR CHILDREN'S STORE

4th TEA ROOMS · SEA-FOOD GRILL · LOUNGE · CHINA · HOUSEFURNISHINGS

3rd DONALDSON VILLAGE · ORIENTAL and DOMESTIC RUGS · FURNITURE · DRAPERIES

2nd WOMEN'S & MISSES APPAREL · BEAUTY SALON · MILLINERY · SHOES · RIDING SHOP

Street ACCESSORIES · PRESCRIPTIONS · RENTAL LIBRARY · FLOWERS · FOOD · FOUNTAINETTE

Basement A COMPLETE STORE ON ONE FLOOR · SHOE SHINING · BEAUTY SHOP · LUNCHROOM

CHAPTER SEVEN

Department Stores

For Minnesota's earliest settlers, shopping was tedious work. Stores sprawled along muddy and crowded blocks on early main streets. Merchants specialized: the men's shirt store was over there, the ladies' millinery down the street, and the cobbler in the next block. After searching through small, cramped stores, hungry shoppers made a separate hike to the corner café.

In the late 1800s, forward-looking merchandisers began combining products. They displayed various items together in one building with separate departments. They added small tearooms and brought in entertainment, including live orchestras. Buyers who crowded into the new department stores were delighted by a veritable indoor bazaar, and shopping became a fun outing rather than a chore.

By the turn of the century, spectacular department stores were going up in city centers worldwide. Building exteriors were glass and iron fantasies embellished with glittery lights and rooftop towers. Palatial interiors of polished marble illuminated by crystal chandeliers dazzled customers, and arcades of classical columns led to light-filled atriums surrounded by balconies overflowing with the latest merchandise.

Although the architecture of midwestern department stores was slightly less exotic than that of their global counterparts, shopping was still an exciting escape from the house. People needed refreshment and a place to meet their friends, and merchants eager to keep customers in their stores hired interior decorators to design fashionable dining rooms. Luxurious tearooms attracted ladies in white gloves, stately grills appealed to men wearing felt hats, and lunch counters provided pie breaks for all. Chefs studied the latest recipes, mostly chicken dishes prepared a number of creative ways—in crispy pastries, in steaming potpies, or as creamy à la king.

Many stores also began to offer entertainment, with some dining-room facilities installing fully equipped theater stages. Grandmothers brought grand-children to breakfast plays, fashionable customers lunched as models sashayed around tables in the latest *haute couture*, and business friends met over fancy cocktails. It was high-style fun in the classiest of surroundings.

In 1956, Edina's Southdale opened as the world's first enclosed, climate-controlled mall, and from that point forward shopping would never be the same. Friends could meet to have lunch not in department stores but in sunny mall courtyards. Many stores downsized or eliminated their in-store restaurants, freeing store managers to concentrate on merchandising. Entertainment appeared in the form of the occasional style show, concert, or holiday display dominating the courtyard.

The new malls echoed patterns of the past with scattered, specialized shops—the shoe store down the aisle, the jewelry shop over there, women's hats by the door—but with big department stores anchoring their corners. Friends still met friends over a bite to eat, foot-weary shoppers picked their favorite in-vogue cafés, and teens identified trendy places to gather for a soda. Mall courtyards became virtual town squares as consumers bought into the vision of entertainment, shopping, and eating, munching away with enthusiasm as they plotted their next purchase.

Menu, Donaldson's Department Store, Minneapolis, 1930s

DONALDSON'S GLASS BLOCK
SEVENTH AND NICOLLET, MINNEAPOLIS

Japanese Room, 1910s (top)
Gentlemen's Cafe, 1910s (above)

Silver Gray Room, 1910s

In the 1890s, Donaldson's Glass Block featured the Upper Midwest's most beautiful department-store dining rooms. The elegant cafés and luxurious banquet halls were designed by John S. Bradstreet, Minnesota's premier decorator at the dawn of the twentieth century. He traveled the world, often stopping in Japan to collect objects and ideas for his projects. The Japanese Room and the Gentlemen's Cafe epitomized Bradstreet's favorite Asian motifs.

First-floor lunch counter, 1951 (above)
Donaldson's Grill, 1948 (left)

For more than one hundred years, Donaldson's Department Stores embraced the newest designs by creating up-to-date dining rooms. The latest styles called for indirect and fluorescent lighting, vinyl upholstery materials, and plastic laminates.

1897 Donaldson & Co. Chicken Timbales

The 1897 Donaldson & Co. Fashion Monthly *featured twenty pages of women's fashions, and the back page offered household tips on how to walk stairs properly, how to polish furniture, and how to prepare the best recipes from the Glass Block restaurants. Chicken timbales is a classic Victorian recipe, and this is how it was written for cooks in 1897. Timbales are served on artfully arranged greens and decorated with edible leaves and fresh flowers.*

1 lump of butter, about the size of an egg

Half a coffee-cupful of stock or sweet milk

1 table-spoonful of chopped parsley

1 level tea-spoonful of salt

1 small salt-spoonful of paprika or white pepper

2 table-spoonfuls of fine bread crumbs

1 Pint—more or less—finely-chopped cooked chicken or turkey bits

2 eggs

Place butter, stock or milk, parsley, salt, paprika or pepper and crumbs in a saucepan and stir until it boils. Add the chopped chicken or turkey bits and take from the fire. Add the eggs, well-beaten, and put the mixture into small greased cups or moulds and set in a pan of hot water that does not reach the tops of the cups. Cover and cook for fifteen or twenty minutes. Turn out upon a hot platter and pour over the timbales a bread or cream sauce.

GOLDEN RULE

SEVENTH AND ROBERT, ST. PAUL

THE "LIGHT AS DAY" BASEMENT OF **THE GOLDEN RULE,** ST. PAUL, MINN.	Delicatessen and Bakery 2000 sq. ft. Toy Department 4500 sq. ft. Crockery Department 9000 sq. ft. Sporting Goods 1000 sq. ft. Hardware and Housefurnishings } 12000 sq. ft. Lunch Room seating capacity 400 The largest Soda Fountain in St. Paul.

Basement shops and café, 1920s

Not only did the Golden Rule claim to be the biggest and best St. Paul department store, it also boasted a delivery department consisting of sixty horses, thirty wagons, and five automobiles. There's more. Inside was the largest soda fountain in St. Paul, a two-thousand-square-foot deli and bakery, and a four-hundred-seat restaurant, all supplied with water from artesian wells located on the property.

Capitol Room, 1950s

In later years, shoppers dined in circular banquettes in a room that expressed the new attitudes of modern proportions and uncluttered spaces. The giant state capitol picture was a forerunner of the oversized photographs and room-sized murals that gained popularity in the 1950s.

OYSTER STEW Ā LA GOLDEN RULE

Lunch at the Golden Rule was reason enough to draw shoppers to downtown St. Paul. The large dining room had an equally sizable menu, always featuring popular oyster stew, made somewhat like this.

2 cups whole milk

1/2 cup cream

1/4 cup butter

1 pint fresh oysters with their liquor (juice)

1 teaspoon salt

Freshly ground pepper

Butter

Oyster crackers

In a saucepan, heat milk and cream until they just start to simmer. In another saucepan, melt butter. Add oysters and cook just until the edges of the oysters begin to curl. Add oysters to the hot milk mixture and heat through but do not boil. Stir in salt and pepper. To each portion, add a pat of butter. Serve with oyster crackers. Makes 6 servings.

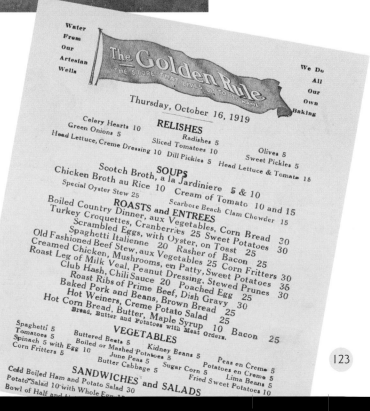

123

DAYTON DRY GOODS COMPANY

SEVENTH AND NICOLLET, MINNEAPOLIS

Dayton Dry Goods Company, 1910 (left)
Tea Room, 1915 (above)
Menu, 1905 (below)

Located in the elegant Dayton Dry Goods Company store, the famous tearooms served customers who in the earliest days arrived by horse and carriage. The hundred-year-old department-store building and its ornamentation in terra cotta have been restored on its original site, now the Nicollet Mall.

Dayton's Sky Room, 1952

Dayton's Sky Room held style shows and special programs on a fully equipped theatrical stage. Diners were surrounded by windows that offered a long-distance "sky view." Though the room still exists, the view has metamorphosed into a scene of modern office towers.

The opposite of the airy Sky Room was the Oak Grill, a clubby retreat of paneled oak, red leather, velvet drapes, and a three-hundred-year-old English fireplace. Both rooms still welcome diners, the Sky Room in a modified version.

TURKEY À LA KING

Department-store restaurants catered to what was known as "lighter fare," with choices such as turkey à la king, a favorite of the ladies. Patty shells are an elegant carrier for the creamy turkey mixture, but more plebian cafés made do with buttered toast points.

1/4 cup sliced fresh mushrooms

1/4 cup chopped red pepper or pimiento

1/4 cup minced onion

5 tablespoons butter, divided

3 tablespoons flour

1 cup chicken or turkey stock

1/4 cup cream

2 cups diced cooked turkey, white meat preferred

1 egg yolk, beaten

1/4 cup frozen peas

1 to 2 tablespoons sherry (optional)

In a sauté pan, melt 2 tablespoons butter. Sauté mushrooms, peppers or pimiento, and onion. Set aside. Melt remaining 3 table-spoons butter in large saucepan. Stir in flour and blend until flour is cooked. Stir in stock until mixture thickens. Stir in cream, bringing the sauce to a slow boil. Add the mushroom mixture and diced turkey. Combine some of the hot sauce with the beaten egg yolk; stir the egg yolk mixture back into the hot sauce, stir-ring until sauce is smooth and thickened. Add peas and sherry, if desired. Stir until peas are heated through. Serve in patty shells or over buttered toast points. Makes 4 to 6 servings.

THE EMPORIUM AND SCHUNEMAN'S

DOWNTOWN ST. PAUL

THE EMPORIUM DEPARTMENT STORE, 7TH, 8TH, ROBERT AND JACKSON STS., SAINT PAUL, MINN. 103475

The Emporium Department Store, Seventh and Robert, St. Paul, 1920s

Tea Room, Emporium, 1937

This huge tearoom served multitudes of shoppers and nearby office workers. It was a study in manmade materials: the counters were early plastics and the upholstery vintage vinyl, chrome sparkled everywhere, and nearly endless acoustical tile flowed freely overhead. Soup and sandwiches were menu standards, and, with a nod to nutrition, countertop baskets of fresh fruit tried to compete with racks of juicy pies.

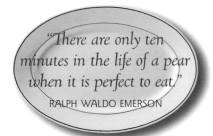

"There are only ten minutes in the life of a pear when it is perfect to eat."
RALPH WALDO EMERSON

Schuneman & Evans Department Store, Wabasha and Sixth, St. Paul, early 1900s

The Schuneman and Evans Department Store was located in one of St. Paul's stately Victorian buildings.

Employees of Schuneman and Evans, 1901

River Room, Schuneman's

Refurbished for modern dining, the River Room had beautiful wall murals depicting the Minnesota, Mississippi, and St. Croix Rivers. The large-pattern carpet in green, pink, and yellow expressed the latest style, and a sea of tables and chairs promised a lively dining experience. Today's shoppers can still meet for lunch in an updated River Room in what is now Marshall Field's.

YOUNG-QUINLAN

901 NICOLLET AVENUE, MINNEAPOLIS

Rendezvous in the Tea Room, 1930s

"One steps from the elevator on the fourth floor into what might be a charming restaurant in the Bois. The blue-green carpet and the wall panels suggest green trees and spring grass, while colorful hangings give the effect of tropical sunlight. Here one may lunch or tea or dine and dance. While artistry in dress is the keynote for the rest of the shop, here is artistry in cuisine." EXCERPT FROM A YOUNG-QUINLAN BROCHURE

Young-Quinlan, 1930s

Elizabeth C. Quinlan was one of the first female merchandising executives in the United States. With her partner, Fred D. Young, she opened the Young-Quinlan women's specialty shop in 1894—the second of its kind in the country.

Advertising promoted the 1926 Young-Quinlan store, "the pride of Nicollet Avenue," as the Northwest's finest specialty shop for "Gentlewomen and their Daughters."

SOUTHDALE

EDINA

Southdale, 1960s

Southdale, the world's first fully enclosed shopping center, introduced a new style of shopping and dining to the world. Snowbound Minnesotans were able to bask in a bright and airy mall courtyard—like an outdoor café on a warm summer day, even in the middle of winter! The Sidewalk Cafe's menu featured the shopper's casserole and soups, salads, and sandwiches. And, in remembrance of the soda fountains of old, a large selection of sundaes and banana splits was available.

Southdale Sidewalk Cafe, 1960s
The Sidewalk Cafe sat amidst the modern architecture of Southdale's Garden Court. Harry Bertoia's sculptured steel "Golden Trees" provided the shade.

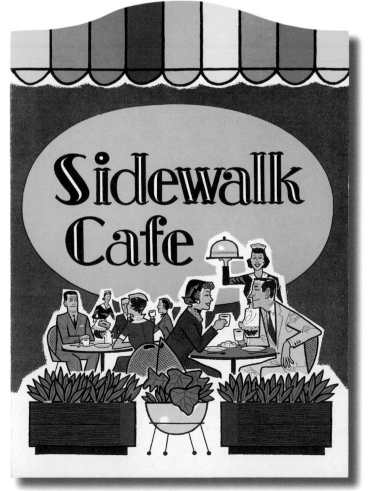

Tired shoppers could reward themselves with colorful fruited Jell-O cubes topped with whipped cream—a classic midwestern treat for a whopping twenty-five cents.

SHOPPER'S CASSEROLE
$1.10
10. Baked Elbow Macaroni and Diced Smoked Ham Au Gratin
Tossed Greens with French Dressing
CHILD SIZE CASSEROLE 80
Small Portion of Featured Casserole on a Plate with Salad, Roll and Butter.
Milk or Coca Cola

desserts

15. Fresh Apple Crumb Pie	.30
16. Bittersweet Chocolate Frosted Layer Cake	.30
17. Lemon Chiffon Pie with Whipped Cream	.35
18. Sidewalk Cafe French Peppermint Stick Ice Cream	.30
19. Old Fashioned Bread Pudding, Lemon Sauce	.25
20. Fruited Jello Cubes Topped with Whipped Cream	.25

Old department-store restaurants, grand and elegant or modern and kitschy, are missed by those who dined there and by those who wish they had. The mall eateries taking their place exhibit a new variety of themes and motifs, clever ideas accomplished through creative design. Stores display the latest in merchandise fashions, and mall dining is a study in the newest restaurant styles. The compatible duo—shopping and eating—will provide solid fun for generations of customers to come.

Dining car warehouse, Great Northern Railroad, 1930

Railroad staff contemplate the storage needs for dinnerware big and small, short and tall.

CHAPTER EIGHT

Movable Feasts

Travel over territorial Minnesota's bumpy roads was hard work. Few took the trip for pleasure. When hunger hit, scattered stagecoach stops and roadside inns provided food and rest. Captive excursionists had but one choice: the innkeeper's supper of the day, which was served at the cook's leisure in the most minimal of environments.

During the same period, river steamboats provided both efficient and joyful transportation. Elaborate and ornately decorated vessels designed as floating palaces made travel easy and fun for would-be sailors. Riverboat décor ranged from comfortable to downright lavish, and on-board meals could be taken in dining rooms, cafés, or ice cream parlors. Passengers feasted on regional cuisine while calliopes pumped out musical hits on the upper deck.

Travel changed dramatically in the 1880s when rail lines met in Utah at the golden spike to unite the East and West Coasts. Excited voyagers could go farther, faster, yet travel in great style and comfort. Leisurely shore-to-shore excursions allowed passengers time to enjoy fine cuisine served in fashionable dining cars. The sheer pleasure of a lulling trip over long distances made journeys unforgettable.

Improving the nation's roadways became a priority after the turn of the century. The multiplying numbers of automobiles and buses added options for travelers. Gas stations installed lunch counters, and moms and pops opened roadside eateries to serve home-cooked meals. Homeowners turned their living rooms into cafés and bedrooms into "tourist rooms," the forerunners of today's bed-and-breakfasts. Small-town hotels and rooming houses remodeled to meet the needs of an ever-expanding mobile population. Along America's new highways, as far as the eye could see, restaurants, motor courts, and travel lodges arose in a building frenzy.

In the 1930s, commercial airlines took to the skies, carrying record numbers of passengers who were served lavish and elegant meals. To compete, railroads designed their trains as sleek, fast streamliners and enlivened their dining cars with colorful appointments. Custom china held eye-catching entrées served by swaying parades of bow-tied waiters.

Midwesterners faced the greatest variety of globetrotting options ever offered. As on-the-move populations multiplied, the sheer number of travel choices—by train, bus, boat, automobile, or airplane—created excitement. For these nomadic diners, meals were quickly cooked to order and flew out of the kitchen lickety-split.

By the 1950s, travel by riverboat and railcar gave way to the speed of jetliners and the intimacy of automobiles. Americans had fallen in love with their cars, and driving and eating became the great vacation pastime. Travelers have always been hungry folks, and their roadside dining choices skyrocketed. The great American drive-in emerged, changing favorite foods and eating habits forever. Motorists couldn't miss "hi-way" cafés with towering signs, rooftops bearing flashing lights, or drive-ins shouting in blinking neon. The movable feast became a hamburger with pickle, french fries, and Coca-Cola.

MEALS ON WHEELS

Popcorn wagon, 1925

Recreationists munch on hot dogs and popcorn in a Twin Cities park.

Lunch wagons served customers during the day and after local cafés closed in the evening. Hot food was prepared inside the vehicle, and diners took a stick-to-the-ribs meal back to work or balanced lunch on their laps outside. When annoyed community members complained about the clattery wagons rolling through the streets, they were ordered closed by 10 P.M. Clever owners unhitched the horses, settled the wagons on permanent sites, and stayed open twenty-four hours.

V. J. Saul lunch wagons pulled up with hot meals morning, noon, and night. This surly crew served ham and eggs, rabbit, oysters, pigs feet, and hot tamales.

V. J. Saul lunch wagons, St. Paul, 1903

Box lunches came to the workplace in the 1920s when automobile and truck travel became routine. Meals were prepared and packaged in a commercial kitchen and then delivered to a business or club meeting or the occasional party or picnic. Twenty-five-cent box lunches included a cup of hot coffee.

Benner's Box Lunch, 750 Grand Avenue, St. Paul, 1925

An early fleet of trucks cornered St. Paul's lunch box market. With this crew of determined cooks and drivers, lunch will be there on time!

STEAMERS ON STEAMERS

At the height of their popularity, steamboats plying the Mississippi River were opulent in the extreme, with bountiful fresh food and grand interior spaces that were extraordinary by any American standard. Produce, fresh fish, and steamers were gathered along the route and cooked to order by chefs flaunting considerable talents. Rivaling anything seen on land, dining rooms in these floating palaces were often ringed with balconies and ornate railings. Walls shimmered with enamel paints, and furnishings invited travelers to enjoy a leisurely riverboat lifestyle.

Dining salon, Harry G. Drees steamboat, 1923

Mississippi River steamers entertained passengers from St. Paul to ports south, while excursion steamers on Lake Superior traveled north along rocky shorelines. Excursions also included lunch set on tables by picture windows or a snack enjoyed on a sunny deck.

Excursion boats, Jackson Street, St. Paul

Tourists ready to board Steamer Sidney, Lake City

Excursion steamer, Fond Du Lac line, Duluth

The Golden Bantam boat provided 1930s pleasure cruises on Big Stone Lake. For passengers' enjoyment, its owner, Big Stone Canning Company, employed an onboard chef with a reputation for preparing great meals in small spaces.

GO GREYHOUND

During the 1910s, Carl Eric Wickman shuttled miners between Iron Range towns in a seven-passenger Hupmobile for fifteen cents a trip. Non-miners soon began hitching rides, and the Mesaba Transportation Company of Hibbing became a thriving business. From these quirky beginnings, the company expanded and changed its name to Northland Greyhound Lines and then to Greyhound Lines. Eventually the distinctive buses carried passengers from coast to coast.

Greyhound Post House, Brainerd, 1950s

Cubby's Cafe, Ortonville, 1950s

The Minneapolis bus depot of 1950 was a masterpiece of streamlined modern design, creating the impression that the building was on the move. Inside, the same graceful curves and sleek surfaces reinforced the fact that passengers were there to travel. Lunch was served at an accelerated pace as the bus warmed up in the garage.

Greyhound station café, Minneapolis

Greyhound station, Minneapolis
Passengers were picked up at the curb in 1925.

Greyhound station, 701 First Avenue North, Minneapolis, 1950

Welcoming movers and shakers of a different sort, this classic depot is now home to the First Avenue nightclub.

afés provided passengers with a place to buy their tickets and space to wait for the bus. Quick meals topped the menu in case the bus arrived early and riders had to leave in a hurry. Soups and sandwiches, pie à la mode, or donuts and coffee fortified voyagers for the journey ahead.

Scenic Hotel, Northome

Northern Triangle bus riders stopped at the Scenic Hotel, where dining rooms—and maybe fresh fish—awaited.

Wendt's Cafe, Hinckley

Lunch was good and service was fast at Wendt's Cafe, where the time and date were prominently displayed so no travelers would miss their Greyhound bus.

Silver Latch Cafe, New Ulm, 1950s

DONUTS

Long bus trips were broken by short stops at roadside stations where passengers quickly purchased something to eat and drink. A donut and a cup of coffee were the usual choice, and some stops, such as the original Tobie's in Hinckley, were famous for their old-fashioned fried dunkers, such as these.

Tobie's, Hinckley, 1940s

3 tablespoons shortening

1 cup sugar

3 eggs

6 cups sifted flour

2 1/2 teaspoons baking powder

3/4 teaspoon each: ground cinnamon, mace, and nutmeg

3/4 teaspoon salt

1 1/2 cups buttermilk or whole milk

2 teaspoons vanilla

Fat for deep frying

Cream shortening and sugar until light and fluffy; add eggs one at a time, beating well after each. Sift dry ingredients and add alternately with milk to the creamed mixture. Chill for 1 hour or longer. Roll dough out onto a lightly floured board to 1/2-inch thickness. Cut with a floured donut cutter. Fry in oil or lard heated to 370 degrees in a deep-fat fryer until golden brown on both sides, turning only once. Drain on paper towels. Makes about 40 donuts.

JUST DRIVE IN

Dining at a drive-in is a uniquely American experience. Initially, café staff toted simple orders to customers waiting in their 1920s automobiles. Sandwiches were wrapped in waxed paper, drinks arrived in the bottle, and, with a hope and a prayer, drivers juggled everything while sitting on their car seats. Eating in an automobile was novel, and soon everyone wanted to join in the fun. When trays were introduced, they teetered on passengers' laps, but it wasn't long before they moved outside to hang on car windows. The new trays balanced a hefty load of hamburgers, french fries, and Coca-Colas.

Wykoff's Oasis Drive-in, Mankato, 1930s

In 1931, the Oasis opened as Mankato's first drive-in restaurant, selling only root beer that summer. Other soft drinks, hot roast beef sandwiches, and ice cream followed the next year. During the busiest months of the summer, thirteen girls and a couple of guys tended to the boisterous crowds. Evenings, a three-piece orchestra played the latest tunes on a rooftop overhang, and the lively music attracted cars by the hundreds, prompting Kato Beer to buy roof space for advertising.

"I can resist everything except temptation."
OSCAR WILDE

Eddy's, St. Cloud, 1949

Eddy's customers knew to "blink lights for service." The twinburger was unique to Eddy's, which also advertised "big yummy hamburgers, frosty foamy root beer, crispy crunchy popcorn, and piping hot coffee."

Shortstop Drive-in, Cokato

Carhops were so popular that a 1940s *Life* magazine cover featured a sassy carhop in a shiny satin uniform. Early drive-ins had been staffed by car-boys, but it was soon discovered that a pretty face sold more burgers, and the girls took over. They were called "carhops" for their exuberant hop onto a car's running board to take the order. Some could twirl on roller skates and not spill a drop of soda.

FROSTY ROOT BEER

During Prohibition root beer was so popular it was sometimes called the national temperance drink. The tart and rooty refreshment provided work and wages for carhops during the summer months. A really good carhop could carry seven glasses gathered by the handles in one hand—and balance burgers with the other!

Emil's, Winona (above)
Lakeview carhop, 1950s (right)

Homemade root beer was the beverage of choice in this 1938 pop stand. When Emil's became the Lakeview drive-in restaurant years later, Winona customers ordered foamy root beer in iced glasses or crispy french fries they dipped into tartar sauce.

ROOT BEER

Root beer is made from a mixture of flavorings, sweeteners, and carbonation. Depending on the brew, it may contain any number of herbs: burdock root, sarsaparilla root, yellow dock root, ginger root, juniper berries, wild cherry bark, or birch bark.

2 ounces sassafras root	4 gallons water, divided
1 ounce dandelion root	5 pounds sugar
1 ounce hops or ginger root	1 cake compressed yeast
2 ounces juniper berries, crushed	2 ounces wintergreen

Wash roots well in cold water; drain. Add hops or ginger root and juniper berries to roots. Pour 2 gallons boiling water over root mixture in a large pan and boil slowly 20 minutes. Strain through flannel bag and return liquid to pan. Add sugar and remaining 2 gallons water. Allow to stand until lukewarm. Dissolve yeast in a little cool water. Add to root liquid along with wintergreen. Stir well. Let settle, then strain again and bottle. Cork tightly. Keep in a warm room 5 to 6 hours, then store in a cool place. Put bottles on ice as required for use.

A is for Allen, W is for Wright. Roy Allen mixed up a batch of creamy root beer in 1919 after purchasing the formula from an Arizona pharmacist. Allen served it at his newly established root-beer stand in Lodi, California. Excited employee Frank Wright loved the taste and immediately became a partner. A&W Root Beer was the most popular beverage served at their rapidly multiplying stands. The A&W formula of herbs, spices, barks, and berries remains a proprietary secret.

A&W, Brainerd, 1955

A&W Root Beer gets top billing over french fries and barbeque in this early root-beer stand.

Ernie Swanson's A&W, Red Wing, 1950s

EAT AND GET GAS

Bim's Cafe and Gas Co-op, Glencoe

Lorntson's Cafe, Beaver Bay

Highway travel had improved immeasurably by the 1940s and 1950s. Automobiles were affordable, wanderlust had captured Americans' hearts, and the romance of the road blossomed into a love affair. Midwesterners wanted to see the country, and gas stations added cafés to provide them with fuel and food on their quest. For weary wayfarers, it was a roadside convenience to fill up the tank and satisfy the hunger pangs at the same time. The famous highway invitation to "Eat and Get Gas" caused gales of laughter in passing cars.

Café and gas station, Burnsville

"You can find your way across this country using burger joints the way a navigator uses stars."
CHARLES KURALT

Café and gas station, Motley

Oak Ridge Cafe, Lincoln

Barndley's Store, Ray

EAT AND SLEEP

Highway cafés soon became modern full-service restaurants, and owners expanded further by adding long rows of motel rooms. Travelers speeding across the country pulled over for a robust meal, parked the car next to a cozy room for the night, and topped off the tank in the morning.

Windy Acres, Cannon Falls, 1950s

Springfield Motel and Rainbow Cafe, Springfield, 1950s

This twenty-four-hour truck stop provided gas, showers, fireproof motel units—and barbecued spare ribs.

Howard Johnson's Motor Lodge, Burnsville

For Americans hitting the highways in unprecedented numbers, nothing could beat the sight of a Howard Johnson's on the horizon. Sleepy travelers could depend on the orange-roofed motor lodges to offer comfortable rooms and consistently good food. Howard Johnson franchised his name and concept in the 1930s. Both the distinctive design and the placement of the eye-catching buildings were carefully planned. Impossible to miss, the buildings themselves became signage, visible from great distances.

It was dependable food quality that appealed most to travelers stopping at a HoJo. Famous Tendersweet fried clams, brown bread, and twenty-eight flavors of ice cream tasted just the same and just as good at every location.

RIDING THE RAILS

Railroad travel was an exercise in equilibrium as passengers negotiated swaying aisles on their way to the dining car. When firmly seated, they saw tables brilliant with crisp white linen and menus featuring game, fish, and produce harvested from the land whizzing past. Waiters provided impeccable service in their starched uniforms. Food wasn't snobbishly gourmet, but it was well prepared, abundant, and delicious, say those who recall railroad's glory days. Dining on the rails as America's changing landscape flew by the windows provided a hypnotic escape for passengers. To the beat of clicking rails, they pursued adventure, explored new territory, or sought fame and fortune.

Dining car, Northern Pacific Railway, 1935

By 1935, dining cars had become modern and colorful to reflect the contemporary definitions of fun and leisure. Travelers going places in their careers and on the train embraced these new designs.

Dining car, Northern Pacific Railway, 1910

Somber and elegant, Victorian rail cars were appropriate for serious travel. George Pullman designed the first dining cars for the Union Pacific Railroad in the 1870s, and they were radiant with rich mahogany paneling, polished brass, soft leather, and fine velvets.

Both national railroads and local short runs, like those offered by Duluth companies, served meals on an amazing variety of custom china.

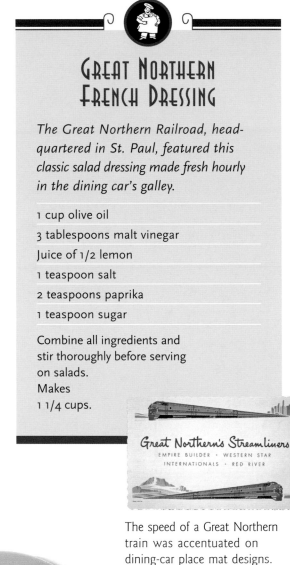

GREAT NORTHERN FRENCH DRESSING

The Great Northern Railroad, headquartered in St. Paul, featured this classic salad dressing made fresh hourly in the dining car's galley.

1 cup olive oil

3 tablespoons malt vinegar

Juice of 1/2 lemon

1 teaspoon salt

2 teaspoons paprika

1 teaspoon sugar

Combine all ingredients and stir thoroughly before serving on salads.
Makes
1 1/4 cups.

The speed of a Great Northern train was accentuated on dining-car place mat designs.

COLORFUL DINING ROOM ON NORTH WESTERN'S FAMOUS "400"

9A-H1863

Dining room, Chicago and North Western Railway, 1935

CHICAGO, MILWAUKEE & ST. PAUL RY.

DINNER

English Beef Broth

Boiled Lake Trout, egg sauce

Leg of Mutton, caper sauce
Jole and Spinach

Roast Beef
Pork, apple sauce
Spring Lamb, mint sauce
Rib Ends of Beef, with browned potatoes

Shrimp Salad, Mayonaise dressing

Baked Beans Boston style

Beef a la Mode
Apple Fritters, brandy sauce

Crabapple Jelly	Queen Olives	Lettuce
Horseradish		Pickled Beets
Boiled or Mashed Potatoes		Stewed Tomatoes
Mashed Turnips	Green Peas	Elgin Corn

Cocoanut Custard Pudding
Apple Pie   Cranberry Pie

Lemon Ice Cream   Assorted Cake   Oranges
Figs   Layer Raisins
    Bent's Crackers   Edam Cheese
French Coffee

— MEALS 75 CENTS. —

PATRONS DESIRING TO RETAIN THIS MENU AS A SOUVENIR ARE AT
LIBERTY TO DO SO.

WINE LIST.

CHAMPAGNES.

Chapin & Gore's Extra Dry, half pint, $1.00	- $3 50	2 00
Mumm's Extra Dry	3 50	2 00
Ruinart Pere & Fils Extra Dry	3 50	2 00
Pommery Sec,	3 50	2 00
Cook's Imperial	2 00	1 25

WHITE WINES

Sauterne	1 25	75
Latour Blanche, bottled at the Chateau, 1870	2 50	1 50

CLARETS.

St. Julien	1 00	50
Pontet Canet	2 00	1 00

WINES, LIQUORS, ETC.

V. S. O. Brandy, half pints, 80 cents, per glass	30
Sour Mash Whisky, half pints, 80 cents, per glass	
Amontillado Sherry, half pints, 50 cents, per glass	
Old Tom Gin, half pints, 50 cents, per glass	
Bass' Pale Ale, per bottle	
Guinness' Dublin Porter, per bottle	
Bedfast Ginger Ale, per bottle	
Hathorn Water, per bottle	
Apollinaris Water, per bottle	
Friedrichshall Bitter Water, per bottle, 35 cents, per glass	
Milwaukee Lager Beer, Pilsener, per pint	
Budweiser Lager Beer, per quart	

CIGARS.

Imported Cigars, selected	10, 12½, 15, 20
Cigarettes, per package	
Fine Cut Tobacco, per package	

Railroads' artfully illustrated menu covers depicted scenes of the countryside, and their meal listings reflected cross-country food preparations. Considering the minimal space available for storage, surprisingly diverse varieties of wines and spirits were stocked on board. Cooking in dining-car kitchens and serving meals seamlessly were balancing acts in more ways than one.

1943

GREAT NORTHERN RAILWAY

ROUTE OF THE EMPIRE BUILDER

SKY-HIGH DINING

M-81—Wold-Chamberlain Field, Minneapolis

Eleanor Roosevelt at Wold-Chamberlain lunch counter, 1937

Wold-Chamberlain Field, Minneapolis, 1940s

Wold-Chamberlain Field was the Twin Cities' first municipal airport. The terminal featured a lunch counter, a small dining room, and a few seats in a waiting room. Passengers having a meal—even famous people like the president's wife—watched planes pull up to the open doors, and when the engines shut down, they paid their bill and climbed aboard.

Dining room and soda fountain, Wold-Chamberlain Field, 1935

Minnesota's Northwest Airways, as it was originally called, required pilots to pick up box lunches and distribute them to passengers during the flight. When stewardesses took over those duties in 1939, the pilots were more than grateful. By 1950, Northwest Orient Airlines served passengers drinks in etched glasses and meals on custom china plates with monogrammed silver flatware. Chopsticks—for exotic Asian dishes— kept diners busy during long overseas flights.

The Minneapolis–St. Paul International Airport, 1960s

The new International Terminal Building at the Minneapolis– St. Paul Airport was dedicated in 1962 and served seven airlines. Travelers who dined in the airport's only restaurant sat by tall windows overlooking the runway. Food, while hot and healthy, took a back seat to the airport activity outside.

SKY-HIGH SIGNAGE

Signage was fabricated in a variety of "look-at-me" neon shapes that hungry customers flying past on the roadways found impossible to ignore. Hamburgers, french fries, and shakes, the mainstay of the drive-in industry, were the magic words on these roadside beacons.

Skyline Supper Club, Albert Lea

McCarthy's Drive-in, St. Cloud, 1960s

Sandy's, Fergus Falls, 1973

Sandy's Drive-in, Rochester

Robbys, Austin, 1950s

Bimbo's Drive Inn Restaurant, Anoka, 1955

King Leo's, Rochester, 1960s

The all-American phrase "I'll have a hamburger, please!" began its rise to popularity shortly before World War II. No other food item has come to represent America or dominate menus over the years like the hamburger. Its origins can be traced to medieval times, when Europeans shredded tough beef and served it cooked or raw. Germans mixed regional spices with the beef, fried it, and called it "Hamburg steak." In the late 1800s the Hamburg steak immigrated to the United States, where it was renamed "Hamburger steak" and then simply the "hamburger" as it's known and loved today.

PORKY'S

Porky's on University was a heavyweight among Twin Cities drive-ins. The lights went out for many years in the 1980s, but a revival in 1990 repaired the classic building and reopened the doors to fans of neon-emblazoned drive-in architecture. Porky's juicy hamburgers and deep-fried onion rings sparked the interest of classic car and hot rod enthusiasts. Now they park their cars in Porky's lot for appreciative fans who admire the restored autos while enjoying a Porky's burger and fries.

Porky's, 1890 University Avenue, St. Paul, 1960s

PORKY'S ONION RINGS

Porky's drive-in on St. Paul's University Avenue has been famous for its onion rings since the day it opened in 1953. When the drive-in reopened in the '90s, onion rings were again made with the original Porky's recipe. The current owners wouldn't reveal their seasoning salt formula but said that Lawry's will make the rings taste like they did in the '50s—salty and wonderful. This recipe is a fraction of the restaurant-sized version.

1 extra-large egg

2 cups whole milk
(important to use whole milk)

2 tablespoons seasoning salt
(or less, to taste)

4 cups plus 1 tablespoon
Gold Medal flour

Extra-large yellow onions

(Note: The original recipe also calls for regular salt, about 5 teaspoons for a recipe of these proportions; use if you like a lot of salt.)

Combine the first 4 ingredients and beat with a wire whip for several minutes, until very smooth. Refrigerate for at least 1 hour. Slice extra-large yellow onions into rounds; break apart into individual rings. Dip rings into batter using a long-handled fork. Drop rings into hot oil, at least 360 degrees. Cook rings until medium golden brown. If desired, sprinkle with more seasoning salt before serving. Serves 6 to 8.

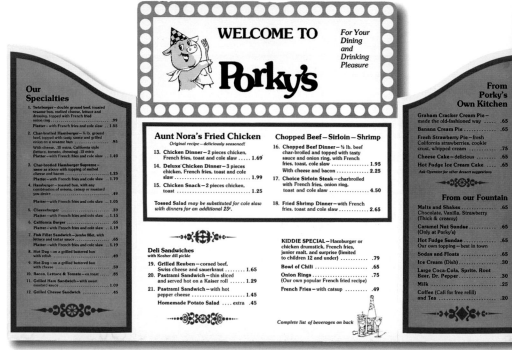

For many years, Porky's in south Minneapolis operated from a drive-in building near Lake Calhoun. The structure was remodeled into Nora's Restaurant, which now serves classic midwestern fare to the pleasure of nostalgic drive-in fans.

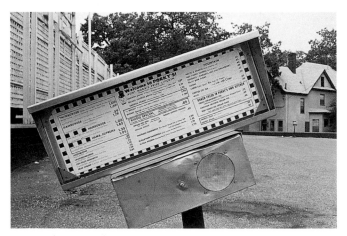

Menu, Porky's, St. Paul, 1970s

Customers studied the menu board and hollered their orders into a squawky box. The speaker system increased profits for drive-ins but not for carhops; eventually they were no longer needed at all.

Porky's beacons called raucously to the parade of vehicles on University Avenue.

Mickey's Dining Car, Ninth and St. Peter, St. Paul, 1930s

Ever-popular diners, like Mickey's in St. Paul, were created to resemble railroad dining cars, which themselves were rarely converted into restaurants. Operating on the same site since 1937, Mickey's is on the National Register of Historic Places. The exterior is classic streamline design, and the interior retains the original pressed metal panels and mahogany walls. Its staff is nearly historic as well: some have been at the grill for decades, flipping hearty 'cakes and eggs for customers perched on the old swivel stools.

Ford Bridge Drive-in, 4556 Forty-sixth Avenue South, Minneapolis, 1950s

Ford Bridge Drive-in employees, 1950s

Band Box, 729 South Tenth Street, Minneapolis

The Band Box was ordered as a unit from a company in Iowa that also made banks and gas stations. It opened in 1934 and though the Minneapolis franchise numbered fourteen at one time, this one is the only survivor.

Today these original diners are rare, treasured by fans of this unique style of architecture and grill cooking.

The delicacy known as sausage (Americans' hot dog) dates back to 1500 B.C. Babylonia. It was also popular in Roman times, until the Catholic Church made sausage eating a sin and Emperor Constantine temporarily banned its consumption. Although Europeans had been serving sausage on a plate beside a pile of sauerkraut, it wasn't until 1897, in Coney Island, New York, that a German pushcart owner, Charles Feltman, laid the first "dog" to rest on a bun. Eureka! Diners could lunch standing up, walking around, or on their way back to work.

THE MUG'S BEEF ROAST SANDWICH

The Mug Drive-in was famous for slow-simmered beef roast sandwiches, the rich broth slightly sweetened with raisins. This version has been cut down from the original formula, which was built on 15 to 25 pounds of beef. Only owners of a drive-in would need a batch that big.

5 pounds of beef roast (chuck or rump roast)
1/4 cup raisins
1/4 cup chopped onion
2 teaspoons salt
1/4 teaspoon pepper

Place beef roast, raisins, onion, salt, and pepper in a Dutch oven or small roaster. Add enough water so the meat is barely submerged. Cover the pan. Roast at 250 degrees for 8 hours (or, to speed things up, at 350 for 3 hours). Remove the meat from the roaster. Save the juice, skimming off any fat. Refrigerate. Let the meat cool and trim off all fat. Shave meat into small pieces. Refrigerate. When ready to serve, heat meat and some juice in a double boiler. Serve on sliced buns. Makes enough for a party.

The Mug, New Ulm, 1950s

FOOD FAST

White Castle, 616 Washington Avenue Southeast, Minneapolis, 1929

Edgar Ingram and J. Walter Anderson created America's oldest continuously running burger chain in Wichita, Kansas, in 1921. The first familiar castle-like structure was constructed from primitive rusticated concrete block and contained a griddle and five counter stools. The more complex and elegant White Castle buildings appeared in later years, enveloped in porcelain-enamel steel paneling that was fire-proof and easy to maintain. The steamy little burgers called "sliders" are square in shape and pierced with holes. "Buy 'em by the sack" is the everlasting White Castle motto.

White Castle, 1945 University Avenue, St. Paul, 1936

This 1948 promotional brochure, die-cut in White Castle's distinctive shape, listed the company's locations, which stretched westward from New York City all the way to St. Paul and Minneapolis.

Maid-Rites

Maid-Rites were one of the Midwest's earliest fast foods, an addictive mixture of ground beef and seasonings served on a bun—not exactly sloppy joes, but in that general vicinity. Customers could doctor their sandwiches with mustard, ketchup, onions, and pickles. This recipe is attributed to a Maid-Rite café in New Ulm. However, most Maid-Rite cafés ordered the distinctive flavor-

ing formula from the company headquarters in Iowa, so this may be a reasonable facsimile of the original. In these cafés, the beef mixture was kept hot in an electric cooker.

3 pounds ground beef (doesn't have to be the lean variety)

3 tablespoons Heinz 57 steak sauce

1 tablespoon salt

1 1/2 teaspoons pepper

1 cup water

Brown beef; drain off excess fat. Add steak sauce, salt, pepper, and water; simmer for 30 minutes. Spoon onto buns. Leftovers can be reheated in the microwave oven.

Dairy Queen, White Bear Lake, 1976

The first Dairy Queen opened in Joliet, Illinois, in 1940. Soft serve, never called ice cream, was "the cone with the curl on top," the first item to cross the counters to customers in early establishments. Malts, shakes, and sundaes, served in wax-coated cardboard containers, followed. Hot foods came much later, in expanded Dairy Queens called Braziers.

McDonald's, Winona, 1970

In the late 1940s, drive-in customers were growing bored with carhop service. They still wanted their hamburgers and Coca-Colas fast—if not in their cars, then close to them. Richard and Maurice McDonald, owners of a San Bernadino, California, drive-in, began thinking of ways to improve their service. In 1948 they opened the first "self-serve" McDonald's, with a menu board and order counter. Before long, they decided to franchise the successful concept. The first buildings were simple square boxes, but the pair soon developed a unique style for their restaurants. In May of 1953, in Phoenix, Arizona, the first illuminated golden arches reaching skyward came to life.

Snuffy's drive-in, location unknown, 1952

Looking forlorn, Snuffy's represents the disappearing neighborhood drive-in. Falling slowly from favor in the 1960s, most have been replaced by fast-food counters and drive-thru service. People still eat in their cars and juggle food on their laps, but they also wish for a carhop to brighten their day.

Bebe Shopp, Minnesota's first Miss America (1948), entertains at a hotel banquet.

CHAPTER NINE

Hotels

For pioneer travelers in mid-America's wild and sometimes dangerous territories, stagecoach stops provided rest and nourishment along the trail. Primitive inns, boarding houses, and saloons offered a bed for the night with a simple meal and not much more. Even so, after arduous journeys over bumpy dirt roads, weary travelers who reached these roadside havens thought they had arrived in paradise.

When Minnesota became a state in 1858, real hotels became an urgent necessity, and up they went in nearly every village, town, and city. Always imposing and often architecturally eccentric, these buildings dominated their main street corners. They became the most important structure in town and the hub of activity in their communities. Large public rooms served as settings for civic meetings, dining rooms hosted social get-togethers, and banquet rooms provided space for celebrations and weddings. Off the lobbies, saloons weathered raucous parties and meeting rooms hosted politicians who rocked podiums pleading for votes.

Menus created in late-nineteenth-century hotel kitchens were astonishing. With only limited resources available to them, cooks managed to produce exotic dishes that often surprised hungry travelers. Local game was prepared with a gourmet twist: green turtle soup, broiled quail *en canapé*, antelope with currant jelly, pheasant larded with truffles, compote of pigeon with mushrooms, goose stuffed with apples, moose with guava jelly, leg of mutton with sauce soubise.

At the dawn of the twentieth century, Minnesota hoteliers built architecturally spectacular landmarks with imaginative dining rooms and banquet halls. Dinner was served on porches and rooftops, in cellars, alleys, and lobbies, or inside casinos and nightclubs. Orchestras coaxed couples to dance, violinists serenaded diners tableside, and organists pumped out music at tea time. Hotel dining was fun, and after dessert it was an easy walk to a room for the night.

By mid-century, hotel restaurants began creating personalities quite apart from the identity of the hotel. The Viking Room, Norse Room, Dutch Room, and Moorish Room piggybacked on dreams of travel destinations hinted at by their names. Some menus were the size of small posters and included culinary themes that impressed visitors and armchair travelers alike.

Banquet rooms and ballrooms designed to be flexible could accommodate events large and small, or any size in between. Hotel kitchens expanded into bigger spaces with hotter ovens and state-of-the-art equipment. Chefs developed gourmet recipes and irresistible food presentations, which armies of uniformed servers delivered in precision marches to banquet tables.

Hotelkeepers knew the *pièce de résistance* was dessert, and they competed to hire the best pastry chefs. Sweets-loving Midwesterners could satisfy their appetites for charlotte russe, claret wine jelly, cream kisses, English plum pudding, and jelly fanchonette. With specialty gourmet meals served in grand rooms and topped off by extravagant desserts, travelers and locals found it easy to ask, "is there room at the inn tonight?"

FRONTIER HOTELS

On early statehood days, travelers and local workers crowded into simple midwestern hotels for a hearty meal and a night's rest. For around fifty cents, they rented a room and were served a big breakfast and an afternoon dinner. This combination became known as the American Plan.

Mankato House, Mankato, 1855

Frontiersmen moseyed in for a night at the Mankato House, and when the dinner bell rang it was to announce veal with dumplings, pork and beans, Irish stew, corned beef with turnips, sauerkraut, marrow fat squash, and string beans. Everyone saved room for cornstarch blancmange, apple pie, and imported French coffee.

Skandinaven House Hotel, Dawson, 1886

Hotel, Marine on St. Croix, 1880

Houses designed to provide room-and-board accommodations were early versions of today's bed-and-breakfasts. Guests appreciated cozy bedrooms and homemade meals, while innkeeping duties kept family members busy.

Skjei's Hotel, Madison, 1899

Names on small-town hotels often reflected the heritage of the community. Dawson's and Madison's Scandinavians could gather at the local inn for neighborhood news and conversation.

Ziebler Hotel, Barnum, late 1800s

Cats kept the critters away in early hotel kitchens. Meals were prepared at sturdy tables and cooked on wood-fired stoves. Washing pots and pans was a heavy chore.

Kitchen, Snelling House, 390 West Seventh Street, St. Paul, 1890

Boarders at Anderson's, Barrett, 1900s

Mealtimes in boarding houses kept kitchen help and servers busy. It was "cook's choice" for the hearty Minnesota fare served daily.

DACOTAH HOUSE GERMAN POTATO SALAD

The most acclaimed and remembered dish in the long history of the Dacotah House was developed by Helena Seiter shortly after the hotel opened in 1859. The recipe was passed on to daughter Emma and then, in 1938, to Cecelia Reimer, who carried on the tradition.

2 pounds red potatoes, cooked with jackets

5 slices bacon, cut in pieces

1 small onion, diced

1 teaspoon salt

1/4 teaspoon pepper

3/4 cup sugar

3/4 cup vinegar

1 1/2 cups water

1 1/2 tablespoons flour

1 1/2 tablespoons cornstarch

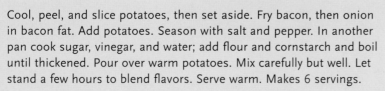

Cool, peel, and slice potatoes, then set aside. Fry bacon, then onion in bacon fat. Add potatoes. Season with salt and pepper. In another pan cook sugar, vinegar, and water; add flour and cornstarch and boil until thickened. Pour over warm potatoes. Mix carefully but well. Let stand a few hours to blend flavors. Serve warm. Makes 6 servings.

Dacotah House Hotel, New Ulm, 1870 (left); Dakota House Hotel, 1890 (above)

The Dacotah House originated as a frontier outpost on the Minnesota River and served as inspection tour headquarters for Generals Sherman and Sheridan. Composer John Philip Sousa and political leader William Jennings Bryan joined the list of famous people, from authors to Minnesota governors, who stayed at the hotel and applauded the great German cooking. As for the infamous, locals speculate that members of the James-Younger gang snoozed in upstairs rooms before the Northfield robbery.

An 1890 remodeling added a third floor, a solid brick exterior, and a spelling change to the name. Salesmen rode the horse-drawn bus from the depot; their trunks and suitcases followed on a buckboard. The hotel served the New Ulm community for 112 years.

TURRETS AND PORCHES

Hotels were landmarks in their towns, and they clamored for attention with quirky architecture and exterior embellishments of gables, turrets, towers, and spires.

Buckaman Hotel, Little Falls, 1890

Columbia Hotel, Ortonville, 1913

Lakeside Hotel, Detroit Lakes, 1890

Hotel Lenhardt, Litchfield, 1910

Dining hall, Hotel Hazelmere, Fairmont, 1910

Summer breezes floated through this open-air dining hall, offering a refreshing change of pace from the standard indoor dining room.

Dining room, Grant House, Rush City, 1915

Built in 1895, the Grant House was considered the finest hostelry between St. Paul and Duluth. Cabinets and plate rails provided china storage as well as decoration.

Calumet Hotel, Pipestone, 1900s

Built of locally quarried Sioux quartzite, the Calumet Hotel is a landmark in one of Minnesota's largest national historic districts.

raparound porches, carved columns, fanciful railings, and decorative fretwork dressed up hotel buildings in Victorian style. Many exteriors included balconies for catching a summer breeze and porches for taking breakfast—two nearly irresistible delights.

Hotel Lyon, Lake City, 1895

The Hotel Lyon's block-long balconies became the epicenter for celebrations in Lake City.

Brunswick Hotel, Faribault, 1885

This coaching party from Minneapolis enjoyed an early version of the weekend getaway, probably staying the night at the Brunswick Hotel.

arly hotel dining rooms were furnished for comfort. Pressed-back and spindle-back chairs were solid and good looking, and tables were covered in starched white cloths that matched the waitresses' aprons.

Foley Hotel, Aitkin, 1908

Waitresses at the Foley Hotel wore the voluminous starched aprons, ruffled collars, and sometimes puffy hats suggestive of a first-rate dining experience.

Grant House, Waseca, 1890s

A room at the Grant House cost two dollars, plus twenty-five cents to use the *indoor* bathroom.

THE SAULPAUGH
MANKATO

Breakfast.

Clam Broth
Salted Wafers
Baked Apples
Fruit
Shredded Wheat with Cream
Boiled or Broiled Salt Mackerel
Broiled Sirloin Steak
Plain or with Mushrooms
Ham
Bacon
Mutton Chops
Broiled Quail en Canape
Fried Oysters
Sausage
Baked Pork and Beans
Hot Boston Brown Bread
Eggs as you like
French Fried Potatoes
Baked Potatoes
Dry and Buttered Toast
Hot Rolls
Corn Muffins
Doughnuts

Palmer House Hotel, Sauk Centre

Writers looking for history visit the Palmer House Hotel, where Sinclair Lewis once bellhopped and worked the front desk. Those hungry for "main street" inspiration will find that the cozy pub and full-service restaurant are still as popular as they were in 1901.

Breakfast in the late 1800s at Mankato's Saulpaugh Hotel sustained a person for a long day. Advertised as the traveling man's headquarters, the hotel made sample rooms available for sales pitches just inside the entrance.

NORTH STAR HOTEL

WACONIA

A horse-drawn wagon-bus met passenger trains at the depot and toted guests back to the North Star Hotel. After checking in at the lobby, guests made arrangements for dinner, and then the kitchen staff got busy. The experience was efficient and downright Minnesota Nice. A flurry of modernization occurred in 1909 when hotel rooms were hooked up to an "apparatus" for hot and cold water and a long-distance telephone was installed. For nearly one hundred years, the North Star was the center of business and social events in the community and its surrounding resort area.

Dining room

Lobby

Kitchen

> "I would like to find a stew that will give me heartburn immediately, instead of at three o'clock in the morning."
> —JOHN BARRYMORE

Golden Grain Belt Beer was unabashedly featured at the North Star buffet. With the bar's location at the entrance to the hotel, customers looking for a fresh brew needed only to open the corner screen door. Minneapolis beer was always on tap and the bar well stocked with liquors, cigars, pop, and cider. A pavilion next door provided live entertainment, orchestras for dancing, and a venue for festive balls. In 1894, a masquerade party was attended by revelers in full costume.

Buffet and bar, late 1800s

HOTEL-STYLE BEEF STEW

Stew was the ubiquitous, clean-out-the-larder, soul-satisfying staple of many a hotel menu. Though it could feature many kinds of meats, this beef version was the most popular. What wasn't served one day tasted even better for the next day's customers.

2 pounds beef stew meat, cut into 1-inch cubes

1/4 cup flour

2 teaspoons salt, divided

1/2 teaspoon pepper, divided

3 tablespoons fat, shortening, or oil

1 quart boiling water

12 small onions

6 medium carrots, cut into chunks

3 ribs celery, cut into 1-inch pieces

1 teaspoon Worcestershire sauce

1 tablespoon vinegar

1 teaspoon sugar

2 bay leaves

Dash of cloves

1/2 teaspoon paprika

Toss beef cubes in a blend of flour, 1 teaspoon salt, and 1/4 teaspoon pepper. In a large pot or casserole, heat fat; add meat and brown on all sides. Add remaining ingredients, mixing well. (If desired, add a clove of garlic, finely chopped.) Cover pot. Place in a 350-degree oven and bake for about 3 hours, or until meat is tender. Remove bay leaves. Season to taste with remaining salt and pepper. Serve over mashed potatoes or cooked noodles. Makes 6 servings.

EARLY TWIN CITIES

Simple frame buildings provided room and board in the fast-growing cities of Minneapolis and St. Paul.

Market Hotel, 434 Wabasha Street, St. Paul, 1886

On a break from the kitchen, aproned cooks joined guests in a pose for posterity.

Seventh Avenue Hotel, 244 Seventh Avenue South, Minneapolis, 1890s

Travelers were picked up at the railroad station in the hotel's depot hack, but for those arriving with their own horses, boarding and safe stable were available behind the Seventh Avenue Hotel.

The Fort Snelling Hotel, West Seventh Street and Fort Snelling Bridge, 1898

The Fort Snelling Hotel housed the Ladies Waiting Room Restaurant and the George T. Harris Saloon. Riders arriving on horseback, by bicycle, or by horse and carriage could order a drink in the saloon, and teetotalers could find sodas and homemade ice cream next door.

After the first bridge to span the Mississippi was completed at Hennepin Avenue in 1855, the Winslow House was the first hotel to be built on the river's east side. Five stories of imposing limestone held 260 rooms, many of which overlooked the crashing Falls of St. Anthony. Visitors from throughout the country flocked to Minneapolis to see nature's rocky spectacle—said to rival Niagara Falls—and to partake in the famous sulfur and magnesia springs behind the hotel.

Winslow House, St. Anthony, 1860

Winslow House guests arriving with their maids, servants, and occasionally even slaves viewed one of the most imposing buildings in the Twin Cities. The dining rooms were luxurious, banquets were extravagant, and the ballroom was rumored to be the largest west of Chicago.

    This dinner menu for the Minnesota Historical Society included can't-eat-just-one pastries as well as puddings that might capture one's fancy in 1856.

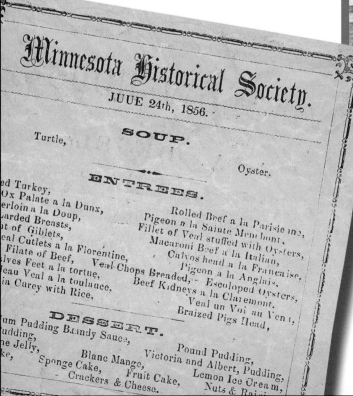

Minnesota Historical Society.

JUNE 24th, 1856.

SOUP.

Turtle,

Oyster.

ENTREES.

d Turkey,
Ox Palate a la Dunx,
erloin a la Doup,
arded Breasts,
at of Giblets,
eal Cutlets a la Florentine,
Filate of Beef, Veal Chops Breaded,
lves Feet a la tortue,
eau Veal a la toulauce,
ia Curey with Rice,

Rolled Beef a la Parisienne,
Pigeon a la Sainte Menehont,
Fillet of Veal stuffed with Oysters,
Macaroni Beef a la Italian,
Calves head a la Francaise,
Pigeon a la Anglais,
Escoloped Oysters,
Beef Kidneys a la Claremont,
Veal un Voi au Vent,
Braized Pigs Head,

DESSERT.

um Pudding Brandy Sauce,
udding,
ne Jelly,
ke,   Blanc Mange,   Victoria and Albert, Pudding,
Sponge Cake,   Fruit Cake,   Lemon Ice Cream,
Crackers & Cheese.   Nuts & Rai

Pound Pudding,

MENUS FROM THE MID-1800S

These rare and fragile bills of fare provide a fascinating picture of elegant pioneer dining in Minneapolis hotels. Breakfast was served from 7 to 10, the afternoon meal was known as "dinner," and the evening meal was often called "tea." Several menus noted, "waiters are provided with wine cards and pencils."

PICTURES, [ALL KINDS

WINE LIST.

CHAMPAGNE.

S. F. & J. H. Schmidt. Madame Cliquot, Reims,............	$5 00
Moet & Chandon— Imperial Green Seal— Heidsick & Co., Reims,........	pts. 5 00
Royl St. Marceaux, Reims....	pts. 2 50
De St. Marceaux & Co., Reims....	5 00
Bine Fitls & Co., Reims— Golden Spray,.............	qts. 5 00
Champagne Rose,..........	qts. 5 00
" "	pts. 2 50
Green Seal..............	hf. pts. 2 50
" "	hf. pts. 2 50
Heidsick, Piper & Co.......	qts. 5 00
De St. Marceaux & Co., Reims—	pts. 2 50
Red Lac.............	qts. 5 00
Fleur De Bouzy.......	qts. 5 00
Verzinay Cabinet........	qts. 5 00
	pts. 2 50

CLARET.

Branduberg & Freres, Bordeaux— St. Emilion, M. A. Leopold & Cie, qts.3 50	
St. Julien..........	qts. 3 50
St. Estephe........	pts. 2 00
Chapeau Lerose......	qts. 3 50
Margaux........	qts. 4 00
J. Merman & Co., Bordeaux— Chateau la Crock, 1851.	qts. 4 00
ges Pauillac 1854	qts. 4 50
te Canet, 1854.	qts. 4 00
	qts. 4 00

LIFORNIA VINE GROWING WINE.

	2 50
	2 50
	2 50

Henkel & C
Deidesheim
Niersteiner
Hochheim
Liebfraus
Marcobr

Sp

Rom
Imp
Lo

Old
Pure Juic

BRA
V. O. P.—A. M. &c., Pal
vintage, 1850.
United Vineyard, Dark,....
Pale....
Alex. Leignette, Pale,....
Dark....

WHISKEY.

Old Rye........
Old Bourbon........

ALE A
Edinb
Ba
R.
Ale

FULLER HOUSE,

STEPHEN LONG, ... PROPRIETOR.

Saint Paul, Saturday, December 20, 1856.

BILL OF FARE.

WINES.

CHAMPAGNE.

Mumm' & Co.,.......3 00
Mumm's Imperial, 3 00
Mumm's Cabinet, 3 00
Chas. Heidsick,....3 00
do Cabinet,.....2 50
Piper Old Heidsick 2 50
Duc de Montabelle 2 50
De Breem't Verz'y, 2 50
Anchor Grasbos, 2 50
A. Du Temple &
Fills Flés de Buzay 2 50
Sparkl'g Catawba, 2 50

BORDEAUX, RED AND WHITE WINES.

St. Esteph Medock, 2 00
Le duc St. Julien, 2 50
Picha de Longavile, 3 00
St. Julien,.........1 50

SPARKLING HOCHEIMER.

Hocheimer,.......2 00
Rudesheimer,.......2 00
Johannesberger,.......2 00
Sparkling Hock
very superior, 3 00
Sparkling Mossell,....
Mu-selle,.......2 50

BILL OF FARE.

SOUP.
Vegetable.

FISH.
Baked Pickerel, Wine Sauce,

BOILED DISHES.
Mutton Caper Sauce, Corned Beef Plain.
Ham, Wine Sauce.

ENTREES.
Culbert Heart, Pork and Beans,
Venison Pie, Hog's Head, Spice Sauce.
Lamb Chops Fried in Batter.

ROAST DISHES.
Beef, Pork, Mutton, Venison, Cranberry Sauce.

RELISHES.
Slaugh, Horse Radish. Beets, Walnuts, Celery

ALL THE VEGETABLES OF THE SEASON.

PASTRY.
Cranberry Pie, Mince Pie, Pumpkin Pie,
Plum Pie, Grape Pie, Brandy Jelly, Orange Jelly.
Indian Pudding, Rice Pudding,

DESSERT.
Raisins, Apples, Almonds, English Walnuts.

BREAKFAST, from 7 to 10 o'clock. TEA, at 6 o'clock.
DINNER, from 1 1-2 to 4 SUPPER, from 7 to 10 o'clock.
SERVANTS AND CHILDREN'S BREAKFAST, 8, DINNER 2 1-2, TEA 6 1-
wine cards and pencil.
Waiters are provided with Fare will be charged...
All articles not on the Bill of

WINES.

BRANDIES.

O. A. & Co., Pale, 2 00
do Dark, 2 00
do Nonpareil, 4 00
Plant,.......2 00

SHERRY.

Amontillado,......2 00
Fine Old Harmony 2 00
H. H. de Bashed, 2 00

PORT,

London Dock......2
Crown,......2
Old White....

CORDI

Anaset...
Morache
Absynt
Curoe

UNION ASSOCIATI
SECOND
GRAND ANNUAL FESTIVAL,
E PLURIBUS UNUM
AT THE
WINSLOW HOUSE,
On Tuesday Evening, January 17th, 1859.
BILL OF FARE.
E. A. DEUEL.
SAINT PA

Menus often included concierge information such as travel schedules, horse and carriage rental rates, and distances to local sights or the next town.

DINING LIGHT

Lighting in hotel kitchens and dining rooms evolved as kerosene lanterns gave way to gas lights, then to gas and electric combinations, and finally to all-electric lighting.

Clark House, Duluth, 1875

Kerosene lanterns that provided illumination for tables at the Clark House were located high on the columns to guard against a bump from a tall passer-by.

Kitchen, Central House, Cold Spring, 1900s

In this kitchen, lanterns provided weak light to the center of the room and made working in the shadows difficult—an unfortunate prototype of many modern kitchens.

Leyendecker Hotel, Paynesville, early 1900s

Early electric lights were installed with cloth-covered cords draped through ceramic insulators that were nailed to the ceiling. Diners saw them as state-of-the-art.

The brand-new gas/electric fixtures were a dynamite design. Electric wires wrapped in fabric were pulled through the gas line— a lethal combination that caused massive explosions! In the era of wooden buildings that could burn to the ground in minutes, these new-fangled fixtures didn't last long.

"Too much of a good thing can be wonderful."
MAE WEST

Dining room, Winona Hotel, Winona, early 1900s

The Winona Hotel had fancy lighting—the gas/electric combination—and everyone crossed fingers against a disaster. Actresses Lillian Gish and Sarah Bernhardt dined in the restaurant during their stays at the hotel and then walked next door to perform at the Opera House.

Dining room, Winona Hotel, 1920s

The room survived to be remodeled into a remarkable Arts and Crafts style. The ceiling was lowered to cover the transom windows, and leaded glass panels and new lights were installed. The original tables and chairs fit right in with the new look.

HOTEL HOLIDAYS

ℋoliday parties filled hotel dining rooms, and chefs outdid themselves providing authentic and traditional dinners. Old-fashioned recipes flavored these turn-of-the-century holiday menu offerings.

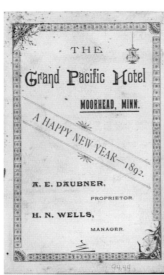

THE
Grand Pacific Hotel
MOORHEAD, MINN.

A HAPPY NEW YEAR—1892.

A. E. DAUBNER,
PROPRIETOR.

H. N. WELLS,
MANAGER.

The Grand Pacific Hotel, Moorhead, 1880s

With a fountain in the lobby, floor-to-ceiling mirrors, gas lighting, and steam heat, the Grand Pacific was the grandest hotel west of the Twin Cities. Guests in the dining rooms or banquet rooms savored seafood and produce brought in daily by train. Rail passengers found themselves inside the Grand Pacific Hotel upon arrival in Moorhead, courtesy of James J. Hill, who located the Great Northern depot next to the lobby. The Grand Pacific Hotel opened with great celebration in 1882 and was lost to history a mere fourteen years later.

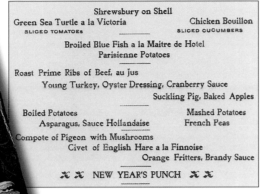

Shrewsbury on Shell
Green Sea Turtle a la Victoria   Chicken Bouillon
SLICED TOMATOES   SLICED CUCUMBERS
Broiled Blue Fish a la Maitre de Hotel
Parisienne Potatoes
Roast Prime Ribs of Beef, au jus
Young Turkey, Oyster Dressing, Cranberry Sauce
Suckling Pig, Baked Apples
Boiled Potatoes   Mashed Potatoes
Asparagus, Sauce Hollandaise   French Peas
Compote of Pigeon with Mushrooms
Civet of English Hare a la Finnoise
Orange Fritters, Brandy Sauce
✕ ✕   NEW YEAR'S PUNCH   ✕ ✕

Hotel Kaddatz, Fergus Falls, 1916
Menu, Hotel Kaddatz, 1915

Thanksgiving Dinner, 1915
COURSE SERVICE
$1.00
Canape Lorenzo
Crisp Celery   Creme Victoria   Queen Olives
Salted Almonds
Broiled Fillet of Whitefish, Parsley Butter
Potatoes Wilson
Croquettes of Sweet Breads, Modern
Neutral Punch
Salpicon of Sea Food Patties 1915
Roasted Goose, with Chestnut Dressing
Candied Sweet Potatoes
Baked Apple   Baked Squash
Head Lettuce and Cucumber Salad
Thousand Island Dressing
Special Thanksgiving Turkey
Giblet Sauce
Mashed Potatoes   Cranberry Sauce   French Peas
Plum Pudding
Hard and Brandy Sauce

PLUM PUDDING

An English classic, plum pudding traveled to the Midwest where it became a hearty ending to already-filling hotel meals. Dark and rich with fruits and nuts, portions of warm pudding were "lightened" with dollops of cream-colored hard sauce reeking of rum or brandy.

1/2 cup flour
1/2 teaspoon baking soda
1/4 teaspoon salt
1 teaspoon cinnamon
1/2 teaspoon nutmeg
1/2 teaspoon cloves
3/4 cup fine dry bread crumbs
1/2 cup butter
3/4 cup firmly packed brown sugar
3 eggs
1 package (8 ounces) pitted prunes
1 package (8 ounces) pitted dates
1 cup raisins
1/2 cup diced candied fruit mixture
1 tablespoon grated orange rind
1 cup chopped pecans or walnuts
1/4 cup brandy or dark rum

TO MAKE PUDDING: Grease an 8-cup mold very well. Sift together flour, soda, salt, and spices. Stir in bread crumbs. Cream butter and brown sugar until light and fluffy. Beat in eggs, one at a time. Blend in flour mixture. Fold in fruits, rind, nuts, and brandy or rum. Pour into mold. Cover tightly (if the mold doesn't have a cover, use several layers of aluminum foil tied tightly with a string).

TO STEAM PUDDING: Place mold in a large kettle. Add boiling water to a depth 2/3 of the mold. Place uncovered kettle on burner and keep water boiling gently at all times. Add hot water as necessary. Steam pudding for 3 1/2 hours, or until firm. Unmold. Serve while still warm, if desired, with a hard sauce made by beating 1/2 cup butter, 1 1/2 cups powdered sugar, and 1 egg, moistened with brandy or rum.

SEVEN SURVIVING STAGECOACH INNS

innesota's oldest hotels date back to stagecoach days. If your coach is ready to roll, choose one (or all) of these surviving hostelries and settle in for a historic heartland experience.

Banquet room, Sawyer House, 1900s

Sawyer House, Stillwater, 1900s

In 1860, the Sawyer House was an imposing inn where Stillwater families held social events and governors, senators, stage celebrities, and wealthy Southerners were frequent guests. The bar was off-limits to women in early days, but the dining rooms were packed right from the start.

In 1927 the Lowell Inn replaced the Sawyer House and quickly became known as "the Mount Vernon of the West." Nelle and Arthur Palmer, vaudeville performers with a flair for theatrics, were the successful new innkeepers. The George Washington Room and Garden Court feature solid American fare and the Matterhorn Room specializes in beef fondue. Hotel room walls are papered with flowers, and teardrop crystals sparkle from the lights.

Lowell Inn, Stillwater, 1930s (inset)
George Washington Room, Lowell Inn, 1930 (above)

Guests arrived at the St. James Hotel by train, by horse and carriage, or on a Mississippi riverboat. Each 1870s sleeping room had a coal-burning stove and a pitcher of water, but the hotel hallmark was home-style cooking—dependable, abundant, and all-Minnesotan. Huge blocks of ice were hauled uphill from the river levee to kitchen iceboxes. Banquet tables held bouquets of shrimp, and cold meats were wrapped to look like calla lilies. The Red Wing Shoe Company restored the historic building in 1977, and rooms today are like a visit to the past, *with* steam heat and running water.

Dining room waiters, St. James Hotel, 1887
St. James Hotel, Red Wing, 1940s (right)

Hubbell House bicycle riders, Mantorville

Frank Mantor and John Hubbell hopped off a stagecoach on the unbroken Minnesota prairie and staked a claim. It was 1854. Frank named the unoccupied hamlet after himself—Mantorville. John built a 16x24-foot log house with a guest room under the eaves and named it the Hubbell House. Two years later, travelers mustered up to a new, three-story limestone Hubbell House, where territorial mail couriers provided entertainment with their descriptions of daily encounters with the natives. Surrounded by knotty pine, today's pioneers can still order bread pudding—and Oreo fudge pie.

Cushing House, Afton, 1860s
(rebuilt after a fire as the Afton House)

In 1680, explorer Daniel Greysolon, Sieur Du Luth, pitched his tent by the St. Croix River and roasted his catfish dinner on a sandbar. The honky-tonk Catfish Saloon in the Afton House Inn honors that event and welcomes tired guests to new old-fashioned rooms upstairs. River rafters and carriage riders have called the Afton House home since 1867.

Schumacher's Hotel, New Prague, 1975

At the turn of the twentieth century in Minnesota's Czech country, architect Cass Gilbert designed the Broz Hotel. Now called Schumacher's Restaurant and Hotel, its dining and guest rooms retain old-world elegance rarely found in the Midwest today.

Archer House, Northfield, 1877

Through the long life of the Archer House, dining choices included a pub, coffee shop, café, and speakeasy. Today the restored inn houses a tavern and restaurant, with rooms upstairs for a nod for the night.

ANDERSON HOUSE LEMON BREAD

The most-requested recipe at Wabasha's Anderson House, this moist and tangy bread frequently starred on the inn's bread platter, passed to eager diners by costumed waitresses.

BREAD:

3/4 cup shortening

1 1/2 cups sugar

3 eggs

2 1/4 cups flour

1/4 teaspoon baking soda

1/4 teaspoon salt

3/4 cup buttermilk

Grated rind of 1 lemon

3/4 cup chopped nuts

GLAZE:

3/4 cup sugar

Juice of 1 lemon

Cream shortening and sugar. Beat in eggs. Add combined dry ingredients. Stir in buttermilk. Add lemon rind and nuts. Divide mixture among 3 greased loaf pans. Bake in a 350-degree oven for 30 to 35 minutes. While still warm, glaze loaves with a mixture of 3/4 cup sugar dissolved in lemon juice. Makes 3 loaves.

Cooks and staff, Anderson House, Wabasha, 1900

Minnesota's oldest inn opened its doors in 1856, and its ornate bedsteads, flowered wallpapers, and patterned carpets have lulled wayfarers to sleep ever since. After a robust dinner from Grandma Anderson's Dutch Kitchens—beginning with hot breads and kugelhof, followed by Dutch-oven steaks or stuffed beef rolls, topped off with Dutch apple pie—guests are going to need a rest! Today's vacationers can rent a cuddly hotel cat to purr them to sleep in a Victorian room upstairs.

HOTEL LENOX

DULUTH

Hotel Lenox, 1900s

The Hotel Lenox maintained state-of-the-art dining facilities in turn-of-the-century Duluth. A large bill of fare challenged the culinary talents of experienced chefs, and dining room servers maintained a professional manner in stately settings.

Kitchen

In one cavernous room, a dozen cooks and bakers stood at the ready to prepare all the items on the Lenox menu in the 1900s.

Dining room

Deeply coffered ceiling panels supported by simple iron columns created a measured environment of warm midwestern style suggestive of the period.

Bar room

A carved mahogany bar, rich leather upholstery, and ornate tin ceiling created a warm atmosphere for bar patrons who, while using the spittoons, might also admire the tile floor.

COLD WEATHER RETREATS

On cold weather, hungry customers and cozy cafés went together like mashed potatoes and gravy, and diners snuggled in for hot meals throughout the day. By the 1930s, hotel cafés and coffee shops became stylish and welcoming, their tables covered in white cotton and the food guaranteed to be down-home good.

Dining room, New Brainerd Hotel, Brainerd, 1940

Art Nouveau, Mission, Art Deco, and Moderne style were all present in the eclectic dining room at the New Brainerd Hotel. Sculptured horses lounged under potted palms, shiny bands streamlined the walls, and niches held vases of flowers—the perfect setting for a 1940s dinner date.

*Dining-room staff, Pokegama Hotel,
Grand Rapids, 1914
Pokegama Hotel Coffee Shop, 1920s*

The Pokegama staff made a snowy visit worthwhile. Cooks dished up steaming meals on hot platters, and waitresses brought along vegetables, potatoes, breads, dessert, and more dessert.

Kitchen staff, La Grand Hotel, Morris, 1920s

By the 1930s, improvements in hotel kitchens, including enhanced ventilation, increased storage space, and faster food preparation, made the cooks happier and serving easier.

Dining room, Brumund Hotel, Thief River Falls, 1920s

Terrace Gardens, Hotel Rockledge, Two Harbors, 1940s

A split-rock fireplace warmed cold hands for an after-lunch round of bridge.

MIDWEST STYLE

On the prairies of the Upper Midwest in the early 1900s, Victorian frills gave way to timber construction suggestive of a building's framework. Finely crafted woods surrounded artful paintings in warm and peaceful colors, and guests dined in comfortable chairs at tables topped with homespun linens.

The Dutch Room and Pipe Organ, National Hotel, 205 Washington Avenue South, Minneapolis

Rembrandt would have loved the Dutch Room. Heroic ceiling beams sheltered diners who appreciated hand-painted murals, collections of beer steins, and artful glass light fixtures. Notes from a pipe organ were music to the ears, and serenades for the palate were served on handsome china plates.

Revere Hotel Cafe, 316–18 Second Avenue South, Minneapolis, 1920s

New Granada Cafe and cafeteria, St. Francis Hotel. Seventh and Wabasha, St. Paul, 1930s

Café, Hotel Sherman, Fourth and Sibley, St. Paul, 1918

Wearing their booster hats, Nonpartisan League members gathered for a banquet in the Sherman Hotel café. Meetings for societies, clubs, organizations, and leagues were the bread and butter of hotel banquet and private dining rooms.

Blue Goose Room, Hotel Rogers, Fourth and Nicollet, Minneapolis, 1910

Anew and distinctly American style of art and architecture was emerging from the heartland in the early twentieth century. Variously called Arts and Crafts, American Craftsman, or Prairie School, the aesthetic became world famous through the work of Frank Lloyd Wright and regionally known thanks to Minnesota architectural firm Purcell and Elmslie.

Cafe Grotto, Hotel Rogers, 1910

The fanciful Cafe Grotto was the perfect Arts and Crafts garden. Leafy branches arched gracefully toward the sky-lighted ceiling, room-sized murals depicted serene hillsides, and iron gates anchored the doorways. Across the lobby, the Blue Goose Room provided a warm and woody retreat in classic Craftsman style, and inlaid tile floors meandered throughout.

Russell Coffee House

Russell Hotel, 16 South Fourth Street, Minneapolis, 1925

TWELVE o'CLOCK DINNER

NOT RESPONSIBLE FOR ARTICLES LOST
NO PERSON SERVED FOR LESS THAN FIFTEEN CENTS
NOTE—FISH, CHOPS, SAUSAGE, FRIED POTATOES AND EGGS ARE COOKED TO ORDER

Jan. 27, '05

SOUP

Clam Chowder 10 Bouillon 20 Cup Beef Tea 5 Bowl10
Beef Broth with Tomatoes....10 Cream of Peas....10

OYSTERS

Blue Points, Half Shell..25
Rockaways, Half Shell..25
Little Neck Clams....25
Oyster Stew............25
Water Stew.............25
Dry Stew..25 on Toast.30
Cream Stew.............30
N. Y. Counts Stew.....35
        "   Fried....35
        "   Raw......35
Escalloped, to order...35

FISH

Fried or Boiled Halibut...15
Finnan Haddie, Boiled or Broiled. Finnan Haddie in Cream 10
Fried Whitefish.........15
...dfish in Cream.......15 Broiled Live Lobster....20
...sh Mackerel.... 5 Cold Boiled Lobster....30-60
...dled Clams..........25 Fried Pike
...d Crapples.   Frog Legs
...ked Whitefish Tomato S'ce10 Fried Smelts......15
                      Boiled Salt Mackerel 10

MEATS

Roast Beef..10 Extra Cut..25 Little Pig Sausage....10
   "   Browned Potatoes..15 Home Made Sausage10
Chicken Hash on Shredded Wheat Toast..........15
Fried Tripe Breaded, Tomato Sauce 15 Welsh Rarebit 20
Hamburger Steak with or without Onions........15
   "   with Fried Onions.....
Frizzled Ham or Beef........10 Broiled Tripe.15
Roast Turkey, Cranberry Sauce
Chicken Patties

RELISHES

Celery 15 Green Onions 10
Lettuce..10 with Egg...15
Sliced Cucumbers......15
Radishes..10 Piccalilli
Sliced To...

HOTEL NICOLLET

WASHINGTON AND HENNEPIN, MINNEAPOLIS

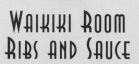

Dining room

An elegant hotel was considered necessary for the growth of urban outposts on the midwestern frontier. The Hotel Nicollet provided first-rate accommodations with eastern elegance in a setting of fine tapestries, wool carpets, marble floors, and period furniture. Beautiful banquet halls and elegant dining rooms hosted the region's most diverse and inspired meals.

Dining room

Minnesota Terrace, 1937

New Hotel Nicollet, Minneapolis, 1930s

In 1923, a larger and more modern Nicollet replaced the original hotel, built in 1858. Diners applauded the addition of live music and entertainment. The dining rooms were so popular that on some evenings tables were known to turn over seven times.

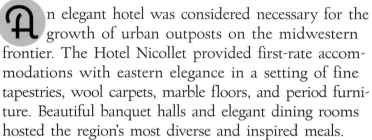

Waikiki Room

The Waikiki Room's atmosphere was authentically South Pacific. Diners sat in chairs from Hong Kong, at tables from Hawaii, and surrounded by Formosan bamboo, Philippine coral, Tahitian flowers, and Samoan decorations. Memories were made while savoring imaginative blendings of seafood or chicken in fruity sauces. And no one would ever forget the rum drinks—tall and frosty, sweet and *sneaky.*

WAIKIKI ROOM RIBS AND SAUCE

Those who couldn't afford a trip to Hawaii got a taste of Polynesian fare under the palm fronds at the Hotel Nicollet's Waikiki Room. Puffy fried shrimp dipped in plum or mustard sauce were a treasured flavor memory. Will Jones, entertainment columnist at the Minneapolis Tribune, created this recipe for the Waikiki's luscious barbecued ribs after being tipped off by an employee (not the chef, who refused to divulge the sauce ingredients).

SAUCE:

1/2 cup soy sauce

1/2 cup honey

Piece of fresh ginger, about walnut size, peeled

1/2 cup ketchup

1/4 teaspoon pepper

1 clove garlic, peeled

RIBS:

4 to 5 pounds lean pork spareribs (baby back preferred)

4 teaspoons salt

1 teaspoon Chinese five-spice powder

Additional honey or sugar

TO MAKE SAUCE: Combine all ingredients in a blender until smooth.

TO PREPARE RIBS: Combine the salt and five-spice powder; rub over all surfaces of ribs. Allow to marinate in the salt mixture for about an hour, refrigerated. Grill the ribs or bake them in a 450-degree oven. After the ribs are about half cooked, baste with the sauce several times. Just before the ribs are done, brush with honey or sprinkle with sugar to form a glaze. Serve hot. Serves 6 to 8 persons as an appetizer; 3 to 4 as an entrée.

THE WEST HOTEL

FIFTH AND HENNEPIN, MINNEAPOLIS

8665. West Hotel, Minneapolis, Minn.

innesota architect LeRoy Buffington designed the West Hotel for Charles and John T. West in 1884. The impressive building was an animated combination of chimneys, dormers, recesses, and balconies anchored by a horizontal band of red and white stripes and massive ground-level columns. The eclectic style continued inside, where a heroic sky-lighted lobby housed an onyx and marble staircase, and dining rooms were wrapped with elaborate Moorish decorations. After five exciting and successful years, proprietor John T. West died suddenly behind the hotel desk. Mrs. Eliza Wood and daughter Helen owned and managed the hotel until it took its place in history fifty years later.

Sunshine Society outside the West Hotel, 1925

The Moorish Room

Lobby, 1890

Delegates to the 1892 National Republican Convention sampled the culinary diversity and liquid refreshment that brought laurels, along with celebrities, to the hotel dining rooms.

165

THE RYAN HOTEL

SIXTH AND ROBERT, ST. PAUL

Dining room, 1890

St. Paul businessmen wanted a new hotel to compete with the grandiose structures on the rise in Minneapolis. Dennis Ryan, newly arrived in St. Paul with a fortune in Utah gold and silver, agreed to finance a magnificent new hostelry. Opening in 1885, the Ryan did not disappoint. Its exterior was an architectural fairyland of undulating walls, towers, spires, balconies, and terra-cotta ornament. Visitors entering the building were astonished to face marble columns and walls embellished with rich Victorian frescoes and luxurious wood paneling. The dining room was the final extravagance, a fanciful, airy puzzle of decorated columns, stenciled walls, painted panels, and ceiling arches, all lit up with bronze and glass chandeliers.

Coffee shop, 1920s

Minnesota Civil Engineers Society banquet, 1913

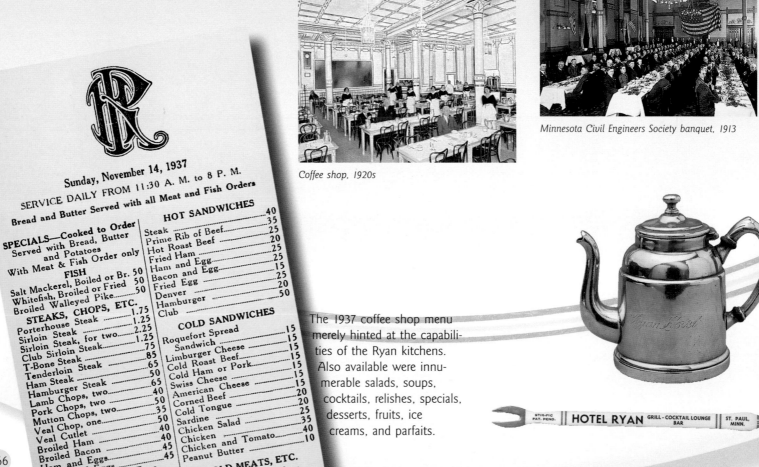

Sunday, November 14, 1937
SERVICE DAILY FROM 11:30 A. M. to 8 P. M.
Bread and Butter Served with all Meat and Fish Orders

SPECIALS—Cooked to Order
Served with Bread, Butter and Potatoes
With Meat & Fish Order only

FISH

Salt Mackerel, Boiled or Br.	.50
Whitefish, Broiled or Fried	.50
Broiled Walleyed Pike	.50

STEAKS, CHOPS, ETC.

Porterhouse Steak	1.75
Sirloin Steak	1.25
Sirloin Steak, for two	2.25
Club Sirloin Steak	1.25
T-Bone Steak	.75
Tenderloin Steak	.65
Ham Steak	.50
Hamburger Steak	.65
Lamb Chops, two	.40
Pork Chops, two	.50
Mutton Chops, two	.35
Veal Chop, one	.50
Veal Cutlet	.40
Broiled Ham	.40
Broiled Bacon	.45
Ham and Eggs	.45
Bacon and Eggs	
Ham or Bacon and Eggs,	.25
Half Order	.50

HOT SANDWICHES

Steak	.40
Prime Rib of Beef	.35
Hot Roast Beef	.25
Fried Ham	.20
Ham and Egg	.25
Bacon and Egg	.25
Fried Egg	.15
Denver	.25
Hamburger	.20
Club	.50

COLD SANDWICHES

Roquefort Spread Sandwich	.15
Limburger Cheese	.15
Cold Roast Beef	.15
Cold Ham or Pork	.15
Swiss Cheese	.15
American Cheese	.15
Corned Beef	.20
Cold Tongue	.20
Sardine	.25
Chicken Salad	.35
Chicken	.35
Chicken and Tomato	.10
Peanut Butter	

COLD MEATS, ETC.
With Potato Salad or Cold Slaw

The 1937 coffee shop menu merely hinted at the capabilities of the Ryan kitchens. Also available were innumerable salads, soups, cocktails, relishes, specials, desserts, fruits, ice creams, and parfaits.

HOTEL RYAN GRILL · COCKTAIL LOUNGE BAR | ST. PAUL, MINN.

THE SAINT PAUL HOTEL

ST. PETER AND FIFTH STREET, ST. PAUL

The Windsor Hotel

John Summers opened his own home to river voyageurs and travelers in 1856. It immediately filled to capacity. In 1871, he moved his house and on the site erected a frame hotel of sixty rooms, the Greenmail House, which burned to the ground in 1877. A year later his Windsor Hotel opened, and it enjoyed a successful run of thirty years.

In the Saint Paul Hotel restaurant, old-fashioned ornate made way for 1930s "enduring modern." Crystal chandeliers were replaced with sleek recessed lights, carved gilded walls gave way to smooth mirrors, and white table linens were folded up in favor of stylish plastic tabletops.

Saint Paul Hotel and Orpheum Theater, 1920s

With the demise of the Windsor Hotel, plans were made to build a million-dollar landmark on the site. Perfectly appointed, the finest equipped and most conveniently arranged hotel in the Northwest, the Saint Paul Hotel opened in 1910.

Architecture and history lovers are grateful for the elegant renovation completed in the 1980s.

Palm Room

Designed as a whimsical, sky-lighted Victorian palm court, this banquet room provided elegant surroundings for private parties and meetings.

Breakfast

Sliced Fresh Pine Apple

Oatmeal   Preserved Figs
              Cracked Wheat
         With Cream

Broiled Whitefish, Montpelier Butter
Sliced Tomatoes   Potato Cakes
                              Sliced Cucumbers
Lamb Fries, Breaded, Tartar Sauce
         Long Branch Potatoes
Sirloin and Tenderloin Steaks, with Chili Sauce
      Baked Potatoes   Rashers of Bacon
Broiled Fresh Mushrooms on Toast, Maitre d'Hotel

Stewed Chicken, Breakfast Style
              Corn Fritters
Oysters—Panned   Fried   Stewed a la Poulette
    Eggs as Ordered
         Vienna Crescents   Spanish Omelets
              Rice and Graham Muffins
Wheat and Corn Griddle Cakes, with Maple Syrup   Brioche
         Honey
    Coffee
         Tea   Currant Jelly
                   Milk
                        Chocolate

Windsor Hotel,
St. Paul, Sunday, April 17, 1892.

RADISSON HOTEL

41 SOUTH SEVENTH STREET, MINNEAPOLIS

The Radisson Hotel was named for Pierre Radisson, one of the earliest explorers of the Minnesota territory. It was a popular choice of business and vacation travelers, who loved its central location and Dayton's dry-goods store next door. Minnesotan Curt Carlson bought the hotel in 1962, eventually covering six continents with more than eight hundred Radisson hotels, inns, and resorts.

The Radisson offered a wide variety of dining choices, ranging from high-fashion rooftops to the rustic sea-level Viking Room.

Teco Inn

The Teco Inn was a glorious showcase of glazed terra cotta with richly colored ceramic murals celebrating scenes from Minnesota and historic events in Minneapolis, the gateway to the great Northwest.

Lounge Pierre, 1930s

Ballroom, 1937

Rooftop Springtime Room, 1930s

Viking Room, 1940s

Cruising at the Viking Room was a popular after-work pastime and holiday tradition. A silver Viking ship sailed from the bar's rafters, and murals painted by renowned Scandinavian artist Arthur Wilberg depicted scenes from Sweden and Norway.

Coffee shop order, 1948

FLAME ROOM HAM STEAK WITH FLAMING COCA-COLA RUM SAUCE

Patterned after smart, small New York City nightclubs, the Flame Room was the place to go for special evenings, especially in later years when the Golden Strings entertained. As with many dishes on the menu, this unique ham with pineapple-cola sauce was served flaming.

2 tablespoons butter

2 sticks cinnamon

6 whole cloves

1 cup crushed pineapple, drained

1/2 cup Coca-Cola

1 lean pre-cooked ham steak

1 ounce dark rum

In a skillet, melt butter. Add cinnamon sticks and cloves, then stir in pineapple and cola. When sauce is steaming and well flavored, remove the cinnamon sticks and cloves. Carefully place the ham steak in the skillet, spooning some sauce over top. Add rum, heating for a minute or so. When serving, ignite the rum for a flaming entrée. Serves 2.

Dining room, Leamington Hotel, Tenth Street and Third Avenue, Minneapolis, 1936

Built in 1910, the Leamington specialized in politicians. Presidents Lyndon Johnson, Richard Nixon, and Jimmy Carter stayed there, and John F. Kennedy slept on his own mattress flown in from the White House. Vice President Hubert H. Humphrey held his election party in the Hall of States with nearly six thousand cheering fans. The dining rooms changed in style over the years, but the food's quality remained constant. The oft-admired Leamington chefs whipped up flavorful dishes ranging from blue-plate lunches to thousand-plate desserts.

LEAMINGTON AND CURTIS HOTELS
DOWNTOWN MINNEAPOLIS

Entertainers in the Hall of States, 1958

Norse Room, 1960s

Smorgasbord fanciers went to the Norse Room for Scandinavian inspiration and traditional northland specialties such as marinated herring and Nova Scotia smoked salmon.

Cardinal Room, Curtis Hotel, Tenth Street and Fourth Avenue, Minneapolis, 1920s

While the Leamington hosted presidential banquets, the Curtis Hotel entertained uncles, grandmas, cousins, and friends. Every Sunday, lines stretched from the lobby to the Cardinal Room as faithful customers waited for a table and to hear the brunch-time organ recital. Apartments in the hotel brought a certain informality to the dining rooms, and chicken salad, lettuce wedges, and gelatin molds were as popular as the steaks and chops.

THE HOTEL DULUTH AND ROCHESTER'S KAHLER HOTEL

In 1925, the Hotel Duluth featured a first-class lobby, banquet rooms, dining rooms, cocktail lounge, and coffee shop. Opening festivities and spirited speeches guaranteed landmark status for the impressive new hostelry. Residents and visitors supported the hotel enthusiastically for more than half a century, after which the building was converted into apartments.

Menu, Black Bear Lounge, Hotel Duluth, 1950s

Duluthians found a favorite place to rendezvous at the Hotel Duluth. After a black bear crashed through a lounge window in the middle of the night and was discovered cleaning out the sugar bowls, the room was renamed the Black Bear Lounge.

Main dining room, Hotel Duluth

Rochester's Mayo Clinic at one time attracted 60,000 patients annually to a city with a population of 15,000, putting hotel accommodations on the critical list. The handsome third Kahler Hotel opened in 1921 with seven hundred guest rooms and five dining areas. It was perfect for hungry patients and their patient friends who had plenty of time and the inclination for finding healthy food.

Café customers ordered menu mainstays of rice and bread puddings—comfort food when it really counted.

Elizabethan Room, Kahler Hotel, 1950s

In this thoroughly English dining room, Whitbread's ale on tap—imported directly from the Samuel Whitbread brewery in London—complemented a dinner of beefeater sirloin steaks or milady filet mignon.

Dining room, Kahler Hotel, 1940s

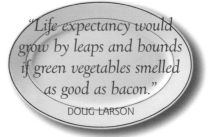

"Life expectancy would grow by leaps and bounds if green vegetables smelled as good as bacon."

DOUG LARSON

HOTEL DINING 1940S STYLE

Commodore Hotel coffee shop,
79 Western Avenue North,
St. Paul, 1930s–1940s

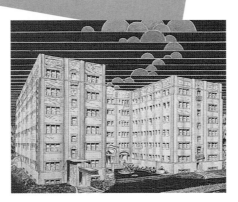

COMMODORE HOTEL
DE LUXE DINNER
CHOICE

CHILLED TOMATO JUICE

GLASS OF WINE · FRUIT COCKTAIL

BROTH WITH BARLEY

FILET OF SOLE, TARTARE SAUCE 85¢

HALF FRIED CHICKEN, CORN FRITTER $1.00

BREADED VEAL CHOP, PAN GRAVY 75¢

FRIED CALVES LIVER AND BACON OR ONIONS 75¢

BROILED TENDERLOIN STEAK, FRESH MUSHROOMS $1.25

BUTTERED WAX BEANS · OR · WHIPPED POTATOES

OR · MASHED SQUASH

HOT ROLLS

GARDEN SALAD, FRENCH DRESSING

PUMPKIN PIE · APPLE DUMPLING

MAROON AND GOLD PARFAIT

MILK · TEA

DINING ROOM HOURS

12.30 TO 2.00 P.M. AND FROM 6.00 TO 8.00 P.M.

NOVEMBER, 13, 1937

F. Scott Fitzgerald and his wife Zelda lived at the Commodore Hotel when their daughter Scottie was born. The restaurant, bar, and coffee shop were Art Deco gems designed by Russian immigrant Werner Wittkamp. Bands on the rooftop garden played swing for women in long gowns and men in tails.

Dinner appetizers circa 1937 included a choice of juice, fruit, broth, or wine.

Hotel Lowry, Wabasha and Fourth Streets, St. Paul

Minnesota Farm Bureau Federation Insurance Division banquet, Hotel Lowry, 1950

The Johnny Gilbert Orchestra performed for a WCCO radio broadcast at the Hotel Lowry in 1940. The practice of booking hotel dining rooms for radio events benefited all concerned by providing a lively radio audience and filling the room for lunch or dinner.

The hotel's white china exhibited a stunning black logo, among the most elegant of all restaurant designs.

BRAISED VEAL WITH PEPPERS AND MUSHROOMS

The Hotel Dyckman was most famous for the Chateau de Paris, but it also served guests in the Carousel Room, where veal with peppers and mushrooms was a menu favorite. Veal was more commonly used in the postwar years, but beef chuck could be substituted, as could cubes of turkey breast.

1 1/2 pounds lean veal, cut in 1-inch cubes

1 medium onion, minced

1/4 cup oil

2 cups sliced mushrooms

2 tablespoons flour

2 cups chicken or beef broth

1 1/2 cups tomato purée

1/2 teaspoon salt

1/4 teaspoon rosemary

1/2 teaspoon sweet basil

2 bay leaves

3 medium bell peppers, any colors, cut into 2-inch squares

Brown veal cubes and onion in oil in a sauté pan or Dutch oven. Add mushrooms and sauté lightly. Stir in flour. Add broth, tomato purée, salt, rosemary, basil, and bay leaves. Cover pan and simmer over low heat until meat is tender, about 2 hours, adding more broth if mixture becomes too thick. About 15 minutes before cooking is finished, add pepper pieces. Serve hot, over mashed potatoes or noodles. Makes 5 to 6 servings.

Chateau de Paris Restaurant, Hotel Dyckman, 29 South Sixth Street, Minneapolis

French restaurants were unusual in midwestern hotels, but the Dyckman housed the very successful Chateau de Paris. It became nationally known for French pâtés, entrées, sautés, and flambés, and for decades metropolitan diners rated it *magnifique*.

COLORFUL 1950s

By the 1950s, hotels sought new customers to check in, and the style to be in was Moderne. Tearing out old-fashioned lobbies and dining rooms seemed the only option. Elegant traditional rooms were replaced with shiny walls, indirect lighting, geometric patterns, chrome, vinyl, and the new hot colors. Postcards in hotel lobbies advertised up-to-date fun awaiting in-vogue and smartly dressed patrons.

SUPER SIXTIES

After World War II, motels were being built along expanding highways in ever-widening suburbs. The old downtown hotels began expensive remodeling projects or closed their doors altogether. The few new hotels constructed during the '50s and '60s were examples of "less is more," and International Style swept through midwestern cities. Restaurants at the tops of hotels reappeared, located under giant geodesic glass domes or surrounded by floor-to-ceiling panoramic windows. Dining tables moved slowly on revolving floors or overlooked hotel swimming pools.

Capp Towers, Nicollet at Thirteenth, Minneapolis, 1960s

Capp Towers, Ninth and Minnesota, St. Paul, 1960s

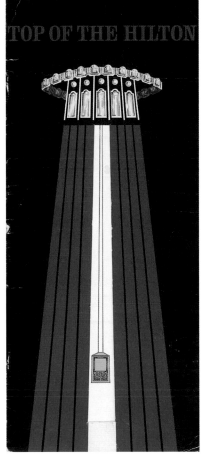

Menu, Top of the Hilton, Kellogg Boulevard at Wabasha Street, St. Paul, 1960s

Northstar Inn, 618 Second Avenue South, Minneapolis, 1960s

Dining rooms surrounded the hotel swimming pool at the Northstar. Anyone want a dip with their chips?

Dinner and an evening getaway at a downtown hotel is still a special event. A romantic weekend for two, a day of shopping and dinner in the lounge, or a mid-week show with a late-night snack—these simple joys are as appealing today as they were a century ago.

Lobster cookout, Minneapolis Golf Club. St. Louis Park, 1950

Ravenous club members line up in anticipation of a succulent lobster dinner at this special event.

CHAPTER TEN

Members Only

For centuries, like-minded people have joined together to share their interests and friendship—to become an extended family of sorts. The roster of club categories is endless, a range of social, benevolent, trade, mystical, ethnic, political, and even criminal associations. Many organizations were started to help members in case of accidents or unemployment, often providing insurance and business connections. Some clubs offered philanthropic outreach to aid veterans, orphans, the sick, and the needy. Other groups played to members' recreational, sporting, and athletic interests.

The most compelling motives for joining a club were the camaraderie, information exchange, and social interaction among members, who endured everything together, whether they were part of secret societies with mysterious initiations or friendly church groups with community bake sales. Who didn't feel kinship with those sharing their interests in the Schubert Club, alumni club, athletic club, or book club? Others joined fraternal groups such as the Independent Order of Odd Fellows, the Ancient Order of Hibernians, the Knights of Pythias, or the Order of the Eastern Star.

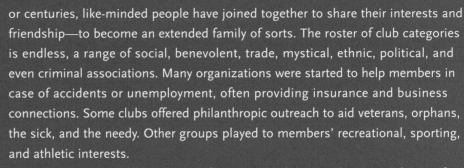

Club architecture enhanced the Minnesota skyline, and some of these structures are benchmarks on city boulevards today. Clubhouses often reached several stories in height, and fluted columns, carved Doric capitals, porches, towers, and turrets embellished their façades. Some buildings stood as stately retreats nestled on country club grounds. Others brought joviality to lake shores with their whimsical structures. Members shared their spacious meeting halls with local populations: wedding parties celebrated until dawn, tutu-ed ballerinas pirouetted at recitals, and fund-raising festivities occasionally raised the rafters.

Club dining facilities rivaled those in the finest hotels and restaurants. Echoing the styles of their English counterparts, some club interiors incorporated sculptured bronze lighting, massive handhewn beams, and linen-fold carved wall panels. Others featured dining areas with bright and frivolous decorations that spoke to members' interests. One thing was certain—club dining had a unique focus that could not be confused with any other dining experience.

The cuisine was sure to match the décor. Business clubs called on chefs to devise rich meals accompanied by fine wines and served on pricey china. Sailing club members may have wanted only a quick sandwich on a thick pottery plate with a cold beer. Women's clubs specialized in fresh salads and flavorful casseroles artfully arranged on flowered plates. Any club worth its salt aspired to use personalized dishes with artistically scripted names or logos fired under the glaze. Image was so uniformly cherished that today more monogrammed collectible china survives from clubs than from any other dining category.

Few of the grand old buildings remain, but for many people club membership is still a cherished goal. Clubs satisfy curiosity, support hobbies, advance avocations, and encourage friendships. A meal shared with kindred spirits, accompanied by conversation centered on common passions, is the best club experience of all.

FRATERNAL AND BENEVOLENT

lub events often featured a meal. When dining rooms were part of association buildings, members met over breakfast, entertained over lunch, and staged events around cocktails or dinner. Some clubs held meetings that were shrouded in ceremony and mystery, but members publicly promoted their charitable and philanthropic projects. Other clubs held meetings at local restaurants. They, too, performed worthy deeds and funded humanitarian programs in the community, often quietly and with little fanfare.

Dining room, Elks Club, Second Avenue South and Seventh Street, Minneapolis, 1920

The Benevolent and Protective Order of Elks was established in 1868, named for the North American animal admired by the founders for its strong and valiant characteristics. Ornately stenciled ceiling beams and scenic murals added mystique to these Arts and Crafts dining rooms.

Green Room, Elks Club, Minneapolis

Elks Hall, Washington and Fourth Street, St. Paul
Exotic architecture heralded the importance of some fraternal organizations.

Dining room, Minnesota Masonic Home, Bloomington

America's first known charitable society was the Freemasons, established in 1733. Fourteen U.S. presidents, including George Washington, were members, as were thirteen signers of the Declaration of Independence. The Masons' auxilliary, the Order of the Eastern Star, was open to women.

American Legion, Moorhead

eavy-gauge commercial china came into use in the 1890s. Clubs and organizations took the cake for using the greatest variety of custom dinnerware. The interlocking rings in the Odd Fellows' logo represent friendship, love, and truth. Other designs made use of stately animals, stylized flowers, scripted names, or ornamental logos and emblems.

Knights of Pythias banquet, North St. Paul, 1898

The Order of Knights of Pythias, dedicated to the cause of universal peace, was founded in 1864. Named for a follower of Pythagoras, the father of Greek philosophy, the group strove for moral uplift and the purification of society through friendship, charity, and benevolence.

177

ATHLETICS AND LEISURE

Ⓘn the early 1900s, leisure time meant big business for clubs and their restaurants. Downtown athletic clubs catered to business people by offering diverse recreational facilities and stately dining spaces. Automobile, boating, and golf clubs were built for members in growing suburbs, and they too offered enchanting dining rooms and cafés.

Main dining room, Minneapolis Athletic Club, 615 Second Avenue South, Minneapolis, 1930s

New Ulm's Turner Hall was established in 1856 by members of the Turnverein—a German association whose development paralleled that of the town itself. Endorsing the Turner philosophy that physical exercise strengthened the mind, the 1866 building featured large gymnasiums, a theater, and classrooms as well as meeting rooms, dining rooms, and an authentic German rathskeller with handpainted scenic murals.

The Dutch Room, Turner Hall, New Ulm, 1920s

Waitresses, St. Paul Athletic Club, 240 Cedar Street, St. Paul, 1915

Minneapolis Athletic Club, 1915

This visually stimulating room was a tile extravaganza. The walls, ceiling, beams, columns, and floor were covered in beautiful—though not acoustically pleasing—ceramics with Native American motifs. Swastikas, an ancient symbol of friendship and good luck, also decorated the room.

Ⓨacht and boat clubs were popular in the land of sky-blue waters. These imaginitive buildings were beacons for sailors. Inside, landlocked galleys offered casual and relaxing meals for the captain and crew.

Clubhouse, White Bear Yacht Club, 1900s

Duluth Yacht Club, 1910

Minnesota Boat Club, Harriet Island, St. Paul, 1960

Lobster cookout, Minneapolis Golf Club, St. Louis Park, 1950

Fiftieth anniversary celebration of the Town and Country Club, 300 Mississippi River Boulevard North, St. Paul, 1938

Built in the late 1800s, the Town and Country Club operates the nation's second-oldest golf course still located on its original site. The club hosts many events, from black-tie parties to country hoedowns.

Thought to be the most common type of club in the United States, golf clubs provided outdoor recreation and elaborate social facilities. Members entertained in elegant lounges and dining rooms, and chefs responded with menus equal to the spectacular vistas of green grass and tall trees.

Party at the Minikahda Club, 3200 Excelsior Boulevard, Minneapolis, 1935

AMERICAN AUTOMOBILE ASSOCIATION

Country clubhouse, Minneapolis Auto Club, Bloomington, 1920s

In 1902, auto enthusiasts in Chicago founded the American Automobile Association to provide road service. The Minneapolis AAA was formed the same year with a mission of "instruction and mutual improvement in the art of automobilism and the literary and social culture of its members." The organization owned an architecturally spectacular country club in Bloomington overlooking the Minnesota River. It was a favorite of auto aficionados, who stopped by for walks in the formal gardens or for dining, live music, and dancing.

Dining-room and kitchen staff outside Minneapolis Auto Club, 1925

Dining room, Minneapolis Auto Club, 1931

179

SOCIAL AND FUN

Social clubs provided interesting dining choices and more. Members could hold business meetings and seminars, play pool in billiard rooms, enjoy a cigar in smoking rooms, or exercise in the gym. Breakfast was served in sunny dining areas, lunch was a buttoned-up affair, and evening cocktail or dinner-dance parties were both formal and fun.

Women's Club, Winona, 1900s

Women's City Club, Third and St. Peter Streets, St. Paul

Dining room, Women's Club, 410 Oak Grove, Minneapolis, 1930

Women's clubs have been popular since the early 1900s. They provide important spaces for professionals to meet over lunch or network for business exchanges, and their artistic initiatives support many cultural activities.

Dining room, Kitchi Gammi Club, Duluth

The Kitchi Gammi Club, named with the Ojibwe term for Lake Superior and organized by Duluth's iron ore magnates in 1883, was one of Minnesota's earliest social clubs. Overlooking the lake, the dining room features paneled wood wainscoting and timbered ceilings.

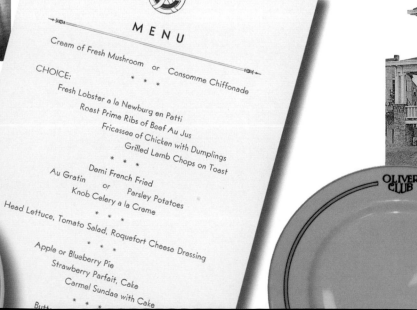

MENU

Cream of Fresh Mushroom or Consomme Chiffonade

CHOICE:
* * *

Fresh Lobster a la Newburg en Patti
Roast Prime Ribs of Beef Au Jus
Fricassee of Chicken with Dumplings
Grilled Lamb Chops on Toast

* * *

Demi French Fried
Au Gratin or Parsley Potatoes
Knob Celery a la Creme

* * *

Head Lettuce, Tomato Salad, Roquefort Cheese Dressing

* * *

Apple or Blueberry Pie
Strawberry Parfait, Cake
Carmel Sundae with Cake

Coffee hour at Unity Church, St. Paul, 1960

Church suppers, lutefisk dinners, pancake breakfasts, after-the-sermon coffees, and youth-group snacks filled church basements with devotees looking to keep body and soul together.

PERFECTION SALAD

"Salad" at early-twentieth-century ladies' soirees was usually jelled. Perfection salad, as served by Hibbing's Brooklyn Club, was considered most elegant. Vegetables were of secondary importance.

1 1/2 tablespoons Knox gelatin

1/4 cup cold water

1 1/2 cups boiling water

2 tablespoons vinegar

2 tablespoons lemon juice

1/3 cup sugar

1/4 teaspoon salt

1/2 cup shredded cabbage

1/4 cup diced celery

1/4 cup diced pimiento

Soak the gelatin in cold water for five minutes. Add boiling water and stir until gelatin is dissolved. Add vinegar and lemon juice, sugar and salt. Cool. When the mixture begins to thicken, add the cabbage, celery, and pimiento. Pour into molds or a shallow pan. Chill; unmold or cut in squares. Makes 6 servings.

Club row, Second Avenue South, Minneapolis

Modeled after the great European guilds and anchoring the city's club row, the Minneapolis Club was incorporated in 1885 and has been in its present building since 1908. A downtown landmark, the club hosts business and social events in an English-inspired environment.

Minnesota Club, Fourth and Cedar, St. Paul, 1914

The Minnesota Club, founded in 1869, occupied this dignified red brick building as its second home. Famed member architect Cass Gilbert selected the gentlemanly furnishings for the dining rooms.

Oliver Club, Hibbing, 1920s

The Oliver Club was available to the Oliver Mining Company's employees and their friends.

innesota boasts numerous clubs tailored to a huge variety of professions, charities, and hobbies. For those with interests ranging from the Tuxedo Club to the Post Office Toboggan Club, there probably is a perfect club connection just around the corner in every Minnesota town.

Dining room, Lake Park Hotel,
Lake Minnetonka, 1875

Early resort diners enjoyed fresh
meals served by seasoned waiters.

CHAPTER ELEVEN

Resorts

Minnesota has always been envied for its healthy climate, comfortable summer weather, and beautiful lakes. In the late 1800s, a midwestern vacation was thought to be the healthiest choice of all, and multitudes of tourists flocked in from distant states. Southern families seeking relief from oppressive heat arrived by riverboat for watery relaxation at spas and lakeside inns. Eastern vacationers escaped crowded cities, boarding fun-filled excursion trains destined for picturesque resorts and grand hotels at the water's edge. Food, relaxation, and play were the triple pleasures of a Minnesota vacation.

Meals in elegant resort hotels helped to define the perfect holiday. Food was served fresh—from the dairy farm next door or from a nearby lake or garden. Dining rooms were large, well appointed, and staffed with experienced servers. Chefs created French entrées, from-scratch breads, bubbly fruit pies, and homemade ice cream. Their culinary skills drew satisfied sighs from even the weariest of vacationers.

While the elegant resorts and their fancy restaurants attracted tourists from other states, Minnesota's residents often had a different vacation in mind. They loaded up their Model Ts and headed "up to the lake" as soon as dirt roads could take them there. Families endured long and sometimes harrowing journeys through sparse countryside, but they soon had their destination in sight. Drivers steered along twin tire tracks, tufts of grass in between, and pulled up to quaint lakeside cabins for a long-awaited summer break.

North-woods resorts served casual meals on breezy porches and in rustic dining rooms, lofty pavilions, and barnlike dining halls. Cooks raided garden plots for fresh vegetables, vine-ripened cantaloupes, and just-dug potatoes. Menu specials featured local fish and game; walleye, fried or breaded, was the all-time favorite. In pine-timbered lodges the coffee was always hot, and next to a gigantic split-rock fireplace a game of checkers awaited.

People relaxed, rested, and enjoyed modest recreation. Cozy beachside cabins provided sheltered hideaways complete with rustic furniture, homespun curtains, and chenille bedspreads. Waterside rows of fishing boats greeted the active guest, while those fancying a stroll in the woods could take along baskets for gathering plump berries. The most energetic patrons warmed up for shuffleboard, rowing, volleyball, and water play. Farther north, fishing, hunting, and hiking were favorite pastimes. And growling stomachs were quieted with a shore lunch cooked over a blazing campfire.

By the 1950s, vacation amusements became more strenuous. Advances in motor boating and water sports encouraged vacationers to play harder and longer. Resorts happily installed equipment and recreational facilities for guests to earn their aches and pains. Meanwhile, dining-room staff geared up for the heightened hunger pangs these activities created.

A vacation appetite, however small or large, responded to the musical serenade of sizzling fish. Creaking oven doors promised crusty pies, and pots gurgled with simmering new potatoes or just-picked vegetables. As tantalizing aromas wafted from kitchen windows, resort guests burst out of their cabins and headed straight for the dining room!

MINNESOTA'S EARLY RESORTS

On the late 1800s, spending time in the sun was thought to be unhealthy. Women wore long skirts and carried parasols on their walks, and men donned suits and starched shirts even to go fishing. Likewise, early resort dining was a somewhat formal affair. White tablecloths notified diners that a vacation could also be a civilized experience, and dressing for dinner was a common practice.

Dining room, Hotel Blake, Alexandria, 1912

Spring Park Villa, Bald Eagle Lake, White Bear Township

Birchmont Hotel, Bemidji

A summer waitress at Hotel Blake remembered gathering flowers from the gardens to make arrangements for her tables and memorizing the menus before serving breakfast, lunch, and dinner. Between meals, she helped clean the rooms and cottages, seven days a week, nearly twelve hours a day. Early quarters for the help were segregated: white chauffeurs slept in the attic, and black drivers had space in the garage.

Guests at this popular resort hotel consorted with millionaire Cornelius Vanderbilt Jr., lawyer Clarence Darrow, doctors William and Charles Mayo, and movie star Rosalind Russell, who regularly ordered her favorite dish—a plate of boiled fish swimming in melted butter.

Pigeon River Hotel, U.S.-Canadian border

Crystal Waters Lodge, Grand Rapids

Lakeside Resort, Whitefish Lake

Pinehurst Lodge, Deer River

Manhattan Beach Lodge, Manhattan Beach

"Watermelon—it's a good fruit. You eat, you drink, you wash your face."
ENRICO CARUSO

Watermelon picnic, 1919

Tuelles Resort, Annandale

SULFUR-SPRING RESORTS

Mudbaden Sulphur Springs Health Resort, north of Jordan

Unusual sulfur springs were discovered near Shakopee and Jordan in the early 1900s. Mud baths made from these waters were thought to provide curative treatments for rheumatism, gout, sciatica, neuralgia, asthma, neuritis, and various skin, kidney, and nervous diseases. Three elaborate health resorts were built, and Minnesota's sulfur-springs industry gained national fame. Thousands of patients seeking treatment began arriving from all over the United States and Canada.

To accommodate the large number of visitors, Mudbaden had its own railway, and passengers arrived at the front door of the Classical Revival–style building. Inside were lounges, sun parlors, sitting rooms, amusement halls, resting rooms, mud rooms, bath rooms, dormitories—more than one hundred rooms in all, plus one hundred and twenty-five private sleeping rooms.

Dining room, Mudbaden, 1925

This spacious room overlooked serene vistas of flower gardens and landscaped grounds. Warm oak paneling and woodwork, plus tables covered in clean white cloths, complemented the restful environment. Up-to-date kitchens offered meals that suited the era's healthy diets.

Mud room, Mudbaden, 1925

Mudbaden employed nearly one hundred people, owned an early x-ray machine, and maintained two surgical operating rooms. Patients simmered in healthy mud until they got hungry; then they headed upstairs to the dining room's steam tables.

Jordan Sulphur Springs and Mud Bath Sanitarium, Jordan, 1910

Jordan Sulphur Springs' chauffeured cars picked up arrivals in Shakopee. Mud-bath resorts employed physicians, surgeons, nurses, chiropractors, lab technicians, masseurs, masseuses, and numerous aides and assistants. Rates in 1927 ranged from thirty-five to forty-five dollars per week for room, meals, and treatment.

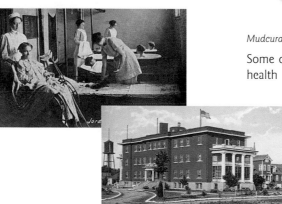

Mudcura Sanitarium, Shakopee, 1916

Some of the buildings have survived, but the health resorts were all gone by the late 1950s.

MINNETONKA STREETCAR BOATS

Of sulfur springs didn't provide a cure, boating on Lake Minnetonka was another healthy option. Bright yellow street-cars brought vacationers and day-trippers from the Twin Cities to the Blue Line Dock in Excelsior. Passengers boarded one of several look-alike "streetcar boats" for scenic lake excursions or for transportation to resorts and ports around the lake.

Stillwater *streetcar boat, 1900s*

Tourists headed out for a cruise around the big lake or for a mealtime treat at a waterside hotel.

Blue Line Boat House and Restaurant, Excelsior, 1900s

Passengers dined at the Blue Line restaurant or bought a picnic lunch for a steamboat stop at Big Island Amusement Park.

Steamboat docks, Big Island, Lake Minnetonka, 1910

Visitors arriving at Big Island, 1910

Picnic at Big Island Amusement Park, 1909

Big Island's pavilions and tables offered shady spots for a picnic before a ride on the carousel or roller coaster.

This silk menu from 1882 announced dinner for the daughter of Senator Washburn, who owned the steamboat *City of St. Louis.* The meal served on board was typical of high-society dinners at "the lake."

MENU.

Consommé a la Royal.
Petit Bouchess au Salpicon.
Broiled Bluefish a la Maitre d'Hotel.
Potatoes Parisienne,
Fillet of Beef larded with Mushrooms,
Asparagus. Baked Mashed Potatoes.
Chicken Croquets, Sauce Bechamel.
Cauliflower.
Lemon Sherbet.
Shrimp Salad.
Mayonnaise Chicken.
Prairie Chicken, Jelly Sauce.
Baked Stuffed Tomatoes.
Charlotte D'Russe, Port Wine Jelly.
Ornamented Cake.
Vanilla Ice Cream,
Bon Bons,
Fruit. Nuts.
Coffee.

CAPTAIN'S TABLE
STUFFED TOMATOES

Stuffed tomatoes sat on many Victorian plates. Their color perked up a dull meal, and they could be stuffed with many creative ingredients. They also traveled well—these were served at Mary C. Washburn's on-board party.

4 large tomatoes

1 cup soft bread crumbs

1/2 cup grated mild Cheddar cheese

1/4 cup finely minced or grated onion

2 slices bacon, fried crisp and crumbled

1/2 teaspoon salt

1/4 teaspoon pepper

Additional Cheddar cheese

Take a very thin slice off the rounded bottom of each tomato so it will sit flat. Slice tomatoes in half through their middles. Into a mixing bowl, scoop the tomato pulp from each half, leaving a tomato shell. Set shells on a baking sheet. Mix tomato pulp with bread crumbs, 1/2 cup cheese, onion, bacon crumbles, salt, and pepper. Mix well. Spoon the stuffing mixture into the tomatoes. Sprinkle with additional cheese. Bake in a 350-degree oven for 25 minutes. Serve hot. Makes 8 servings.

LAKE MINNETONKA

Lake Minnetonka's tourism boom of the late 1800s surpassed all others in the state's history. Steam trains puffed along rail lines to Wayzata. Coaches arrived packed with excited tourists accompanied by steamer trunks, playful children, helpful nannies, and noisy commotion. Throughout the summer months, vacationers by the thousands crowded into the few dozen hotels located on the lake.

Lake Park Hotel, Lake Minnetonka.
J. W. HUTCHINSON, Proprietor.

Verandah, Lake Park Hotel, Lake Minnetonka, 1880s

The Lake Park Hotel, later called the Tonka Bay Hotel, was one of the largest on the lake—its dining room could seat four hundred people. Sweet milk products, fruits, and vegetables came from hotel-owned dairy barns, orchards, and gardens. Victorians flocked to the broad verandahs with their sweeping views of the lower lake, spending vacation days reading, playing billiards, watching theater productions, or laughing at minstrel troupes.

DINNER,

Tuesday, Aug. 21, 1883.

SOUP.
Pearl Barley.
FISH.
Baked Croppies, Genoese Sauce.
BOILED.
Ham.   Corned Beef and Cabbage.
ROASTS.
Beef.   Veal with Dressing.
Lamb, Mint Sauce.
ENTREES.
Tenderloin of Beef a-la-Jardiniere.
Fricasse of Veal a-la-Allemande.
Spigette of Macaroni au Parmison.
VEGETABLES.
Mashed Potatoes.   Boiled Potatoes.   New Corn.
Squash.   Sugar Beets.   Cabbage.
MYONAISE.
Lobster.   Cucumbers.   Tomatoes.
PASTRY.
Rice-Pudding, Cream Sauce.
Grape Pie.   Peach Pie.   Fruit Cake.   Pound Cake.
Jelly Roll.   Assorted Cake.   Grape Jelly.
DESSERT.
Assorted Nuts.   Raisins.   Fruit.
Water Melon.   Vanilla Ice Cream.
Crackers.   Cheese.
TEA.   COFFEE.
Lunches for evening parties must be ordered before 8:30 P. M.

Hotel Lafayette, Minnetonka Beach, 1890s

As soon as it opened, James J. Hill's Hotel Lafayette was *the* place to be seen. A multifaceted structure, resplendent with turrets, gables, and porches, it was the largest resort of its kind anywhere in the West, and Hill's trains stopped at its door six times a day. Plush red carpets were rolled out for former presidents, generals, governors, earls, lords, and diplomats, all of whom dined on lavish feasts in elegant rooms overlooking the lake. Live dinner bands entertained sailing parties, and business clubs toasted and roasted in the dining rooms. But on a cold and fateful day in 1897, the fabulous fourteen-year-old Hotel Lafayette and all its elaborate furnishings burned to the ground in less than an hour.

HOTEL·LAFAYETTE

JULY 4TH 1893

Many vacationers arrived at Lake Minnetonka by rail, streetcar, or steamboat; then they simply walked to the hotel or were driven by horse and buggy. On the Excelsior side of the lake, holidays were relaxed—wraparound porches caught summer breezes, and guests in rocking chairs sipped on refreshing drinks or enjoyed a leisurely chicken dinner at a wicker table.

Porch dining room, Hotel del Otero, Spring Park

The last of the big hotels on the lake, the Hotel del Otero tempted travelers to unwind with lunch in the porch dining room. In the evenings, swingers took to the big dance floor. Entertainment pavilions, picnic pergolas, and fishing docks amused guests until 1945, when the Hotel del Otero succumbed to a Fourth of July fire.

Hotel St. Louis and boat dock, Deephaven, 1908

Hotel carriages gathered guests at the Deephaven depot and brought them to the luxurious Hotel St. Louis. State-of-the-art electric lights, indoor plumbing, and a five-mile system of electric bells serving two hundred rooms impressed even the most sophisticated guests. When the hotel began hosting lawn-tennis tournaments, players in white flannels and straw hats retired to the dining rooms to verbally replay their matches over dinner.

Pergola, Hotel del Otero, 1905

Excelsior Bay Hotel, Lake Minnetonka, 1925

The basics in resort dining—southern fried chicken and fresh fish dinners—beckoned famished boaters cruising on the lake.

HOTEL ST. LOUIS, MINN.
LAKE MINNETONKA,
NATIONAL HOTEL COMPANY, REEVE & WILCOX

DINNER

Cream of Rice

Consomme Royal
Gherkins
Tomatoes
Olives

Baked Black Bass, Tomato Sauce
Shoestring Potatoes

Philadelphia Broilers, on Toast

Corn Fritters, Maple Syrup

Prime Rib Roast Beef, au Jus

Macedonia Salad

Boiled Potatoes
Green Peas

Mashed Potatoes
Corn, on Cob
Plum Pie
Cocoanut Pudding
Assorted Cakes
Nuts

Apple Pie
Vanilla Ice Cream
Watermelon
Crackers and Wafers

Fruits
Coffee
Brick and American Cheese
Milk
Tea

Extra charge for meals served in rooms or fruits taken from the tables.
WEDNESDAY, AUGUST 15, 1900.

Hotel St. Louis, 1881

When the Model T became popular early in the twentieth century, vacationers hit the road to discover what lay beyond the big lake. Eventually the grand hotels on Lake Minnetonka closed their doors, and every one, great and small, gave way to private cottages and cabins.

HARD CHOICES

minnesota's relaxation came in distinct styles. Guests at big and glamorous resorts settled into lakeside sanctuaries that offered metropolitan amusements and sophisticated dining. Those preferring north-woods lodges and cabins nestled into forest retreats with native wildlife and home-cooked meals. Which to choose?

Chik-wauk cook

Chik-wauk Lodge

Chik-wauk cabin, Grand Marais, 1930s

Built in the 1930s at the end of the Gunflint Trail, Chik-wauk Lodge was the ultimate in native fieldstone and timber construction. Veteran cooks served lake-caught fish hot off the stove to guests gathered at cozy tables by a roaring fire. Well fed, they cuddled in woodsy cabins where entertainment was provided by romping deer and the call of the loon.

Women fishing, Underwood, 1910s

Boys with their catch, 1900s

Interlaken Inn, Fairmont, 1920s

Interlaken's dining rooms and open-air porches were tended by students from Gustavus Adolphus College. Chefs came from the Twin Cities or as far away as California to prepare fish fillets in French sauces, filling the popular dining rooms all four seasons. Each guest room had a porch overlooking Hall Lake, and hippodrome horse races were held on a quarter-mile track in front of the building.

INTERLAKEN INN Menu
Sunday, May 26, 1929

Dining Room open from 12 p. m. to 2 p. m.; 5:30 p. m. to 7 p. m.

CELERY

GREEN ONIONS

VEGETABLE SOUP RADISHES

ROAST CHICKEN
ROAST LOIN OF PORK

TENDERLOIN STEAK DRESSING
APPLE SAUCE

CREAMED CORN
MASHED POTATOES

NEW STRING BEANS
HOT ROLLS

COMBINATION SALAD

APPLE PIE

ICE CREAM STRAWBERRY SHORT CAKE
WITH CAKE

COFFEE

TEA MILK

Price of Dinner 75c

Phone 3302 For Reservations

ON THE TRAIL

Bumpy two-lane roads heading north were often as primitive as the destinations themselves. Even so, remote woodland cabins with simple furnishings and a few amenities seemed like paradise.

"DINING ROOM," VERMILLION TRAIL LODGE, McCOMBER, MINN.

Vermillion Trail Lodge, McComber, 1940s

Cooking in this kitchen couldn't have been easy. A constant supply of wood fired up the big cast-iron stove and the icebox sat out on the porch. The coffee urns held enough for the whole camp, and hikers marched into the spacious room for chicken-and-biscuit lunches or afternoon snacks by the fireplace.

"KITCHEN," VERMILLION TRAIL LODGE, McCOMBER, MINN.

North Shore Hotel, near Tofte, 1940s

Herter's of Waseca became one of the nation's first mail-order catalogue companies in 1893. Its slightly exaggerated descriptions advertised hundreds of products that campers and hunters just couldn't resist. Herter's historical recipe book was published in 1969 with an ambitious assortment of campsite goodies like Cattail Salad with Confederate Baked Potatoes and, cooked over a wood fire in a cast-iron frying pan, Prince Albert's Buckingham Palace Brown Gravy, Cheese Sauce Antoine Van Dyck, Black Watch Scottish Hunters Sandwich, Maria Luisa Roquefort Stuffed Chopped Beef, Mohawk Corn, and Church Builder Chicken.

Little Marais Lodge and Store, 1930s

Old timers in Little Marais pumped their gas, sat down for lunch, and settled up in the store.

DINING IN THE LOGS

Quintessential resort dining rooms were packaged in native timber aged to a golden glow. Post-and-beam construction created lofty rafters of rugged jack pine, and walls of peeled logs, chinked and varnished, nestled up to fireplaces of hefty split rock.

Sawbill Lodge builder, 1934

Sawbill Lodge, near Lutsen

National Forest Lodge, Isabella, 1940s

Hungry Jack Lodge, Grand Marais, 1937

Hamilton's Island Park Lodge, Park Rapids, 1940s

Birch Point Inn, Tower, 1920s

Klose to Nature Kamp, near Hackensack, 1925

Canadian Border Lodge, near Ely, 1940s

192

Cascade Lodge, near Grand Marais

Merit Lodge, Walker

Nelson's Resort, Crane Lake

Cooks and waitresses, Lake Sylvia, 1920s

Resort vacation days ended with fresh fish sizzling on a platter, served with a smile.

Snowbank Lodge, Ely

Northern Pine Lodge, Park Rapids

"Personally I stay away from natural foods. At my age I need all the preservatives I can get."
GEORGE BURNS

GRAND VIEW LODGE

GULL LAKE

Grand View Lodge, Gull Lake, Brainerd, 1940s

Historic Grand View Lodge dates to World War I, when M. V. Baker started a real-estate promotion to sell lots on Gull Lake. Business was so brisk he needed a lodge to house prospective clients. The lodge opened in 1921 with a dining room, lounge, dance floor, and guest rooms. It has remained virtually unchanged for more than eighty years. Grand View has been owned by three generations of the Cote family since 1937. Many of them have greeted Paul Newman as their guest during the Brainerd auto races.

Sherwood Forest Lodge, Gull Lake, Brainerd, 1920s

A trainload of logs on its way to Duluth was abandoned at the Nisswa railroad station, where enterprising Mrs. Williams bought the logs for a dollar each. With a plan sketched on a plank and two talented Scandinavian builders, the logs were lifted into place by horsepower to create Sherwood Forest. Opened as a resort in 1925, the lodge has a cavernous lobby, broad wraparound porches, and a dining room with a piano loft. Chefs offered to prepare and serve a guest's catch of the day.

Sinclair Lewis spent the summer of 1941 writing in a Sherwood Forest cabin. Waitress Doryce Anderson remembered that he drove in with his black chauffeur, wrote only at night, slept most of the day, and partied all evening, sometimes with Jean Harlow and Bing Crosby, who were on holiday at the nearby Breezy Point Resort. Sherwood Forest was eventually purchased by neighboring Grand View Lodge.

GRAND VIEW LODGE BEER-BATTERED WALLEYE AND TARTAR SAUCE

Nearly 40 percent of all dining-room orders at Grand View Lodge were, and still are, for walleye. Chefs offer it prepared many ways, but beer-battered is the all-time favorite.

WALLEYE:

8 walleye fillets, 8 ounces each

3 cups pilsner beer

1 3/4 cups cornstarch

1 tablespoon kosher salt

1 teaspoon granulated garlic

1 teaspoon white pepper

1 3/4 cups flour

Additional flour for dredging

Oil

Combine beer and dry ingredients in a bowl; mix thoroughly. Dredge the walleye fillets in flour, then dip in the beer batter. Cook in 375-degree oil for 4 to 5 minutes. Makes 8 servings.

TARTAR SAUCE:

1 cup mayonnaise

Juice of 2 lemons

1/4 cup sweet pickle relish

2 tablespoons capers

1 tablespoon yellow mustard

1 teaspoon salt

1/2 teaspoon black pepper

Mix ingredients. Chill until served.

GRAND VIEW LODGE ON GULL LAKE NEAR BRAINERD, MINN., P. O. NISSWA, MINN.

BREEZY POINT

PEQUOT LAKES

A veteran of the Spanish-American War and fresh from service in World War I, Captain Billy Fawcett created a civilian career publishing magazines—from mysteries, movies, and gardening to photography, crime, humor, and romance. The risqué magazine *Captain Billy's Whiz Bang* was so successful that by 1921 Fawcett purchased a home and eighty acres of land on Big Pelican Lake. Cabins for friends soon followed, and then an enormous lodge and dining hall designed by Foshay Tower architectural firm Magney and Tusler. The magnificent resort opened on June 10, 1925, on what became widely known as the Riviera of the North.

Breezy Point Lodge, 1930s

Seventy-two railroad flatcars transported huge Norway pine logs to workers who spent two years erecting the massive Breezy Point Lodge. Its dining room could seat up to a thousand people and included a sweeping stage for the orchestra. At both ends were split-rock fireplaces, eleven feet wide, five feet thick, and forty-two feet high. In 1959, as helpless Minnesotans watched in horror, the spectacular old Breezy Point Lodge burned to the ground.

The Breezy Point Orchestra—"A Sterling Troupe of Mirthful Troubadours"—provided music for after-dinner dancing every evening

Breezy Point's table service was worthy of celebrity attention. Movie stars Lionel Barrymore, Joan Crawford, John Wayne, Jack Benny, Rosalind Russell, Gene Autry, Clark Gable, Clara Bow, Carole Lombard, Delores Del Rio, and Jack Dempsey were only a few who signed the guest register.

Dining room employees, 1930s

Ruttger's Bay Lake Lodge, Deerwood, 1950s

Ruttger's Pine Beach Lodge, Brainerd, 1940s

Joseph and Josephine Ruttger opened their first lodge in 1898 on Bay Lake, establishing one of Minnesota's earliest resorts. In 1900, weekly room, board, and boat rental cost fishermen five dollars, which increased to twenty-four by 1920.

In 1922, son Alec hired a crew of lumberjacks and carpenters to build a new log dining room. With horse and chain, man and bucksaw, native poplar logs were harvested from the woods of the nearby Devil's Washboard. The log dining hall was dedicated with a special Ruttger chicken dinner. Four Ruttger sons joined the business, and soon there were five resorts in northern Minnesota that bore the family name. Joseph and Josephine would be proud of their great-grandchildren, now tending the original resort, where they *still* serve chicken dinners.

Ruttger's Blueberry Buckle

As the resort's first chef, Josephine Ruttger handed down her favorite recipes to her family. Made with pails full of dewy blueberries fresh from the woods, this buckle would have made any vacation day warm and sunny.

BATTER:

3/4 cup sugar

1/4 cup soft shortening

1 egg

1/2 cup milk

2 cups flour

2 teaspoons baking powder

1/2 teaspoon salt

1 cup blueberries

TOPPING:

1/2 cup sugar

1/3 cup sifted flour

1/2 teaspoon cinnamon

1/4 cup soft butter

Mix together 3/4 cup sugar, shortening, and egg. Stir in milk. Sift together and stir in 2 cups flour, baking powder, and salt. Carefully blend in blueberries. Spread batter in a greased and floured 9x9-inch pan. Mix together topping ingredients and sprinkle over batter. Bake 45 to 50 minutes in a 375-degree oven. Serve warm. Makes 9 servings.

Norway Ridge Resort, Pequot Lakes, 1950s
Cook Bob Newman by the kitchen door, 1948

Dockside shouts of "let's do ribs!" could mean only one place: Norway Ridge on Lake Ossawinnamakee. Since the 1940s, this piney room has been the place for ribs and walleye, both prepared with secret recipes. The resort has evolved into a restaurant with enlarged dining rooms, but the cooks smoke the ribs and batter the walleye in the same old way.

Izaty's Lodge, Onamia, 1950s

Izaty's Lodge, built in 1922, was named for a Dakota Indian village located on the shores of Mille Lacs Lake. Fishermen and swimmers were coaxed into a safe harbor, where they could enjoy picture-window views of the wild and windy lake and a hot dinner in the dining room.

Madden Lodge dining room, Gull Lake, Brainerd, 1950s

The 1950s Madden Lodge and dining room were classic Minnesota Nice. Tables and chairs were made of native pine, handhewn and pegged together, and pine planks covered the walls and floors. A roaring fire and curio cabinets with shelves of dishes provided warmth and ambiance to the dining room. Members of the Madden family have been hosting vacationers on Gull Lake since the 1930s.

Roland Strand ice fishing on Lake O'Brien, 1950s

Merrill Cragun planned his resort of eight cabins the day before the bombing of Pearl Harbor. Even with gas rationing and shortages, the new resort managed to survive. The original dining room's pine paneling and scalloped valance design reappears throughout the huge resort, maintained by the second generation, Dutch and Irma Cragun.

Cragun's, Gull Lake, Brainerd, 1940s

ISLAND VIEW LODGE APPLE PIE WITH CHEESE PASTRY

Irma Cragun saved the kitchen notes and recipes from Island View Lodge when it became part of Cragun's resort. This recipe from 1947 was marked up with notes and "this one's a keeper" checks. The cheese laces right through the crust in this delicious apple pie.

CRUST:

2 cups sifted all-purpose flour, divided

1/4 cup water

1/2 cup Crisco shortening

1/2 cup grated Cheddar cheese

1 teaspoon salt

FILLING:

2 tablespoons flour

1/8 teaspoon salt

3/4 to 1 cup sugar (depending on sweetness of apples)

1 teaspoon cinnamon

4 to 5 cups peeled and sliced apples

1 tablespoon lemon juice

2 tablespoons butter

TO MAKE CRUST: Mix 1/3 cup flour and 1/4 cup water to a paste; set aside. Cut shortening and cheese into remaining flour and salt until the size of peas; add flour paste. Mix

together into a ball and roll out for 2-crust pie. Fit one crust into bottom of a 9-inch pie pan, reserving top crust.

TO MAKE FILLING: Combine flour, salt, sugar, and cinnamon. Spread half of the mixture over the pastry-lined pan. Add apples; sprinkle remainder of flour mixture over the apples. Sprinkle with lemon juice and dot with butter. Fit and seal upper crust. Bake on lower shelf in a 425-degree oven for 30 to 40 minutes.

CANOE COUNTRY

Gunflint Lodge, Grand Marais

In the wilderness land of fur traders, hunters, and fishermen, the Gunflint Lodge began life with five cabins, a little lodge dining room, and a store for guests and local Indians. When Justine Kerfoot first arrived at the lodge in 1927, the kitchen held a gigantic six-foot-wide wood-burning stove, an icebox filled with lake ice, and a water pump connected to a spring deep beneath the room. Justine declared the kitchen the heart of the lodge, and she lovingly proceeded to make her dining-room meals as famous as her shore lunches. The Gunflint Lodge grew and grew.

Justine Kerfoot prepares a shore lunch, 1930s

BURNTSIDE LODGE TOMATO ASPIC

Second-generation members of the LaMontagne family may be serving this time-honored tangy tomato aspic to hungry hunters and would-be trailblazers today.

4 cups tomato or V8 juice

1/4 cup chopped celery leaves

1/3 cup chopped onion

1 teaspoon salt

2 tablespoons brown sugar

2 small bay leaves

4 whole cloves

1 clove garlic

1 cup dry lemon Jell-O

3 tablespoons fresh lemon juice

1 cup finely chopped celery

1/3 cup chopped onion

1/4 cup chopped green pepper

Simmer tomato or V8 juice, celery leaves, 1/3 cup onion, salt, brown sugar, bay leaves, cloves, and garlic for 5 minutes and strain over Jell-O. Add lemon juice. Stir until gelatin is dissolved and smooth. Place in refrigerator until syrupy; then add celery, 1/3 cup onion, and green pepper. Put in mold and chill overnight or 8 hours. Makes 8 servings.

Got to the woods a little bit late
Everyone was looking for the dinner plate
All except the bugs, their food had arrived
Fresh from the city, right on time
We were the "Blue Plate Special"
We were the "Catch of the Day"
We were sodium free, USDA-positive, no sugar added
Camping at last, beautiful site
Drinking coffee in the firelight

FROM "TALKING CAMPING," BY CHARLIE MAGUIRE

Burntside Lodge, Ely, 1940s (above)
Burntside Lodge waitresses, 1926 (left)

When the Brownell Outing Company built a major addition to its hunting camp at the turn of the century, it was renamed Burntside Lodge. The company also put up sturdy log cabins, most of which are still there, still beautiful, and remarkably well preserved. The charming old dining room, staffed by perky uniformed waitresses in 1926, continues to welcome diners.

THE NORTH SHORE

Original Lutsen Resort, Lutsen, 1930s

Lutsen Resort, 1950s

In 1885, Swedish immigrant Charles Axel Nelson established Lutsen, which is now the state's oldest operating resort. Overlooking Lake Superior, the dining room served herring fillets from the lake and fried chicken passed around on family-style platters.

Original Lutsen dining room, 1930s

In 1952, Minnesota architect Edwin Lundie designed a new Lutsen Lodge of timber-frame construction in the rustic Scandinavian tradition. The interior is a celebration of Lundie's attention to detail. Admirers gather by the stone fireplace to enjoy wood paneling, massive beams, and fanciful carvings that weave throughout the lobby and into the dining room. The menu still offers herring, now called bluefin, and fried chicken, plus Swedish meatballs, rye bread, and many other classic resort dishes.

Dining room, Lutsen Lodge, 1950s

Dining room, Naniboujou Lodge, near Grand Marais, 1950s

In the 1920s, a great lodge was built to house an exclusive hunting club. It was named Naniboujou for the forest spirit who, according to Cree Indian lore, watches over hunters and travelers. Members were famous sports figures and celebrities of the era, including Jack Dempsey, Babe Ruth, Ring Lardner, and all their friends, who were charter members until the 1929 stock market crash. But the forest spirit must have been watching over Naniboujou Lodge, for it survived the depression and many hard times to be enjoyed by generations of thankful admirers.

The magnificent dining hall is the main attraction at Naniboujou. Comprehension comes slowly in the commanding presence of Cree Indian designs, the two-hundred-ton native rock fireplace, and the awesome brilliance of colors and patterns overhead. It is a magical place. Diners are offered sumptuous meals, artfully arranged and watched over by the historic lodge's keepers, Tim and Nancy Ramey.

Naniboujou Corn Pudding

That grand dame of the North Shore, Naniboujou Lodge has always presented top-rate food influenced by local ingredients and a touch of creativity. This vegetable side dish, a perennial hit with guests, is best when made with summer's fresh sweet corn. This recipe also appears in the cookbook Dining in the Spirit of Naniboujou.

2 large eggs
1 1/4 cups half-and-half
1 1/4 cups cream
2 tablespoons brown sugar
1/2 teaspoon nutmeg
2 teaspoons salt
1/2 teaspoon pepper
6 cups corn kernels
(preferably fresh off the cob)
1/4 cup chopped chives

In a large mixing bowl, beat eggs well. Add half-and-half, cream, sugar, nutmeg, salt, and pepper, mixing well. Stir in corn. Pour mixture into a buttered 8x8-inch baking dish. Bake in a 375-degree oven for 45 minutes or until set. (For a better result, place the baking dish in a larger pan and add hot water to half the depth of the baking dish before putting in the oven.) Sprinkle with chives when serving. At Naniboujou, portions of the pudding are served on red cabbage leaves. Makes 8 servings.

RESORT STYLE, 1950S

Tourists knew they were on a Minnesota vacation when they found the resort dining room with its big windows overlooking the lake.

Edgewater Beach, Detroit Lakes

Barnett's Life of Riley Resort, Cook

Swedmark Lodge, Bemidji

Birkeland's Bay Lake Lodge, Deerwood

Hotel Chase, Walker

GRANDMA KALDAHL'S HEAVENLY BROWN BREAD

Fair Hills Resort overlooking Pelican Lake near Detroit Lakes is justly famous for walleye and prime rib, but it's the celebrated rye-graham bread that returning guests hanker to find in their breadbaskets. Loretta Warren, one of Fair Hills' longest-tenured chefs, shared this classic Scandinavian bread recipe, which the resort's founders, the Kaldahl family, served there from its earliest days.

2 tablespoons (or 2 packages) dry yeast

2/3 cup lukewarm water

1 teaspoon sugar

4 cups water, divided

1/2 cup shortening

1 cup sugar

1 1/2 tablespoons salt

1/2 cup dark molasses

1 cup rye flour

2 cups graham flour

7 to 8 cups white flour

Combine yeast with 2/3 cup lukewarm water and 1 teaspoon sugar; allow to soak for 10 minutes. Heat 2 cups water to boiling; pour over a combination of shortening, sugar, salt, and molasses in a mixing bowl, stirring to dissolve shortening. Add remaining 2 cups of cold water and cool mixture to lukewarm. Thoroughly combine rye and graham flours. When liquid is lukewarm, add dissolved yeast and stir in mixed dark flours. Then add 7 to 8 cups white flour to make a kneadable medium-stiff dough.

Knead dough well. Allow dough to rest for 10 minutes, then knead it down. Let rise, covered, in a warm place until doubled in size. Knead down again, cover, and let rise again.

Shape dough into 4 loaves; place in greased bread pans. Let rise until double in bulk or until a depression remains when the dough is lightly touched with a finger. Bake loaves at 375 degrees for 20 minutes; reduce heat to 325 degrees and continue to bake for another 25 minutes. Makes 4 loaves.

Fair Hills Resort, Detroit Lakes, 1950s

200

As Minnesota resort guests became more physically active in the 1950s, proprietors found ways to accommodate increasingly energetic customers. Guests arrived wearing well-worn blue jeans, tennis shoes, and T-shirts to sit at big tables holding heartland fare. Shared tales of heroic activities guaranteed lively conversation, all observed by quixotic decorations of watchful animals, mounted fish, and bearskin rugs.

John, Dean, and Ann Koutsky boating on Leech Lake, 1950s

Squaw Point Resort, Hillman

Judd's Resort, Bena

An elegant deer head guarded the booths at Victoria Lodge, where a modern jukebox replaced the warm and crackling fire.

Victoria Lodge, Lake Victoria

Rockwood Lodge, Grand Marais

Thunder Lake Lodge, near Remer

Peters' Sunset Beach Hotel, Glenwood

The historic Sunset Beach lodge has sheltered vacationers since 1914. The Minnewaska dining room provides shade and sustenance for beach-weary sun worshippers.

Snowbank Lodge, Ely

Douglas Lodge

ITASCA STATE PARK, PARK RAPIDS

The first structure to be built in the Itasca State Park system, Douglas Lodge was designed in 1905 in the popular rustic style of gabled roofs and peeled logs on a split-stone foundation. The lodge has provided tourists with rooms, lounges, and dining facilities for nearly one hundred years. In 1949, for two people per day, a room in the lodge cost $2.50, a room with a bathroom $3.75, and a one-bedroom cabin with a fireplace $5.50.

Employees, 1953

Kitchen staff

Early dining room building, 1913

Douglas Lodge, 1900s
Looking into the dining room, 1920

The Shenango Company designed lady's-slipper china for Douglas Lodge during the 1930s. The great seal of the State of Minnesota dates to 1858, and the lady's-slipper became the official state flower in 1892. Today these beautiful dishes, reproduced by Syracuse China, are sold in Itasca's gift shops.

MINNESOTA STATE FLOWER
MOCCASIN FLOWER

Itasca State Park
LAKE ITASCA, MINNESOTA
Source of the Mississippi

"Good Morning!"
Club Breakfast

PLEASE ORDER BY NUMBER
Now Serving Food Where Prices Appear

No. 1 Fruit or Cereal, Toast and Coffee
No. 2 Ham, Bacon or Sausage, (1) Egg, (2) Hot Cakes, Coffee
No. 3 Hot Cakes with Ham, Bacon or Sausage and Coffee
No. 4 Two Eggs, Hot Cakes and Coffee
No. 5 Waffles with Ham, Bacon or Sausage and Coffee
No. 6 Ham, Bacon or Sausage, 2 Eggs, Toast and Coffee
No. 7 One Egg, 2 Hot Cakes, 2 Eggs, Toast and Coffee
No. 8 Waffles, One Egg, Toast and Coffee
No. 9 Two Eggs Any Style, Toast and C...

Itasca Butter Cookies

These cookies, served with ice cream, were the traditional dessert during the early days at Douglas Lodge.

1 pound butter

2 1/2 cups sugar

3 eggs

1 teaspoon cream of tartar

1 teaspoon vanilla

1/2 teaspoon salt

5 cups flour

1 teaspoon soda

Cream butter and sugar together. Mix in all remaining ingredients. Make into broomstick-sized rolls and wrap in wax paper. Freeze. Slice thin while still frozen. Space on cookie sheets and bake in 350-degree oven for 8 to 10 minutes. Makes about 12 dozen cookies.

Frank Squires, Douglas Lodge cook

Boys washing dishes at camp, 1935

When dinner is done and the tables are cleared, the dishes washed and put away, memories of meals with friends will endure.

ourishment may be a necessity, but an extraordinary amount of creativity and energy has been devoted to our food since the first cooking fire. Just as our ancestors did thousands of years ago, we pay attention to what we eat, where we eat, and with whom we eat. Memorable flavors in friendly environments will surely be meaningful for all time.

PHOTO CREDITS

Illustrations, artifacts, and recipes appear in this book courtesy of the following individuals and repositories:

Anderson House, Wabasha: Anderson House staff and recipe, 159

Erma J. Andrews: Erick Johnson, 7; Columbia Restaurant menu, 7

Big Stone County Historical Museum. Photographed by Sherman Studio, Ortonville, MN: Golden Bantam plate, 131; Cubby's Cafe, 132

Blue Earth County Historical Society: Mankato Candy Kitchen, 110; Wykoff's Oasis

Society: J. C. Arnold Soda Water Fountain, 100; Palace of Sweets (Oscar E. Sando), 102

Clay County Historical Society: Hagen and Olson's Soda Shop, 101; Walgreen's menu, 119; Grand Pacific Hotel photo and menu, 157

Cokato Historical Society: John Christofferson's Store and Restaurant, 63; Cokato Pantry, 67; Shortstop Drive-In, 134

Gust Akerlund Collection, Cokato

Freeborn County Historical Museum: Hazel's Steak House, 11; Ideal Cafe, 63; B. & J. Lunch menu, 63

General Mills Archives: General Mills cafeteria, 96

Georgia Boosalis George: Minneapolis Fruit Store photos, 105; Lankis Cafe, 105

Thomas W. Given: Prom Ballroom photos, 58

Goodhue County Historical Society: Berg's Bakery and Restaurant, 4; Little Cafe, 74; Corner Cafe, 74; Joe's Restaurant, 74; Blue Bird Cafe, 74; Swanson's Bakery, 103; Palace of Sweets, 103; Marigold Dairy Bar, 109; Ernie Swanson's A&W, 135; St. James Hotel staff, 158

Grant County Historical Society: Palm Restaurant, 62; Albert Anderson's, 62, 148–49; Wendell Cafe, 68; Solberg's Store, 102; R. E. Shauer menu, 107; bakery, lunch counter, and soda fountain, 108

Hennepin History Museum: The Buckhorn, 14 (top and bottom); Gmitro's menu, 20; Stouffer's menu, 27; Harry's Cafe bar, 30; Freddie's Café menu, 31, 210; John's Place menu, 44; Flame menu, 54; Axel's Lunch Room, 62; Rainbow Café menu, 80; Young-Quinlan menu, 126; Seventh Avenue Hotel, 153; Winslow House photo, 153; Russell Hotel menu and dishes, 163; Nicollet Hotel dining room, 164 (top); West Hotel Moorish Room, 165; *Stillwater* streetcar boat, 187

Cushing House, 159

Hubbell House: Hubbell House, 159

Itasca County Historical Society: Pokegama Hotel staff, 161

Robert R. Johnson: White Star photo, 51 (top)

Kamrowski Family: Sunlight Bakery and Cafe, 68

Kandiyohi County Historical Society: Deutche's, 3; Spudnut Shop, 76

Ken Wright Studio: W. T. Grant Store, 116

Kozlak Family: Jax photo and recipe, 22

Robert W. Laing: Covered Wagon ashtray, 15

Lake Superior Railroad Museum: dishes, 138–39

Lexington, St. Paul: Lexington photos and dishes, 25

Jack Lindstrom: Grandma Miller's sketch, 91; color for Donaldson's menu, 120

Ronald A. Lyschik: Black and White Cafe, 72

Mark and Dawn McGinley: matchbooks, 6, 10, 26, 53, 69, 70, 72, 79, 80, 107, 173; Crabtree's Kitchen photo, place mat, and dishes, 82; YPS Church dishes, 181; *Bull Cook* book, 191

Mancini's: Mancini's, 24

Marshall Field's: Dayton's tea room and menu, 124

Martin County Historical Society: Interlaken Inn photo and menu, 190

Michael's: Michael's, 26

Francis Miller/Timepix: *Life* cover, 134

Minneapolis Public Library, Minneapolis Collection: Charlie's Cafe Exceptionale photos and menu, ix, 33; The Grill, 3; Bergsing Café menu, 6; Childs menu, 7; McCarthy's menu, 21; Stouffer's waitresses, 27; Harry's Cafe menu, 30; Harry's Cafe menu, 30; Nankin Cafe photo and menu (1933), 34, 42; New Palace Cafe, 65; Lilac Lanes Cafe place mat, 80; Forum menu, 93; Becky's Cafeteria ad, 94; Donaldson's Department Store menu, 120; Dayton's Sky Room, 124; Young-Quinlan logo, 126; Great Northern Railway menu, 139; Hotel Nicollet menu, 164; Curtis Hotel menu, 169; Minneapolis Athletic Club (1915), 178; *City of St. Louis* menu, 187; Lake Park Hotel menu, 188; Hotel Lafayette menu, 188

Minneapolis Star: Miller's Cafeteria (1964), 91

Fountain Room, St. Paul Hotel

Drive-in, 134; Mankato House, 148; Saulpaugh menu, 151

Maria G. Boosalis, Ph.D., and Nick T. Boosalis: Avalon Cafe, 105

William G. Boosalis: The Olympia, 104

Dean Borghorst: 620 Club menu, 20; Dutro's postcard, 20; Teco Inn, 168

Breezy Point Resort: Breezy Point Resort brochure and employees, ii–iii, 195

Brown County Historical Society: Eibner's photos, menu, and artifacts, 39, 113; Silver Latch Cafe, 133; The Mug, 143; Dacotah House Hotel, 149; Dutch Room, Turner Hall, 178

Burntside Lodge Collection, Iron Range Research Center: Burntside Lodge waitresses and recipe, 198

Café di Napoli: Café di Napoli photos, 41

Carlton County Historical Society: Ziebler Hotel, 149

Carver County Historical Society: North Star Hotel dining room, lobby, and kitchen, 152

Chippewa County Historical

Historical Society: Ann's Cafe, 66; Sweet Shop, 76

Cook County Historical Society: Campers Home Cafe, 84; Le Sage's Cafe photo and menu, 84; Edgewater Inn, 84; Tony's Eat, 84; Sjoberg Dairy, 109; Chik-wauk cook, 190; Little Marais Lodge, 191; Sawbill Lodge, 192; Gunflint Lodge cooks, 198; Justine Kerfoot, 198

Cottonwood County Historical Society: White Front Cafe, 63; Villa Restaurant, 102

Irma Cragun: Cragun's photo and recipe, 197

Douglas County Historical Society: Garfield Cafe, 63; Candy Kitchen, 110; Hotel Blake, 184–85; Victoria Lodge, 201

Duluth Tribune: Miller's Cafeteria waitresses, 91

Edina Historical Society: Convention Grill, 80

Family of Lee Nelson Engstrand: Lee M. Nelson, 56

Excelsior–Lake Minnetonka Historical Society: Anchor Inn, 78; Log Cabin Cafe, 78

Rapid River Logging Camp, Park Rapids

Hibbing Historical Society: DelMonico's, 4; Androy take-out cartons, 43; Canelake's Cafe photo and menu, 112; Oliver Club plate, 180

The Historic Afton House Inn and the Afton Historical Society:

Magic Aquarium Bar, Moorhead

Minnesota Historical Society.
Photography by Peter Latner:
place mats, 16–17; Scandia
Kitchen place mat (1998.210.24),
36; House of Sweden place mat
(1998.210.53), 37; Heidelberg place
mat (1998.210.26), 39; John's Place
table (1993.7.6), 44; Road Buddy's
place mat (1998.210.36), 47;

*The Cavalier Room,
Minneapolis Athletic Club*

Diamond Jim's logo
(1998.210.68), 58; Brokerage
Coffee Shop menu (1994.27.1),
66; Nybo's place mat
(1998.210.37), 74; Akre's place mat
(1990.149.23), 82; Van's Cafe place
mat (1998.210.5), 83; Great
Northern place mat (1998.210.43),
138; Christmas '85 menu, 157; St.
James plate (68.252.40), 158;
Hotel Nicollet Glass (1987.225.2),
164; Ruttger's dishes, 196;
Douglas Lodge creamer
(1987.172.1), 202; Douglas Lodge
menu (1987.172.7), 202; Ryan
Hotel menus, 208, 209

Brenda Moberg, Itasca State Park:
Douglas Lodge employees,
kitchen staff, and cook, 202

Mower County Historical Society:
Woolworth's, Austin, 117;
Robby's, 141

**Murray County Historical Society
and Museum:** Iona Restaurant, 2;
Chandler restaurant, 2; Royal
Cafe, 63

**Northeast Minnesota Historical
Center:** Delmonico Cafe menu,
5; Arrowhead Cafeteria menu,
90; Hotel Lenox photos, 160;
Hotel Duluth, 170; Black Bear
Lounge menu, 170

Northfield Historical Society:
Archer House, 159

Norway Ridge Supper Club: Cook
Bob Newman, 196

O'Gara's: O'Gara's Bar and
Grill, 46

**Olmsted County Historical
Society:** Keystone Restaurant, 4;
Michael's, 26; Grand Cafe, 66;
Austin's, 86; Holland's photo, ad,
and menu, 94; Princess Confec-
tionary and Cafe, 111; *Rigby's
Reliable Candy Teacher*, 111; Hafner's
recipe book and hat, 111; Kresge,
Rochester, 116; Sandy's Drive-in,
141; King Leo's, 141

Eleanor Ostman: Blue Horse
glass, 32; Waikiki Room nap·
kin, 164

**Otter Tail County Historical
Society:** Sandy's (*Fergus Falls
Journal* photograph by Harley
Oyloe), 141; Hotel Kaddatz
menu, 157

Palmer House Hotel: Palmer
House Hotel, 151

***Park Region Echo* (Alexandria):**
Candy Kitchen ad, 110

**Pennington County Historical
Society:** Rex Cafe, 101; Ben
Franklin, 116; Woolworth's
waitress and lunch counter,
Thief River Falls, 117

Peters' Sunset Beach Lodge:
Peters' Sunset Beach Hotel, 201

**Pipestone County Historical
Society:** Gano's, 63

Private Collection: fountain spigot, 99; ice cream glasses,
106–107; Baltimore Dairy plate
and ice cream dish, 109

Ramsey County Historical Society:
Hollyhocks Inn, 6; The
Connoisseur, 86

Ruttger's Bay Lake Lodge:
Blueberry Buckle recipe, 196

Ryan Family: Covered Wagon
photos, 15

The Saint Paul Companies, Inc.:
Saint Paul Fire and Marine
cafeteria (from *The Saint Paul
Letter*, centennial issue, 1953), 97

Scott County Historical Society:
St. Paul House (photograph by
LeRoy Lebens), 55; St. Paul
House credit card, 55; Riviera
photo and ad, 55

Mrs. Doris Serlin: Serlin's Cafe, 81

Terri Siderakos: Colonial Inn,
20–21

Family of Helen Skepper-Matson:
Helen Skepper at Montgomery
Wards, 114

Copyright 2002 **Star
Tribune/Minneapolis–St. Paul:**
Miller's Cafeteria, 91; Becky's
Cafeteria, 94

Stearns History Museum: Gohl's
Place, 62; Quality Lunch, 63;
Pan's Cafe photo and ad, 72; B.
F. Carter Soda Fountain, 100;
McCarthy's Drive-in, 141; Maid-
Rite logo, 144; Central House,
156; Leyendecker Hotel, 156

**Myron Hall Photo, Stearns History
Museum:** Dan Marsh Cafe, 60,
77; Sheper's Cafe, 76; Eddy's, 134

Stevens County Historical Society:
Palm Cafe, 110; La Grand
Hotel, 161

Track 16 Gallery, www.track16.com,
Santa Monica, CA: NSP dishes,
97; Montgomery Ward dishes, 114

Vescio Family: Vescio's menu, 40

Wadena County Historical Society:
City Restaurant, 2; Finney's
Cafe photos, 69

Waseca County Historical Society:
Grant House, 151

**Washington County Historical
Society:** Hotel Crookston menu,
157; West Hotel menu, 165

**Wayzata Historical Society,
Minnesota Historical Society collection:** Hart's Cafe sign, 78

**Wayzata Historical Society, Western
Hennepin County Pioneer Museum,
Long Lake:** Buckhorn matches
and menu, 14; Hart's Cafe, 78

Weston Family: Fuji-Ya
Restaurant, 47

Winona County Historical Society:
cooks, 10; Oaks Night Club
stage, 57; Hot Fish Shop menu,
74; Cunningham's Steak Shop,
76; Lauer and Son Drug Store,
101; Emil's, 135; Lakeview
carhop, 135; McDonald's, 145;
Winona Hotel, 156 (left)

Wright County Historical Society:
Minneapolis Brewing
Company, Delano Branch, 50;
Delano Cafe, 68; Danielson
Cafe, 76

Wrinkle Inc: Band Box, 143

Nine Boy Indian Curry at the Rosewood Room, Northstar Inn, Minneapolis, 1960s

Most of the postcards used in this book are from the personal collection of Kathryn Strand Koutsky.

Unless otherwise indicated, all photos are from the collections
of the Minnesota Historical Society.

Unless otherwise indicated in the above credits, all china is
from the personal collection of Linda Koutsky and all silver is
from the collection of Lisa Koutsky Sten. Photography by Eric
Mortenson, MHS.

Many of the recipes from Minneapolis restaurants are from
*Recipes of the Month: Famous Foods from Famous Places in the Minneapolis
Area* (Minneapolis Gas Company Home Service Department, 1953).

RECIPE INDEX

Restaurant employees, Minneapolis, 1915

Baker at the Hotel Nicollet, 1920

Banquet preparation, 1949

*Bellhops at the Hotel Nicollet,
Minneapolis, 1924*

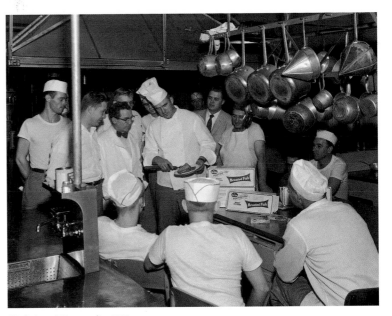

Chef class, Minneapolis, 1955

CHARLIE'S CAFE EXCEPTIONALE POTATO SALAD

*Many recipes have floated around for
Charlie's "exceptionale" potato salad, but
Louise Saunders, who ran the famed
Minneapolis restaurant after her husband's
demise, explained the true formula. You can
make homemade dressing, which they did
at Charlie's, or use a good bottled brand for
this home-size batch.*

HOMEMADE MAYONNAISE:

1 pasteurized egg yolk

1 teaspoon dry mustard

1 teaspoon granulated sugar

1/4 teaspoon salt

1/8 teaspoon cayenne pepper

2 tablespoons lemon juice or vinegar

1 cup vegetable oil

SALAD:

5 medium potatoes, freshly cooked and peeled

1 teaspoon salt

1/4 teaspoon white pepper

2 or more tablespoons chopped green onion

1 to 2 tablespoons finely chopped red bell pepper

3 hard-cooked eggs, diced (or more to taste)

TO MAKE MAYONNAISE: In a blender, combine
egg yolk, mustard, sugar, salt, pepper, and 1
tablespoon lemon juice or vinegar. Blend at
medium speed, adding oil in a thin stream
until mixture thickens. Add remaining lemon
juice or vinegar. Makes 1 3/4 cups.

TO MAKE SALAD: Dice potatoes into a large
bowl. Sprinkle with salt and pepper. Add
onion, red pepper, and eggs. Stir in about 1
1/4 cups dressing, adding more if needed
(Charlie's was a very creamy potato salad).
Mix gently. Chill 2 hours. Makes 6 servings.

INDEX

Menu, Hotel Ryan, St. Paul

Menu, Ryan Hotel, St. Paul, 1887

Menu, Curtis Hotel, Minneapolis, 1929

Menu, Waikiki Room, Hotel Nicollet, Minneapolis

*Menu. Tempo, 2027 East Franklin Avenue.
Minneapolis*

Menu. Erie Jr., Detroit Lakes

RESTAURANTS STILL IN BUSINESS

It's a daunting task to determine which historic eating places have endured the ravages of time and survived into the twenty-first century. Some restaurants appearing in this book are still open for business—in one way or another. Many retain their original wood wainscoting or vintage linoleum floors, others have new names or owners, some have gone modern, and a few operate in entirely new buildings on the same old spot. Cheers to them for surviving at all!

Afton House, Afton
Anderson House, Wabasha
Archer House, Northfield
Band Box, Minneapolis
Bar Harbor, Nisswa
Barnett's Life of Riley Resort,
 Cook
Betty's Pies, Two Harbors
Birchmont Hotel, Bemidji
Black and White Cafe,
 Little Falls
Blue Goose Inn, Garrison
Breezy Point, Pequot Lakes
Burntside Lodge, Ely
Café di Napoli, Minneapolis
Calumet Hotel, Pipestone
Canelake's, Hibbing
Capp Towers, Minneapolis
 (Millennium Hotel)
Cascade Lodge, Grand Marais
Castle Royal, St. Paul
Cecil's, St. Paul
Chatterbox Bar and Cafe,
 St. Paul (Costello's)
Convention Grill, Edina
Cragun's, Brainerd
Dayton's Sky Room and
 Oak Grill, Minneapolis
 (Marshall Field's)
Douglas Lodge, Park Rapids
East Bay Hotel, Grand Marais

Fair Hills Resort, Detroit Lakes
The Forum Cafeteria,
 Minneapolis (Goodfellow's)
Fuji-Ya, Minneapolis
Grand View Lodge, Brainerd
Gunflint Lodge, Grand Marais
Handicraft Guild Tea Room,
 Minneapolis (Hell's Kitchen)
The Hilton's Carousel Room,
 St. Paul (Radisson)
Hubbell House, Mantorville
Hungry Jack Lodge,
 Grand Marais
Izaty's Lodge, Onamia
Jax Cafe, Minneapolis
Joe's Pickwick Tavern, Duluth
Judd's Resort, Bena
Kahler Hotel, Rochester
Kaiserhoff Restaurant,
 New Ulm
Kitchi Gammi Club, Duluth
Lakeview Drive-in, Winona
The Lexington, St. Paul
Lowell Inn, Stillwater
Lutsen Resort, Lutsen
Madden Lodge, Brainerd
Mancini's, St. Paul
Manhattan Beach Lodge,
 Manhattan Beach
Meister's, Scandia
Michael's, Rochester

Mickey's Dining Car, St. Paul
Minikahda Club, Minneapolis
Minneapolis Athletic Club,
 Minneapolis (Grand Hotel)
Minneapolis Club, Minneapolis
Minneapolis Golf Club,
 St. Louis Park
Minneapolis–St. Paul
 International Airport
Morey's, Stillwater (Savories)
Munsingwear cafeteria,
 Minneapolis (The Atrium,
 International Market
 Square)
Murray's, Minneapolis
Naniboujou Lodge,
 Grand Marais
Nelson's Resort, Crane Lake
Northern Pine Lodge,
 Park Rapids
Norway Ridge Resort,
 Pequot Lakes
O'Gara's Bar and Grill, St. Paul
Parker House, Mendota (Axel's)
Peter's Grill, Minneapolis
Peters' Sunset Beach Hotel,
 Glenwood
Porky's, St. Paul
Radisson Hotel, Minneapolis
Rathskeller, Minnesota State
 Capitol cafeteria, St. Paul

Rockwood Lodge,
 Grand Marais
Rustic Inn, Two Harbors
Ruttger's Bay Lake Lodge,
 Deerwood
St. James Hotel, Red Wing
The Saint Paul Hotel, St. Paul
Sawbill Lodge, Lutsen
Schumacher's Hotel,
 New Prague
Schuneman's River Room,
 St. Paul (Marshall Field's)
Scrlin's Cafe, St. Paul
Sherwood Forest Lodge,
 Brainerd
Snowbank Lodge, Ely
Thunder Lake Lodge, Remer
Tobie's, Hinckley
Totino's, Minneapolis
Town and Country Club,
 St. Paul
Turner Hall, New Ulm
Van's Cafe, Brainerd
Vertin's Cafe, Ely
Vescio's, Minneapolis
Women's Club, Minneapolis
Wong's, Rochester
Yarusso Brothers, St. Paul

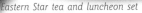

Eastern Star tea and luncheon set

SUGGESTED READING

- Anderson, Will. *Where Have You Gone, Starlight Cafe?: America's Golden Era Roadside Restaurants.* Portland, Maine: Anderson and Sons Publishing Company, 1998.

- Calloway, Stephen. *The Elements of Style: A Practical Encyclopedia of Interior Architectural Details from 1485 to the Present.* Rev. Ed. New York: Simon and Schuster, 1997.

- Heimann, Jim. *May I Take Your Order?: American Menu Design 1920–1960.* San Francisco: Chronicle Books, 1998.

- Mariani, John F. *America Eats Out: An Illustrated History of Restaurants, Taverns, Coffee Shops, Speakeasies, and Other Establishments That Have Fed Us for 350 Years.* New York: William Morrow & Company, Inc., 1991.

- Millett, Larry. *Lost Twin Cities.* St. Paul: Minnesota Historical Society Press, 1992.

- Witzel, Michael Karl. *The American Diner.* St. Paul: Motorbooks International, 1999.

- Witzel, Michael Karl. *The American Drive-In.* St. Paul: Motorbooks International, 1994.

Rose Halleck Boosalis tallying up the day's receipts at the Olympia Confectionary, 1903

Throughout the one hundred years covered in *Minnesota Eats Out*, state residents were blessed with thousands of dining choices. We hope that you were reminded of favorite cafés and restaurants as you paged through this book, but we are painfully aware that many admired eateries were not included on these crowded pages. The large number of photographs and artifacts in private collections and historical society archives throughout the state simply overwhelmed us. And sadly, despite vigorous searching, images were never found for many additional treasured and meaningful community dining places.

Local historical societies are the best places to preserve your antique photographs and historic artifacts for future researchers and fact-finding residents. Historical societies and museums provided us with invaluable resources on Minnesota dining history and furnished many of the photographs that animate these pages. We are grateful for their existence and for their staff's well-informed assistance, which made *Minnesota Eats Out* a fascinating experience for us.

Thank you for your patronage!